An Introduction to Quality Management and Engineering

An Introduction to Quality Management and Engineering

Based on the American Society for Quality's Certified Quality
Engineer Body of Knowledge

by

Victor E. Sower, Ph.D., C.Q.E.

Michael J. Savoie, Ph.D., C.Q.E.

and

Stephen Renick, B.S.

Prentice Hall Upper Saddle River, NJ 07458

Library of Congress Cataloging-in-Publication Data

Sower, Victor E.
    An Introduction to quality management and engineering : based on the American Society for Quality's certified quality engineer body of knowledge / by Victor E. Sower, Michael J. Savoie, and Stephen Renick.
        p.   cm.
    Includes bibliographical references and index.
    ISBN 0-13-936841-8
    1. Quality control. 2. Production management—Quality control. I. Savoie, Michael J. II. Renick, Stephen. III. Title.
TS156.S669   1998
658.5′62—dc21   98-24946
                                                                                                                        CIP

Production editor: BookMasters, Inc.
Editor-in-chief: Marcia Horton
Managing editor: Eileen Clark
Assistant vice president of production and manufacturing: David W. Riccardi
Cover designer: Bruce Kenselaar
Manufacturing buyer: Trudy Pisciotti
Editorial assistant: Dolores Mars
Art Director: Jayne Conte

©1999 by Prentice-Hall, Inc.
Simon & Schuster / A Viacom Company
Upper Saddle River, New Jersey 07458

The author and publisher of this book have used their best efforts in preparing this book. These efforts include the development, research, and testing of the theories and programs to determine their effectiveness. The author and publisher make no warranty of any kind, expressed or implied, with regard to these programs or the documentation contained in this book. The author and publisher shall not be liable in any event for incidental or consequential damages in connection with, or arising out of, the furnishing, performance, or use of these programs.

Printed in the United States of America

10 9 8 7 6 5 4 3 2 1

ISBN: 0-13-936841-8

Prentice-Hall International (UK) Limited, *London*
Prentice-Hall of Australia Pty. Limited, *Sydney*
Prentice-Hall Canada Inc., *Toronto*
Prentice-Hall Hispanoamericana, S.A., *Mexico*
Prentice-Hall of India Private Limited, *New Delhi*
Prentice-Hall of Japan, Inc., *Tokyo*
Simon & Schuster Asia Pte. Ltd., *Singapore*
Editora Prentice-Hall do Brasil, Ltda., *Rio de Janeiro*

Brief Contents

Contents

Acknowledgments

The authors are grateful to a number of our colleagues for their assistance in the development of this book. Dr. Gerald Kohers reviewed and provided helpful comments and suggestions for several chapters and provided invaluable assistance with the production of the photographs included in this book. Mr. Matthew Bent, Dr. Ross Lovell, Dr. Mitchell Muehsam, Dr. Valerie Muehsam, Lt. Dirk Renick, Ms. Rachel Renick, and Dr. George Walker reviewed several chapters, and their suggestions resulted in a number of substantial improvements. Two of our graduate students, Ms. Emily Behrend and Mr. Chris Sower, evaluated the beta versions of the testing program and made helpful suggestions for improvement. Ms. Katie Bent suggested changes in some of the questions in the testing program. Five anonymous reviewers also made many suggestions which improved the quality of this book. Our wives, Judy Sower, Rena Savoie, and Barbara Renick, took over some of our responsibilities at home to provide us with additional time to work on the manuscript. Many of our students used draft versions of parts of the book in their studies and provided helpful feedback. A number of other family members, friends, and colleagues in both the academic and business communities contributed in some way to the production of this book. To all, our thanks. Thanks too to all at Prentice Hall and BookMasters who have helped in the production of this book. Despite the best efforts of all involved, some errors may have crept into the book. We, the authors, are responsible for those errors.

We are dedicated to the process of continuous improvement. We welcome comments and suggestions that readers may have for future editions of this book.

Victor E. Sower [mgt_ves@shsu.edu]
Michael J. Savoie [msavoie@gsm.udallas.edu]
Stephen Renick [srenick@airmail.net]

Introduction

This book is intended for use in college classrooms and in the workplace of the quality professional. It is an introduction to the quality engineering body of knowledge. In addition to providing an introduction to each topic, the book contains extensive references to specialized resources which provide significantly more depth of coverage. Entire books are available covering the material in each chapter of this book. This book is designed to be a gateway to that more extensive knowledge. In addition, this book provides a grounding in the fundamentals of each topic.

The book is appropriate for use as the primary text in an introductory quality engineering course at the associates level in the quality technician curriculum and at the baccalaureate and graduate levels in the industrial technology, engineering, and management curricula. It may also be used as a secondary text in introduction to engineering, process engineering, and quality management courses. In classes where the students have at least one semester of statistics, the first two chapters may be assigned as a review of probability and statistics.

Because this book covers the American Society for Quality (ASQ) Certified Quality Engineer (CQE) body of knowledge, it is an excellent first resource to use in preparing for the CQE examination. Because it does not contain questions from previous CQE examinations, it may be taken into the examination room and used during the examination.

The computerized testing program provides a library of examination questions similar to those that may be encountered on the CQE examination. Upon completion of a computerized examination, the student is provided a summary of the results by category. Detailed information is provided for missed questions including specific references to be studied to remediate the lack of understanding of material represented by that question. One approach to mastering the material would be to read each chapter, address the end-of-chapter Discussion Questions and Problems, and then test for mastery using the computerized testing program.

Because of the extensive documentation of more specialized sources, this book is an excellent resource for quality professionals. The chapters in this book provide overviews of each segment of the CQE body of knowledge and clear directions to resources which cover the material in greater detail. Using this book can thus result in significant *search time* savings for quality professionals.

Fundamentals

CHAPTER 1

Basic Probability Concepts

CHAPTER OBJECTIVES

This chapter introduces the following topics:

- Basic probability concepts including independence, mutual exclusiveness, random variables, and discrete and continuous probability distributions
- Examples of formulas for calculating the probability of occurrence of events
- The concept of expected value and how it is calculated using probability analysis

INTRODUCTION

It is said that the only things certain in life are death and taxes. That implies that everything else is uncertain. Probability is defined as the chance that an event will occur.[1] It is expressed as a number between 0 and 1 inclusive. A probability of 0 indicates there is no chance that an event will occur. A probability of 1 indicates that the event will happen with certainty. The probability of one's eventual death thus is 1, but the probability of one's death taking place tomorrow would be less than 1 (one hopes). The probability of a resident of the United States having to pay taxes of some sort (e.g., sales taxes, income taxes) is 1, but the probability of having to pay a certain specified amount in total taxes would be less than 1.

We encounter probability every day. The weather forecaster predicts a 40 percent chance of rain. That means that there is a probability of 0.40 that rain will occur, not that 40 percent of the viewers will experience rain. We are told that there is a 1 in 6 million chance of winning the lottery if we purchase one ticket. That means that there is a 0.0000001667 probability (1.667×10^{-7}) of winning the lottery by purchasing one ticket. Both the "odds" on sporting events and the chances of filling an inside straight in a casino card game are expressions of probability.

Probability is prominent in the quality field, too. If we select a sample of 10 defective units from a lot containing 100 units, what is the chance (probability) that we selected the only 10 defective units in the lot—that the 90 unsampled units are acceptable? When we make a decision based upon a statistical analysis, what is the probability of being wrong? When we say that a lot consisting of 100 male students has a mean height of 70.5 inches based upon the measurement of a sample of 10 students drawn from that lot, what is the probability that the true mean height of the lot is exactly 70.5 inches? These are questions involving probability.

BASIC PROBABILITY CONCEPTS

Probability is important in quality control because it provides a mechanism for quantifying and analyzing uncertainties associated with future events. Probability is expressed as a number which lies between 1.0 (certainty that an event will occur) and 0.0 (impossibility of occurrence). A convenient definition of probability is one based on a relative frequency interpretation: If an event E can occur in some number (x) cases out of a total of n possible and equally probable cases, the probability that the event will occur is:

$$P(E) = \frac{x}{n} = \frac{\text{number of successful cases/}}{\text{total number of possible cases}} \qquad (1.1)$$

where $P(E)$ is an expression which means the probability of the occurrence of event E.

EXAMPLE 1.1

Consider the case of a lot consisting of 100 parts from which a single part is selected at random (by *random*, we mean that each part has an equal chance of being selected). Suppose that the lot contains a total of 12 defectives (i.e., 12 defective parts). Then, the probability of drawing a single part that is defective (the event) is 12 (the number of "successful" draws—i.e., number of defective parts in the lot) divided by 100 (the total number of possible parts).

$$P(\text{selecting a defective part in single draw}) = \frac{12}{100} = 0.12$$

The following rules are used to solve probability problems.

RULE 1:   If $P(E)$ is the probability that event E will occur, then the probability that E will not occur is $1 - P(E)$.

This situation is illustrated in Figure 1.1. The total area inside the rectangle represents all the possible cases. The area inside the circle represents all the cases where event E can occur. The total area inside the rectangle minus the area inside the circle represents all the cases where event E cannot occur.

Using Example 1.1, the probability of selecting a conforming part (i.e., a part that is not defective) on a single draw is 1 minus the probability of selecting a defective part in a single draw.

$$P(\text{conforming part in single draw}) = 1 - 0.12 = 0.88$$

Joint probability is the probability of two events occurring simultaneously.

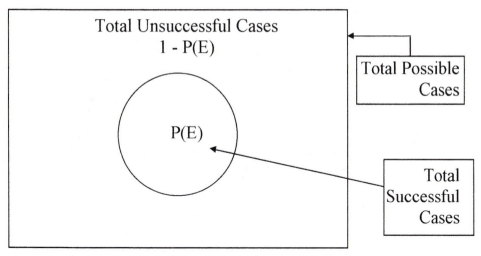

FIGURE 1.1   Relative frequency interpretation of probability.

EXAMPLE 1.2

An example of joint probability would be the probability of selecting a male student who is also a mathematics major in a single sample of 1 from a class of 100 students which contains 25 male students and 10 mathematics majors, 5 of whom are both male and mathematics majors. Since only 5 students in the population are both male and mathematics majors, the probability of selecting a male student who is a mathematics major is $\frac{5}{100} = 0.05$.

We can also determine the probabilities of either of two events occurring. This is written as $P(E1 \text{ or } E2)$, which is calculated using Rule 2.

RULE 2:   If $E1$ and $E2$ are two events, then the probability that either $E1$ or $E2$ occurs is:

$$P(E1 \text{ or } E2) = P(E1) + P(E2) - P(E1 \text{ and } E2) \qquad (1.2)$$

In Figure 1.2, the area inside both circles represents the probability of $E1$ or $E2$ occurring, but the overlapping area, representing $P(E1 \text{ and } E2)$, is counted twice (once with $E1$ and once with $E2$). Therefore, to calculate $P(E1 \text{ or } E2)$, $P(E1 \text{ and } E2)$ must be subtracted. Using the previous example:

$$P(\text{male or math major}) = P(\text{male}) + P(\text{math major})$$
$$- [P(\text{male and math major})]$$
$$P(\text{male or math major}) = 0.25 + 0.10 - 0.05 = 0.30$$

A special case of this rule applies when $E1$ and $E2$ cannot occur simultaneously. When this is the case, we describe $E1$ and $E2$ as being *mutually exclusive* of each other. Two items are said to be mutually exclusive when the probability of both items occurring simultaneously is zero, as shown in Figure 1.3. Then $P(E1 \text{ and } E2) = 0.0$ and Rule 2 becomes:

$$P(E1 \text{ or } E2) = P(E1) + P(E2) \qquad (1.3)$$

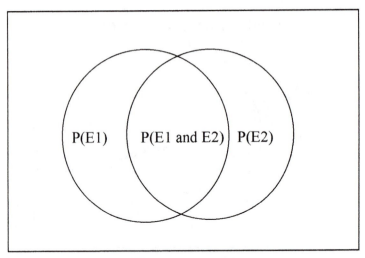

FIGURE 1.2 Joint probability.

EXAMPLE 1.3

An example of mutual exclusivity would be the probability of selecting a mathematics major and a statistics major in a single sample of 1 from a class of 100 students which contains 8 statistics majors and 10 mathematics majors. There are no double majors in the class. The probability of selecting 1 student who is both a mathematics and a statistics major is 0. The probability of selecting 1 student who is either a mathematics major or a statistics major is:

$$P(\text{stat or math major}) = P(\text{stat major}) + P(\text{math major}) = 0.08 + 0.10 = 0.18$$

Another useful equation deals with conditional probability. Conditional probability is the probability that an event ($E1$) will occur given that another event ($E2$) has already occurred. This concept is expressed as $P(E1|E2)$ and is calculated as:

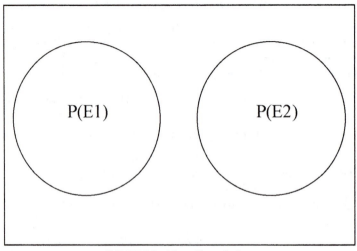

FIGURE 1.3 Mutually exclusive.

$$P(E1|E2) = \frac{P(E1 \text{ and } E2)}{P(E2)} \tag{1.4}$$

Conditional probability can be illustrated using Example 1.2. Given that the sample selected from the class is male, the probability that he is also a mathematics major is:

$$P(\text{math major}|\text{male}) = \frac{0.05}{0.25} = 0.20$$

This can be confirmed using the relative frequency approach. There are 25 male students in the class—5 of whom are mathematics majors. Given that the student selected is male, the probability of that male student also being a mathematics major is $\frac{5}{25} = 0.20$.

The *multiplicative rule* can be used to determine the probability of two events occurring simultaneously.

$$P(E1 \text{ and } E2) = P(E1) \times P(E2|E1) \quad \text{or}$$
$$P(E1 \text{ and } E2) = P(E2) \times P(E1|E2) \tag{1.5}$$

In other words, the probability of two events, $E1$ and $E2$, occurring together is equal to the probability that event 1 ($E1$) will occur times the probability that event 2 ($E2$) will occur *given* that event 1 has already occurred.

A special case of this rule occurs when the two events are *independent* of each other. That is, both items may occur separately or together, but neither relies on the other to determine its probability of occurring. Two events are independent if the occurrence of one event does not change the probability of the occurrence of the other event. If $E1$ and $E2$ are independent of each other, then the probability of one event occurring given that the other has occurred is:

$$P(E2|E1) = P(E2) \quad \text{and} \quad P(E1|E2) = P(E1) \tag{1.6}$$

And if $E1$ and $E2$ are independent of each other, then the probability of both $E1$ and $E2$ occurring is:

$$P(E1 \text{ and } E2) = P(E1) \times P(E2) \tag{1.7}$$

EXAMPLE 1.4

A complex system consists of two major subsystems that operate independently. The probability of successful performance of the first subsystem ($S1$) is 0.95. The corresponding probability for the second subsystem ($S2$) is 0.90. Both subsystems must operate successfully in order to achieve total system success. The probability of the successful operation of the total system, therefore, is calculated as follows:

$$P(S1 \text{ and } S2) = P(S1) \times P(S2) = 0.95 \times 0.90 = 0.8550$$

All the rules have been presented in terms of 2 events. However, each can be expanded to include any number of events.

EXAMPLE 1.5

Assume that we add a third independent subsystem to Example 1.4. This third subsystem (*S*3) operates in serial with the other 2 systems (thus, all 3 systems must operate in order for the system to operate successfully). If the probability of *S*3 = 0.99, what is the probability of the system to operate successfully as a whole?

$$P(S1 \text{ and } S2 \text{ and } S3) = P(S1) \times P(S2) \times P(S3) = 0.95 \times 0.90 \times 0.99 = 0.8465$$

Probability Experiments

A probability experiment is performed when a random process is observed and the results from the process are recorded. For example, we could perform an experiment of rolling a single die and recording the outcome (a value of 1,2,3,4,5, or 6) obtained from one roll. The values that represent all possible outcomes (1 through 6) are said to be mutually exclusive and collectively exhaustive. The term *mutually exclusive* means that only one value can be observed in any one roll. The term *collectively exhaustive* means that only this set of possible outcomes can occur. An event may be defined as a collection of sample outcomes. For example, we might roll a die 1,000 times to observe the number of times that each of the 6 possible outcomes occurs. One event might be 150 ones, 165 twos, 164 threes, 156 fours, 171 fives, and 194 sixes.

Random Variables and Probability Distributions

The collectively exhaustive set of outcomes from an experiment makes up a *sample space*. A mathematical function that assigns numerical values to every possible outcome in a sample space is called a *random variable*. A random variable can be either *discrete* or *continuous,* depending on the specific numerical values it may assume.

A *discrete random variable* can take on only distinct values. An example would be the number of defects observed in a sample. A *continuous random variable* can take on any real value over a specified interval of real numbers. An example would be the diameters of bearings being manufactured in a factory. Of course, the actual observed values for the variable are limited by the precision of the measuring device. In theory, however, this would still be a continuous random variable.

A *probability distribution* represents a theoretical model of the relative frequency of a random variable. The *probability density function* is the equation that allows us to calculate the probabilities for all values of the random variable. Relating probability distributions to the random variables that they represent allows us to classify the distributions as either discrete or continuous.

Discrete Probability Distributions

A *discrete probability distribution* is a table, graph, or equation that relates values of the discrete random variable to associated probabilities. Discrete probability distributions are frequently encountered in statistical quality control.[2] These include the uniform, hypergeometric, binomial, Poisson, and Pascal distributions.

TABLE 1.1   Probabilities of All Possible Outcomes
of the Roll of a Single Die

x	$f(x)$	
1	1/6	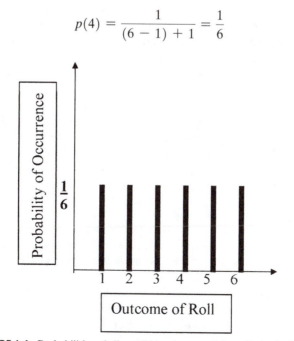
2	1/6	
3	1/6	
4	1/6	
5	1/6	
6	1/6	

The *uniform distribution* is used to model the taking of a random sample from a population where each discrete value of x has the same probability of occurrence. For example, the uniform distribution would be used to determine the probability of obtaining an outcome x on a single roll of a fair die. The values of possible outcomes, x, and the function describing the outcomes' probability of occurrence, $f(x)$, are shown in Table 1.1. These data can also be represented in graphical format as shown in Figure 1.4.

The probability density function for the uniform distribution is:

$$p(x) = \frac{1}{(b - a) + 1} \tag{1.8}$$

where the possible values of the random variable x fall between a and b. In the case of the single roll of a die, the probability density function can be used to determine the probability of obtaining a particular value. For example, the probability of obtaining a 4 on a single roll of a die is:

$$p(4) = \frac{1}{(6 - 1) + 1} = \frac{1}{6}$$

FIGURE 1.4   Probabilities of all possible outcomes of the roll of a single die.

The *hypergeometric distribution* is used to model the taking of a random sample from a finite population without replacement. For example, this model can be used to determine the probability of selecting x defective items in a sample of size n taken without replacement from a population of size N which contains D defective units.

The *binomial distribution* is used to model the taking of a random sample from an infinite population and where the outcome of each observation is either a "success" or a "failure." For example, this model can be used to determine the probability of selecting x defective units in a random sample of size n taken from a very large population of units which contains a fraction defective of p.

The *Poisson distribution* is used to model the probability that a unit taken from a population where the number of defects per unit is λ contains x number of defects.

For a discrete probability distribution, two conditions must hold:

- All probabilities must be greater than or equal to zero.
- The sum of all values of the random variable x must equal 1.

The uses of the hypergeometric, binomial, and Poisson distributions will be discussed further in Chapter 2.

Continuous Probability Distributions

Continuous probability distributions are extremely important distributions in statistical quality control applications. Examples include the normal, exponential, gamma, and Weibull distributions. A continuous random variable takes on all real values over some specified interval. Thus, we cannot calculate the probability of a specific value. Instead, we must talk about the probability that the random variable takes on some value within the interval. The function that describes the probability of ranges of values of a continuous random variable is called a *probability density function,* the uses of which will be discussed in Chapter 2.

The *normal distribution* is very widely used in quality control. It is the basis for the x-bar chart. The *exponential distribution* is used to model component and system reliability. The normal and exponential distributions will be discussed further in Chapter 2. The *gamma distribution* is used in reliability engineering in cases where redundant components are used. The *Weibull distribution* is also used in reliability engineering to model time to failure for components and systems.

Expected Value

An extremely useful concept is that of the *expected value* of a random variable. Many statistical relationships and formulas depend on the use of this concept. The expected value of a random variable can be defined as its probability-weighted average value. As an example of the expected value calculation for a discrete variable, let us extend the previous probability example using a single fair die. If a game of chance pays $0.50 for each dot that appears when the single die is rolled (i.e., $0.50 for a 1, $1.00 for a 2, $1.50 for a 3, and so on), what will be the expected value of the amount that the player will receive?

Expected value $E(x) = 1/6(\$0.50) + 1/6(\$1.00) + 1/6(\$1.50) + 1/6(\$2.00) + 1/6(\$2.50) + 1/6(\$3.00)$

$$E(x) = \$1.75$$

Therefore, the long-run average winnings per roll of a single die would be $1.75.

SUMMARY

This chapter dealt with basic probability concepts. It provided an introduction to probability and its importance to the practicing quality engineer. The chapter serves as a primer for Chapter 2, which deals in depth with several of the topics introduced here.

This chapter has provided a basic understanding of the terms associated with probability analysis. The basic rules of probability analysis and their application were discussed. The effects of independence and mutual exclusivity on the probability rules were also discussed. An introduction to probability density functions was provided using the uniform distribution as the model. This concept will be built upon in Chapter 2 using other discrete and continuous probability distributions.

DISCUSSION QUESTIONS

1. Discuss what is meant by the term *mutually exclusive.*
2. Discuss the difference between a discrete random variable and a continuous random variable. Include an example of each.
3. Discuss what is meant by the term *probability distribution.*
4. Under what circumstances is the hypergeometric distribution the appropriate sampling distribution?
5. The rolling of a single die is an example of an event that would be appropriately modeled using which probability distribution? Explain.
6. Discuss what is meant by the term *expected value of a random variable.*

PROBLEMS

1. An assembly line manufactures in lots of 200 parts. Suppose a lot contains a total of 12 defectives (i.e., 12 defective parts). What is the probability of drawing from the lot a single part that is defective? What is the probability of drawing from the lot a single part that is not defective?
2. As part of a quality audit, a paint factory pulls a random sample of product from 2 different production lines. The sample consists of 100 units, 45 red samples and 55 blue samples. If 10 samples fail to meet specifications, what is the probability that a single sample of 1 will be:
   (a) red
   (b) red and defective
   (c) blue and defective
   (d) defective

3. Using the random sample in Problem 2, what is the probability that a single sample of one will be:

(a) red or defective

(b) blue or defective

(c) red or blue

4. A navigation device on an airliner consists of two major subsystems that operate independently. The probability of successful performance of the first subsystem is 0.99. The corresponding probability for the second subsystem is 0.95. Both subsystems must operate successfully in order to achieve total system success. What is the probability of the successful operation of the total system?

5. In an attempt to ensure continuous operation, a third independent subsystem is added to the navigation device in Problem 4. This third subsystem operates in serial with the other two systems (thus, all three systems must operate in order for the system to operate successfully). If the probability of the third system is 0.99, has the probability of the system as a whole successfully operating improved or not? Explain your answer.

NOTES

1. Kvanli, A. H., C. S. Guynes, & R. J. Pavur. *Introduction to Business Statistics,* 4th ed. St. Paul, MN: West, 1996, p. 104.

2. Montgomery, D. C. *Introduction to Statistical Quality Control,* 3rd ed. New York: Wiley, 1996, pp. 51–68.

SUGGESTED READINGS

Duncan, A. J. *Quality Control and Industrial Statistics,* 5th ed. Homewood, IL: Irwin, 1986, chap. 2, pp. 15–39.

Evans, J. R., & W. M. Lindsay. *The Management and Control of Quality,* 3rd ed. St. Paul, MN: West, 1996, pp. 628–626.

Grant, E. L., & R. S. Leavenworth. *Statistical Quality Control,* 7th ed. New York: McGraw-Hill, 1996, chap. 5, pp. 163–222.

Juran, J. M., & F. M. Gryna. *Quality Planning and Analysis,* 2nd ed. New York: McGraw-Hill, 1980, pp. 40–54.

Kvanli, A. H., C. S. Guynes, & R. J. Pavur. *Introduction to Business Statistics,* 4th ed. St. Paul, MN: West, 1996, chaps. 4 & 5, pp. 104–185.

Montgomery, D. C. *Introduction to Statistical Quality Control,* 3rd ed. New York: Wiley, 1996, pp. 51–70.

Render, B., & R. M. Stair. *Quantitative Analysis for Management,* 6th ed. Upper Saddle River, NJ: Prentice Hall, 1997, pp. 69–98.

CHAPTER 2

Fundamentals of Statistics

CHAPTER OBJECTIVES

This chapter introduces the following concepts:

- Statistical terms and concepts
- Distributions
- Statistical inference
- Correlation and regression analysis

INTRODUCTION

Walter Shewhart, the father of statistical quality control, justified the necessity for quality professionals to know statistics by quoting from two contemporaries:

> It is therefore important to every technician who is dealing with problems of manufacturing control to know the laws of statistics and to be able to apply them correctly to his problem.[1]

> Statistical research is a logical method for the control of operations, for the research engineer, the plant superintendent, and the production executive.[2]

W. Edwards Deming was also an advocate of statistical thinking:

> Only with the proper use of statistical methods can people minimize confusion in the presence of variation. Statistical methods help to understand processes, to bring them under control, and then improve them.[3]

Statistics is important to the quality engineer for its ability to turn data into information. Statistics provides the basis for accurately describing sets of data and for making inferences about populations based upon sample information. It provides the basis for determining whether a process is behaving predictably. It provides a means for determining whether relationships exist and how strong those relationships are.

This chapter is perhaps the most ambitious in this book. It reduces an entire book-length topic to a single chapter and is intended to provide a foundation upon which deeper knowledge of the subject can be built. The chapter introduces the terminology of statistics and discusses some of the more important discrete and continuous distributions, statistical inference, and correlation and regression analysis. Later chapters will apply these concepts to real-world situations. The format is intended to link the conceptual world of statistics to the real world of statistical analysis.

TERMS AND CONCEPTS

The language of statistics is at first foreign, but later comforting. The comfort is in the precision of the language. With few words, statisticians can convey enormous amounts of information.

EXAMPLE 2.1

Consider the case of an engineer who is assigned to determine the height of all the 150 male employees in a plant. The collection of all 150 male employees is referred to as the *population*. Since we can count the elements in this population, it is referred to as a *finite population*.

> DEFINITION: A population is "the totality of items or units of material under consideration."[4]

The engineer measures and records the height of each employee as he reports for duty. Each measurement is called an *observation* or an *observed value*.

> DEFINITION: An observation or observed value is "the particular value of a characteristic determined as a result of a test or measurement."[5]

All the height observations made by the engineer are recorded in Table 2.1.

TABLE 2.1   Unorganized Data—Heights of Male Employees

66	73	70	69	73
69	65	75	67	74
71	69	71	75	71
74	67	68	72	67
77	64	65	71	70
64	74	70	69	75
68	72	72	65	72
70	68	74	68	66
67	66	76	71	72
75	76	65	73	70
72	73	66	75	71
70	70	68	72	74
67	65	71	67	68
69	67	73	69	69
76	71	74	71	71
66	69	72	70	74
68	73	71	68	69
70	75	73	69	71
72	69	71	73	70
71	71	68	70	73
70	73	69	71	74
74	72	71	68	69
72	68	74	73	71
66	70	72	71	72
68	71	71	69	74
70	74	68	74	71
74	73	70	72	70
73	67	72	69	73
72	69	74	71	72
68	70	71	70	73

It is difficult to draw any conclusions from the data in Table 2.1 because the data are unorganized. Determining the height of a "typical" employee, or the height of the tallest or shortest employee, is not a simple task. But organizing the data into a frequency table, Table 2.2, reveals this information at a glance.

TABLE 2.2   Frequency Table—
Height of Male Employees

Height	Frequency
64	2
65	5
66	6
67	8
68	14
69	16
70	18
71	24
72	17
73	15
74	15
75	6
76	3
77	1

For example, we can say that there are more employees that are 71 inches tall than any other height. This is referred to as the *mode* and is a measure of central tendency of the data set.

DEFINITION: The mode is "the most frequent value of the variable."[6]

We can also see that the range of heights is $77 - 64 = 13$ inches. The *range* is a measure of the dispersion of the data set.

DEFINITION: The range is "a measure of dispersion which is the difference between the largest observed value and the smallest observed value in a given sample."[7]

A *frequency histogram* of the data is even more revealing. As Figure 2.1 shows, the employee heights are rather evenly distributed on either side of the mode.

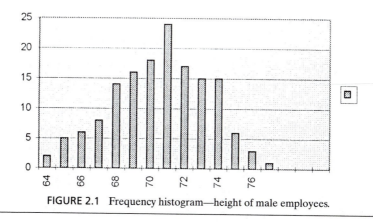

FIGURE 2.1   Frequency histogram—height of male employees.

Levels of Measurement

In basic statistics, there are four levels (or scales) of data measurement. They are (in order from weakest to strongest): nominal, ordinal, interval, and ratio.

Nominal Measurement. Nominal measurement consists of classifying data into mutually exclusive and collectively exhaustive categories. Numerical values may be assigned to the data, but the magnitude of the number has no meaning other than to distinguish one item from another. An example of a nominal measure would be assigning the number 1 to represent females and the number 0 to represent males.

Ordinal Measurement. Ordinal measurement consists of not only classifying data into categories, but ordering or ranking the data as well, so that the magnitude of the number has a relative meaning in terms of a measurement being larger or smaller than another measurement. An example of an ordinal measure would be rank-ordering 10 companies within an industry on the basis of their sales.

Interval Measurement. Interval measurement not only classifies and ranks data, but establishes a unit of measurement, so that we can say *how much* larger or smaller one measurement is than another because the intervals between consecutive values are equal. The scale of measurement may have a zero point, but it will be an arbitrarily determined one. An example of interval measurement is the measurement of temperature. The Fahrenheit and Celsius scales are both used to measure temperature and both have different zero points. Because there is no natural zero point, 50 degrees is not twice as hot as 25 degrees on either scale.

Ratio Measurement. Ratio measurement is similar to an interval measurement except that a ratio scale must also start from an absolute zero point. For example, a 10-year-old is twice as old as a 5-year-old, because age is measured from an absolute zero point (the day of exit from the womb). The previous example of measuring male employee height is an example of a ratio measure—the height scale has an absolute zero point.

DESCRIPTIVE STATISTICS

Descriptive statistics are used to describe and summarize data. Table 2.1 (in Example 2.1) illustrates that raw data are often difficult to understand. Simply arranging the data into an organized form (Table 2.2) provides us with knowledge about the test sample.

Descriptive statistics allow us to understand the properties of data and the various summary measures computed from the data. There are two types of data—quantitative and qualitative. Quantitative data have three main descriptive measures:

- Central tendency
- Dispersion or variation
- Shape

Measures of Central Tendency

Central tendency refers to the examination of data to determine about which point most of the data are centered or to determine the most frequently occurring data value. One of the most commonly used measures of central tendency is the mode. The mode, which is the value that occurs with the greatest frequency, was already discussed in Example 2.1. Another commonly used measure of central tendency is the *median*.

> **DEFINITION:**   The median is the positional average or the center point of a set of ordered observations—half of the observations are below the median, and half are above the median.

EXAMPLE 2.2

A farmer harvests 9 watermelons on a given day and weighs them all. The 9 weights in pounds are arrayed from smallest to largest:

$$9 \quad 10 \quad 11 \quad 12 \quad 15 \quad 16 \quad 16 \quad 16 \quad 51$$

The median in this case is 15—the center value of the set of 9 observations. Had there been an even number of observations, the median would have been the average of the 2 center values.

The most popular measure of central tendency is the *arithmetic mean* or average.

> **DEFINITION:**   The arithmetic mean is "a measure of central tendency or location which is the sum of the observations divided by the number of observations."[8]

The mean of a population, μ, is defined as the sum of the observations divided by the number of observations in the population, N.

$$\mu = \frac{\Sigma x}{N} \tag{2.1}$$

The mean of a sample, $\bar{x}$, is defined as the sum of the observations divided by the number of observations in the sample, n.

$$\bar{x} = \frac{\Sigma x}{n} \tag{2.2}$$

In the case of Example 2.2, the 9 observations represent a population—the entire day's output of watermelons. Therefore we use Equation (2.1) to calculate the value of the population mean as $\frac{156}{9} = 17.3$. Notice the effect of the single very large melon on the measures of central tendency. It has no effect on the mode (16) and it has no effect on the median (15), but it causes the mean to be higher than the median. In fact, only one melon is as heavy as or heavier than the mean. The abnormally large value, 51, is referred to as an *outlier*.

DEFINITION: An outlier is an observation that is unusually larger or smaller than the other values in a data set.

When outliers are present, the median is frequently a better measure of central tendency than the mean because, unlike the mean, the median is not affected by extreme values.

Measures of Dispersion or Variation

Variation is a measure of the spread of the data (shown in Figure 2.2). Measures of variation include the range, the standard deviation, and the variance. The range measures the distance between the two extreme points in the data set, while the variance and standard deviation measure the dispersion of the data about the mean.

We discussed the range in Example 2.1. The range of the population in Example 2.2 is $51 - 9 = 42$. The range is easy to calculate but is heavily influenced by the presence of outliers. A better measure of dispersion is the *variance*.

DEFINITION: The variance is "a measure of the variability (dispersion) of observations based upon the mean of the squared deviations from the arithmetic mean."[9]

One would think a simple measure of dispersion could be calculated by simply averaging the deviations from the mean. In the case of Example 2.2, those deviations would be:

$$-8.3 \quad -7.3 \quad -6.3 \quad -5.3 \quad -2.3 \quad -1.3 \quad -1.3 \quad -1.3 \quad +33.7$$

The sum of the deviations is 0.3. The average deviation is $\dfrac{0.3}{9} = 0.033$ (nonzero due to rounding). This does not reflect the true average deviation from the mean because the negative deviations cancel the positive deviations. For this reason we use the variance, which is the sum of the *squared* deviations from the mean divided by the number of observations in the population. The variance of a population, σ^2, is defined as:

$$\sigma^2 = \frac{\Sigma(x - \mu)^2}{N} \tag{2.3}$$

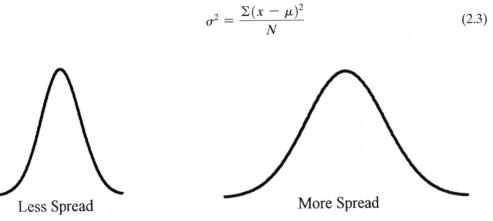

Less Spread   More Spread

FIGURE 2.2   Differences in the spread of the data.

The variance of a sample, s^2, is defined as:

$$s^2 = \frac{\Sigma(x - \bar{x})^2}{n - 1} \tag{2.4}$$

Since the 9 observations in Example 2.2 represent a population, we use Equation (2.3) to calculate the value of the population variance as $\dfrac{1,336.01}{9} = 148.45$.

The positive square root of the variance is called the standard deviation. In the case of Example 2.2, the population standard deviation is $\sigma = 12.18$. An advantage of the standard deviation over the variance is that it is in the same units as the observations—in this case pounds.

These measures are only valid when using interval or ratio data. If the data are nominal or ordinal, other nonparametric measures are needed.

Measures of Shape

The two main measures of shape, *skewness* and *kurtosis,* measure the symmetry and the peakedness of the data set (distribution).

DEFINITION: Skewness is "a measure of the symmetry of a distribution."[10]

A perfectly symmetrical distribution has a skewness coefficient of 0. A positive skewness coefficient indicates that the mean is larger than the median (skewed right). A negative skewness indicates that the median is larger than the mean (skewed left).

DEFINITION: Kurtosis is "a measure of the shape of a distribution."[11] A negative value for kurtosis indicates that the distribution is more peaked (has shorter tails) than the normal distribution.

DISTRIBUTIONS

In Chapter 1 a number of discrete and continuous distributions were introduced. In this section the use in statistics of those and other distributions is discussed.

Important Discrete Distributions

The Hypergeometric Distribution.   Consider the height data from Table 2.2. Assume that the company is sending 5 of its employees to a training program to qualify them as commercial test pilots. One of the qualifications of the program is that students not be over 75 inches in height. From Table 2.2 we can see that 4 of our 150 employees do not conform to this requirement. What is the probability that in a random sample of 10 employees taken from this population, there will be 2 or fewer employees who are too tall to qualify for the program (nonconforming)? Since we are taking a random sample from a finite population without replacement, and the population is classified according to conformance or nonconformance to the height standard, the hypergeometric distribution is the appropriate discrete distribution to use to model this situation.

The mean of the hypergeometric distribution is:

$$\mu = \frac{nD}{N} \tag{2.5}$$

and the variance is:

$$\sigma^2 = \frac{nD}{N}\left(1 - \frac{D}{N}\right)\left(\frac{N-n}{N-1}\right) \tag{2.6}$$

The probability density function for the hypergeometric distribution is:

$$p(x) = \frac{\begin{bmatrix} D \\ x \end{bmatrix}\begin{bmatrix} N-D \\ n-x \end{bmatrix}}{\begin{bmatrix} N \\ n \end{bmatrix}} \tag{2.7}$$

where N is the total number of items in the population, n is the sample size, D is the number of items in the population which fall into the classification of interest, and x is a hypergeometric random variable representing the number of items in the sample which fall into the classification of interest. The notation $\begin{bmatrix} a \\ b \end{bmatrix}$ represents the number of combinations of a items taken b at a time and is calculated:

$$\begin{bmatrix} a \\ b \end{bmatrix} = \frac{a!}{b!(a-b)!} \tag{2.8}$$

Using the probability density function we can determine the probability of there being fewer than 2 employees who do not conform to the height standard in a random sample of 10 taken from the population as $p(x=0) + p(x=1)$. Using the probability density function:

$$p(x=0) = \frac{\begin{bmatrix} 4 \\ 0 \end{bmatrix}\begin{bmatrix} 150-4 \\ 10-0 \end{bmatrix}}{\begin{bmatrix} 150 \\ 10 \end{bmatrix}} = 0.757$$

$$p(x=1) = \frac{\begin{bmatrix} 4 \\ 1 \end{bmatrix}\begin{bmatrix} 150-4 \\ 10-1 \end{bmatrix}}{\begin{bmatrix} 150 \\ 10 \end{bmatrix}} = 0.221$$

Therefore, $p(x<2) = 0.757 + 0.221 = 0.978$.

The Binomial Distribution.   Consider the case of a forester who is harvesting trees from a 10,000-acre site. The site was planted 10 years ago with new, fast-growth hybrid seedlings. The trees are being harvested for use in making paper. Recently, it has been found that the hybrid has a genetic defect that causes 2.0 percent of the trees to be unsuitable for paper making. The distribution of defective trees is random throughout the forest. The trees are harvested in discrete lots of 100. Any individual lot which contains 3 or fewer of the defective trees would be suitable for use. Lots containing more than 3 of the defective trees would create defective paper if used without sorting. The forester wishes to determine the probability of a given lot containing more than 3 defective trees. Since we are sampling an infinite population with a known fraction defective, p, the binomial distribution is the appropriate discrete distribution to use to model this situation.

The mean of the binomial distribution is:

$$\mu = np \tag{2.9}$$

and the variance is:

$$\sigma^2 = np(1 - p) \tag{2.10}$$

The probability density function for the binomial distribution is:

$$p(x) = \begin{bmatrix} n \\ x \end{bmatrix} p^x (1 - p)^{n-x} \tag{2.11}$$

where n is the sample size, p is the proportion of defective trees in the population, and x is a binomial random variable representing the number of items in the sample which fall into the classification of interest.

Using the probability density function we can calculate the probability that there will be 3 or fewer defective trees in a lot (sample) of 100:

$$P(x = 0) = \begin{bmatrix} 100 \\ 0 \end{bmatrix} (0.02)^0 (1 - 0.02)^{100-0} = 0.00265$$

$$P(x = 1) = \begin{bmatrix} 100 \\ 1 \end{bmatrix} (0.02)^1 (1 - 0.02)^{100-1} = 0.27065$$

$$P(x = 2) = \begin{bmatrix} 100 \\ 2 \end{bmatrix} (0.02)^2 (1 - 0.02)^{100-2} = 0.27341$$

$$P(x = 3) = \begin{bmatrix} 100 \\ 3 \end{bmatrix} (0.02)^3 (1 - 0.02)^{100-3} = 0.18228$$

Therefore, $p(x \leq 3) = 0.00265 + 0.27065 + 0.27341 + 0.18228 = 0.72889$. Then the probability of a given lot containing more than 3 defective trees is:

$$P(x > 3) = 1 - p(x \leq 3) = 1 - 0.72889 = 0.27111$$

The Poisson Distribution.   Consider the case of an automobile manufacturer who produces vehicles for the mass market. Part of the final inspection process involves inspecting the finish of the vehicles. The internal specification says that vehicles may have up to 5 minor defects in the paint finish and still be considered acceptable. Vehicles with more than 5 minor defects in the finish are classified as nonconforming. Past history indicates that the number of minor paint finish defects per vehicle is Poisson distributed and the long-run mean number of defects per vehicle from the process is 2. What is the probability that a vehicle randomly selected from this process will contain 5 or fewer minor paint finish defects?

The Poisson distribution is the applicable distribution to use to answer this question. The mean and variance of the Poisson distribution are both equal to the parameter λ. The mean is:

$$\mu = \lambda \tag{2.12}$$

and the variance is:

$$\sigma^2 = \lambda \tag{2.13}$$

The probability density function for the Poisson distribution is:

$$p(x) = \frac{e^{-\lambda}\lambda^x}{x!} \tag{2.14}$$

where e is the base of the natural logarithms ($e = 2.71828$). Using the probability density function we can calculate the probability that there will be 5 or fewer minor paint finish defects in a randomly selected vehicle from this process:

$$p(x \le 5) = \sum_{x=0}^{5} \frac{e^{-2}2^x}{x!} = 0.1353 + 0.2727 + 0.2707 + 0.1804 + 0.0902 + 0.0361$$

$$= 0.9834$$

Important Continuous Distributions

The Normal Distribution.   A definitive study has determined that the heights of males residing in the town of This are normally distributed with a mean of 71 inches and a variance of 3 inches. The special notation which is often used to express this information is $x \sim N(71, 3)$. What is the probability of selecting one male This town resident at random who is 76 inches or more in height? This question can be addressed using the normal distribution.

The normal distribution, often referred to as the *bell curve,* is a symmetric continuous distribution where the mean, median, and mode are equal. Under the assumption of normality, the *empirical rule* applies (see Figure 2.3).

1. Approximately 68 percent of the data values fall between $\mu + 1\sigma$ and $\mu - 1\sigma$.
2. Approximately 95 percent of the data values fall between $\mu + 2\sigma$ and $\mu - 2\sigma$.
3. Approximately 99.7 percent of the data values fall between $\mu + 3\sigma$ and $\mu - 3\sigma$.

The mean of the normal distribution is given by Equation (2.1) and the variance by Equation (2.3). The probability density function for the normal distribution is:

$$f(x) = \frac{1}{\sigma\sqrt{2\pi}} e^{\frac{-1}{2}\left(\frac{x-\mu}{\sigma}\right)^2}$$

(2.15)

where e is the base of the natural logarithms ($e = 2.71828$). We could use the probability density function to calculate the probability that a single male randomly selected from the population of This town's male residents will be at least 76 inches tall. However, it is easier and more common to use the standard normal distribution table (Appendix B). By using the formula:

$$z = \frac{x - \mu}{\sigma}$$

(2.16)

we can convert the $N(\mu, \sigma^2)$ random variable into an $N(0, 1)$ random variable. This process is known as *standardization*. Addressing the question posed:

$$\mu = 71 \quad \text{and} \quad \sigma = \sqrt{3} = 1.7321$$

Using Equation (2.16):

$$z = \frac{76 - 71}{1.7321} = 2.89$$

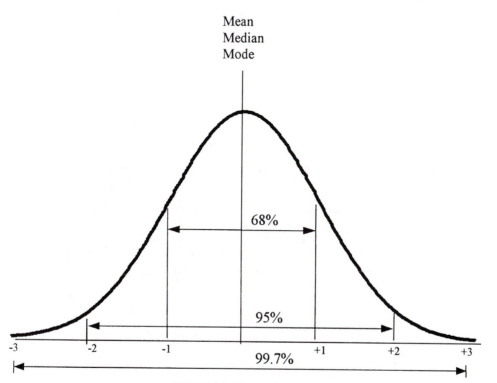

FIGURE 2.3   The empirical rule.

Using the standard normal distribution table in Appendix B, we find that the probability of x (76) being to the left of $z = 2.89$ is 0.9981. This is the probability that the single random sample taken from this population will be 76 inches tall or *shorter*. The probability that the individual will be 76 inches tall or *taller* is:

$$1 - 0.9981 = 0.0019$$

Because of its name and its widespread applicability, some believe that being normally distributed is the natural (normal) state of things. This is erroneous, and care must be taken in assuming normality. The central limit theorem is often used as a justification of the approximate normality of a distribution. The central limit theorem states that the distribution of sample means taken from a population will be approximately normally distributed.[12] This approximation is valid for samples taken from populations which are approximately normal if the sample size is at least 3 or 4.[13] The approximation is reasonably valid for any population if the sample size is at least 30.[14]

The Exponential Distribution.   You are contemplating the purchase of an electrical component for a critical application. The supplier states that the mean time to failure, (MTTF—discussed in Chapter 8) is 5,000 hours. You wish to estimate the probability that a given component will not fail prior to 6,000 hours. The appropriate distribution to model this situation is the exponential distribution.

The mean of the exponential distribution is:

$$\mu = \frac{1}{\lambda} \tag{2.17}$$

and the variance is:

$$\sigma^2 = \frac{1}{\lambda^2} \tag{2.18}$$

The probability density function for the exponential distribution is:

$$f(x) = \lambda e^{-\lambda x} \tag{2.19}$$

where λ is a constant that is greater than or equal to zero (called the failure rate), and e is the base of the natural logarithms ($e = 2.71828$). The reciprocal of the failure rate, $\frac{1}{\lambda}$, is called the mean time to failure (MTTF) for nonrepairable items or mean time between failure (MTBF) for repairable items.

The probability that the exponential random variable X is greater than or equal to a specific value of x can be determined by:

$$P(X \geq x) = e^{\frac{-x}{\text{MTTF}}} \tag{2.20}$$

Using Equation (2.20) we can determine the probability of no failures before 6,000 hours:

$$p(\text{no failure prior to 6,000 hours}) = e^{\frac{-6,000}{5,000}} = 0.3012$$

STATISTICAL INFERENCE

Statistical inference involves attributing to an entire population the significant characteristics observed and measured in a sample from that population. An example would be using the sample statistics $\bar{x}$ and s to estimate the population parameters μ and σ.

EXAMPLE 2.3

A random sample of 100 parts was selected from a process. The lengths of these parts were measured, and the sample mean ($\bar{x}$) was calculated to be 4.521 cm. The best estimate we can make of the mean length (population mean, μ) of parts produced by this process would be 4.521.

Hypothesis Testing

> **DEFINITION:** Hypothesis tests (or significance tests) are "a method of deciding with certain predetermined risks of error (1) whether the population associated with a sample differs from the one that has been specified; (2) whether the populations associated with each of two samples differ; or (3) whether the populations associated with each of more than two samples differ."[15]

The general process of hypothesis testing will be introduced using the test for means where α is known.

Suppose that, based upon long-run testing of parts from this process, we knew that the length of the parts produced is normally distributed with a mean of 4.450 and a standard deviation of 0.500. Can we infer from the sample data in Example 2.3 that the process mean is unchanged at 4.450? We state this problem as a pair of hypotheses.

> **DEFINITION:** The null hypothesis (H_0) states that "there is no difference (null) between the population of the sample and the specified population (or between the populations associated with each sample). The null hypothesis can never be proved true. It can, however, be shown, with specified risks of error, to be untrue."[16]

> **DEFINITION:** The alternative hypothesis (H_a) is the "hypothesis that is accepted if the null hypothesis is disproved."[17]

In conducting hypothesis testing we must determine how much risk of making the wrong decision we are willing to accept. Rejecting H_0 when it is true is called a Type I error. The probability of making a Type I error is referred to as α. Failing to reject H_0 when it is false is called a Type II error. The probability of making a Type II error is referred to as β. α and β are related. The smaller α is, the larger β becomes for a given sample size. So in practice we only specify the value of α. We choose a large value for α if the cost associated with a Type II error is large relative to the cost of a Type I error and a small value for α if the situation is reversed. The α that is selected is referred to as the *level of significance*.

In the case of our example the null hypothesis is:

$$H_0: \quad \mu = 4.450$$

The alternative hypothesis can be expressed in one of two ways:

$$H_a: \quad \mu \neq 4.450 \quad \text{(two-tailed test)}$$
$$H_a: \quad \mu > 4.450 \quad \text{(one-tailed test)}$$

The test statistic [based on Equation (2.16)] is:

$$z = \frac{\bar{x} - \mu_0}{\sigma/\sqrt{n}} \tag{2.21}$$

where μ_0 is the hypothesized value of μ (from H_0). The value of the test statistic for Example 2.3 is:

$$z = \frac{4.521 - 4.450}{0.50/\sqrt{100}} = 1.42$$

If we select an $\alpha = 0.05$, and use the one-tailed test, we find in the table in Appendix B that the value of $z_{1-0.05} = z_{0.95} = 1.645$. Since the test statistic value of 1.42 is smaller than 1.645, we fail to reject H_0 and cannot conclude from the sample results that the process mean has shifted to a value greater than 4.450.

This section provides an introduction to the concept of hypothesis testing. The reader is referred to the suggested readings for information about specific hypothesis tests (e.g., for comparison of means, comparison of variances).

CORRELATION AND SIMPLE LINEAR REGRESSION ANALYSIS

Correlation Analysis

Bivariate data consist of data for two variables for each observation. Correlation analysis allows the estimation of the linear relationship between the two variables.

For example, a manufacturer wishes to determine if there is a linear relationship between annual sales of kitchen sinks and annual issuance of residential building permits. Data collected covering the past 10 years are shown in Table 2.3.

A scatter diagram (discussed in Chapter 3) can be used to graphically evaluate the relationship between two variables, but it is difficult to evaluate the strength of the relationship using a scatter diagram. To measure the strength of the relationship, the *correlation coefficient* is used.

DEFINITION: The correlation coefficient is a "number between −1 and 1 that indicates the degree of linear relationship between two sets of numbers."[18] A

TABLE 2.3   Kitchen Sink Sales and Building Permits Issued

Year	Sink Sales	Building Permits
1985	2,056,000	2,730,000
1986	2,137,000	2,755,000
1987	2,155,000	2,812,000
1988	2,237,000	2,815,000
1989	2,250,000	2,835,000
1990	2,374,000	2,945,000
1991	2,405,000	3,102,000
1992	2,451,000	3,200,000
1993	2,515,000	3,305,000
1994	2,603,000	3,453,000

correlation coefficient of -1 indicates a perfect negative (inverse) linear relationship; a correlation coefficient of $+1$ indicates a perfect positive linear relationship. A correlation coefficient of 0 indicates no linear relationship between the variables.

The correlation coefficient r is calculated:

$$r_{xy} = \frac{n\Sigma XY - \Sigma X \Sigma Y}{\sqrt{[n\Sigma X^2 - (\Sigma X)^2][n\Sigma Y^2 - (\Sigma Y)^2]}} \tag{2.22}$$

Putting the data from Table 2.3 into Equation (2.22) results in a value of $r_{xy} = 0.9626$, which indicates a strong positive correlation between annual sales of kitchen sinks and annual issuance of residential building permits. Correlation analysis cannot be used to establish cause and effect. The results of the analysis of the data in Table 2.3 show only that they move together, not that one is the cause of the movement of the other.

Simple Linear Regression Analysis

While correlation provides a measure of the linear relationship between two variables, simple linear regression determines "the *function* that indicates the linear relationship between two variables."[19] This function can be used as a model to predict the behavior of a dependent variable, Y, based on the behavior of one independent variable. Therefore, linear regression does posit a cause and effect relationship between the independent and dependent variables. Equation (2.23) shows the form of the simple linear regression model.

$$Y = b_0 + b_1 X + \epsilon \tag{2.23}$$

where b_0 is the Y intercept of the regression line, b_1 is the slope of the regression line, and ϵ is the error term (or the random part of the model).

The slope is calculated:

$$b_1 = \frac{n(\Sigma xy) - (\Sigma x)(\Sigma y)}{n(\Sigma x^2) - (\Sigma x)^2} \tag{2.24}$$

where n is the number of paired observations.

The Y intercept is calculated:

$$b_0 = \frac{\Sigma y - b\Sigma x}{n} \qquad (2.25)$$

Using the data in Table 2.3 and Equations (2.24) and (2.25), a linear model is obtained:

Annual sink sales $= 290.071 + 0.67716(\text{annual residential building permits})$

When using regression, the correlation coefficient r is calculated using Equation (2.22). The square of the correlation coefficient, r^2, is called the *coefficient of determination.*

> **DEFINITION:** The coefficient of determination is that "part of the variance for one variable that can be explained by its linear relationship with a second variable."[20]

The correlation coefficient r has already been calculated as 0.9626. The coefficient of determination, r^2, then is $(0.9626)^2 = 0.9266$. This is interpreted to mean that 92.66 percent of the variation in the sales of kitchen sinks can be explained by the variation in the issue of residential building permits.

Assumptions.   Three assumptions must be satisfied in order to use regression analysis:

1. Variations around the regression line are random. This can be observed visually by observing a plot of the data and the regression line.
2. Deviations of the points around the regression line should be normally distributed.
3. The errors are independent of each other.

SUMMARY

This chapter introduced the terminology of statistics and discussed some of the distributions of particular importance in the quality field. An introduction was provided to descriptive and inferential statistics. Hypothesis testing, correlation, and regression analysis were discussed. The information in this chapter should be viewed as a foundation upon which to build a thorough knowledge of statistics. The reader is referred to the specialized sources listed in the Suggested Readings for more comprehensive discussions of these topics. Future chapters will apply the formulas and concepts from this chapter to solve real-world problems.

DISCUSSION QUESTIONS

1. What is the difference between a population and a sample?
2. List and define three measures of central tendency.
3. Define and give examples of nominal, ordinal, interval, and ratio measurements.
4. When would the median be a better measure of central tendency than the mean?

5. Why is the variance a better measure of dispersion than the range?
6. Discuss the appropriate applications of the hypergeometric and the binomial distributions.
7. What is the empirical rule?
8. Discuss the difference between discrete and continuous distributions.
9. What is the null hypothesis?
10. What does a correlation coefficient of 0 imply?
11. Discuss the assumptions that must be satisfied in order to use regression analysis.

PROBLEMS

Measurements were taken during the afternoon shift at a pipe fitting plant. The following data were collected on the length of the cuttings:

Cutting Number	Size (inches)	Cutting Number	Size (inches)
1	6.01	10	6.02
2	5.99	11	6.01
3	5.96	12	6.12
4	5.98	13	5.99
5	6.02	14	5.98
6	5.99	15	5.97
7	6.00	16	6.02
8	6.12	17	6.01
9	6.02	18	6.00

1. Rearrange the table into a frequency table.
2. Plot the data on a frequency histogram.
3. What level of measurement was used to gather the data—nominal, ordinal, interval, or ratio?
4. Determine the mean, median, and mode of the population.
5. What is the range of the values in the population?
6. What is the variance of the cuttings?
7. What type of distribution do you think is represented by these data? Support your answer.

NOTES

1. Springer, J. *Anwendungen der Mathematischen Statistik auf Probleme der Massenfabrikation.* Berlin, 1927; in Shewhart, W. A. *Economic Control of Quality of Manufactured Product.* New York: Van Nostrand, 1931; as cited in Sower, V. E., J. Motwani, & M. J. Savoie. *Classic Readings in Operations Management.* Ft. Worth, TX: Dryden, 1995, p. 193.
2. Daeves, K. H. "The Utilization of Statistics," *Testing,* March, 1924; in Shewhart, W. A. *Economic Control of Quality of Manufactured Product.* New York: Van Nostrand, 1931; as cited in Sower, V. E., J. Motwani, & M. J. Savoie. *Classic Readings in Operations Management.* Ft. Worth, TX: Dryden, 1995, p. 193.

3. Walton, M. *The Deming Management Method.* New York: Perigee, 1986, p. 96.

4. ASQC Statistics Division. *Glossary & Tables for Statistical Quality Control.* Milwaukee, WI: ASQC Quality Press, 1983, p. 3.

5. Ibid., p. 3.

6. Ibid., p. 18.

7. Ibid., p. 21.

8. Ibid., p. 17.

9. Ibid., p. 19.

10. Ibid., pp. 22–23.

11. Ibid., p. 23.

12. Duncan, A. J. *Quality Control and Industrial Statistics,* 5th ed. Homewood, IL: Irwin, 1986, p. 136.

13. Montgomery, D. C. *Introduction to Statistical Quality Control,* 3rd ed. New York: Wiley, 1996, p. 62.

14. Kvanli, A. H., C. S. Guynes, & R. J. Pavur. *Introduction to Business Statistics,* 4th ed. St. Paul, MI; West, 1996, p. 232.

15. ASQC Statistics Division, pp. 97–98.

16. Ibid., p. 98.

17. Ibid., p. 98.

18. Ibid., pp. 23–24.

19. Ibid., p. 24.

20. Ibid., p. 24.

SUGGESTED READINGS

ASQC Statistics Division. *Glossary & Tables for Statistical Quality Control.* Milwaukee, WI: ASQC Quality Press, 1983.

Christensen, H. B., & the Statistics Instructional Development Team, Brigham Young University. *Statistics Step by Step.* Boston: Houghton Mifflin Company, 1977.

Conover, W. J. *Practical Nonparametric Statistics,* 2nd ed. New York: Wiley, 1980.

Duncan, A. J. *Quality Control and Industrial Statistics,* 5th ed. Homewood, IL: Irwin, 1986.

Juran, J. M., and F. M. Gryna, Jr. *Quality Planning and Analysis,* 3rd ed. New York: McGraw-Hill, 1990.

Kenet, R., & S. Zacks. *Modern Industrial Statistics: The Design and Control of Quality and Reliability.* Pacific Grove, CA: Duxbury Press, 1998.

Kvanli, A. H., C. S. Guynes, & R. J. Pavur. *Introduction to Business Statistics,* 4th ed. West, St. Paul, MI: 1996.

Montgomery, D. C. *Introduction to Statistical Quality Control,* 3rd ed. New York: Wiley, 1996, Chapters 2 and 3.

Montgomery, D. C., G. Runger, & N. Hubele. *Engineering Statistics.* New York: Wiley, 1998.

Vining, G. G. *Statistical Methods for Engineers.* Pacific Grove, CA: Duxbury Press, 1998.

CHAPTER 3

Quality Improvement Tools

CHAPTER OBJECTIVES

This chapter introduces the following topics:

- The problem-solving process
- The seven tools of quality
- The seven management tools
- Quality Function Deployment

INTRODUCTION

Quality engineers are often engaged in a process that is called *problem solving*. This process is better defined as consisting of seven separate stages: symptom recognition, fact finding, problem identification, idea generation, solution development, plan implementation, and follow-up. There are a number of tools available to the quality engineer that are effective in each of these stages. This chapter will focus on seven quality tools (the seven tools of quality) and seven management tools (seven new tools of quality) and how they can be used in each stage of the problem-solving process.

The chapter ends with a discussion of Quality Function Deployment (QFD). Quality Function Deployment is a valuable tool for ensuring that customer requirements are taken into consideration during the design process.

THE PROBLEM-SOLVING PROCESS

Evans and Lindsay[1] describe a six-step problem-solving process which is adapted from creative problem-solving concepts developed by Osborn[2] and by Parnes et al.[3] The model developed in this chapter is based upon the Evans and Lindsay model but with a seventh step added. Figure 3.1 illustrates this model.

Symptom recognition involves understanding how the system works and how it should be performing. A symptom is an inconsistency between how the system is expected to perform and how it is actually performing. Tools which are useful in the recognition of symptoms are flow charts, run charts, and process control charts.

In the *fact-finding* step, data must be collected for analysis to provide insight into the nature of the problem which is creating the symptoms. Check sheets and run charts are useful in this step.

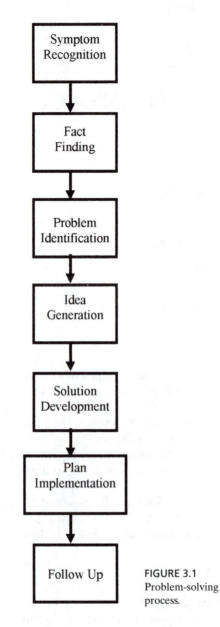

FIGURE 3.1
Problem-solving
process.

Problem identification involves sorting out the real problem from the symptoms created by that problem. Flow charts, check sheets, and Pareto analysis are useful tools in the problem identification step. In this step, data are collected in order to better understand the causal system and relationships involved in the problem.

Idea generation is directed toward determining the possible causes for the problem (root cause analysis) and *developing alternative courses of corrective action* to address the problem. Cause and effect diagrams and scatter diagrams are useful in this step.

In the *solution development step,* alternative ideas for addressing the problem are evaluated and the best course of action is selected for implementation.

Plan implementation is the step in which the selected course of action is actually put into effect. The seven management tools are useful in this step.

While the plan implementation step is often seen as the last step in the problem-solving process, an additional step, *follow-up,* has been added to this model. That is because "the best laid schemes o' mice an' men gang aft agley."[4] Follow-up is important to ensure that the solution implemented has had the desired effect. Process control charts and run charts are useful in this stage.

THE SEVEN TOOLS OF QUALITY

The seven tools of quality are relatively simple but very powerful tools which every quality engineer should master. Indeed these tools are routinely used by individuals and groups throughout organizations to address all sorts of problems. The tools, shown in Figure 3.2, are:

Flow chart

Run chart

Process control chart

Check sheet

Pareto diagram

Cause and effect diagram

Scatter diagram

Flow charts are used to define and to understand a process. ASQ defines a flow chart as "a graphical representation of the steps in a process. Flowcharts are drawn to better understand processes. The flowchart is one of the seven tools of quality."[5] There are conventions for the use of flow chart symbols (for example, see Galloway[6]); however, the consistent use of a given convention contributes more to understanding than the selection of a particular convention.

Flow charts can be produced easily by hand using templates, although most modern presentation software and word processors enable the creation of professional-looking flow charts quickly and with little effort. Specialized software packages are also available for all seven tools of quality.

Flow charts facilitate an analysis of the steps in a process to determine relationships between the steps. An example would be the precedence relationship between steps—which step(s) must precede which other step(s). Flow charts provide a means of visually depicting the steps and interrelationships without struggling through a lengthy textual description. This becomes more important the more complex the process becomes.

Flow charts facilitate the process of continuous improvement. Questions about which steps are value-adding and which are not are clarified by a flow chart. "Why is this step here?" and "What can we do to eliminate the need for this step?" are questions that flow charts facilitate. Figure 3.3 is a flow chart of a chemical batch process. Someone working to improve the process might question whether the

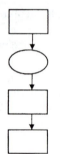

Flow Chart

Run Chart

Control Chart

Check Sheet

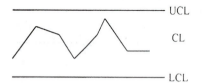

Pareto Diagram

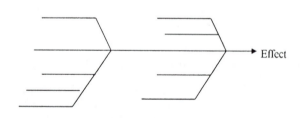

Effect

Cause and Effect Diagram

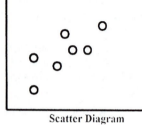

Scatter Diagram

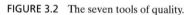

FIGURE 3.2   The seven tools of quality.

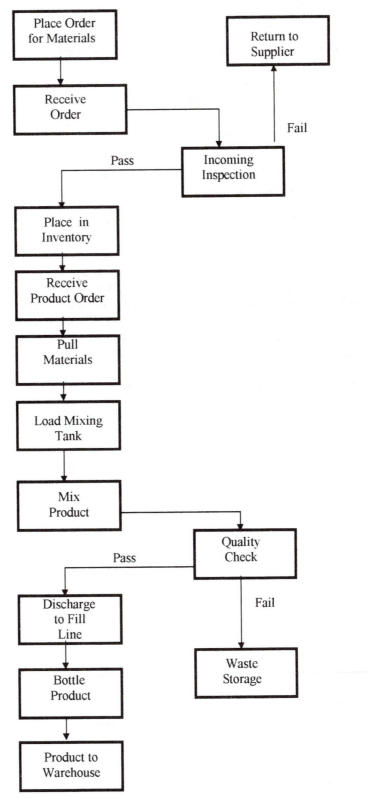

FIGURE 3.3 Mystery Chemical Inc. mixing process.

(non-value-adding) incoming material inspection could be eliminated by using supplier certification. Could improved control of the mixing process reduce the number of batches sent to waste storage?

A *run chart* is a graphical representation of the variation in a measurable characteristic over time. The measurable characteristic is represented on the vertical axis, and the time periods are represented on the horizontal axis. Run charts are useful in providing an indication of a possible shift in the characteristic being plotted. Figure 3.4 shows a run chart that Mystery Chemical uses to track rejections of product after mixing. The run chart provides evidence of a troubling rising trend in the percentage of chemical batches which are rejected and consigned to the waste storage tank. The use of the run chart alone provides no statistical evidence that the apparent trend is due to anything other than random variation alone.

The same data plotted on a *process control chart* (Figure 3.5—in this case a proportion defective or *p*-chart) provide clear evidence that the manufacturing process is out of control. The control chart (which is discussed in more detail in Chapter 4) is a tool which provides a means of determining what type of variation is present in a process and whether the process is performing predictably. It looks much like the run chart but with additional lines. These lines are the upper control limit (UCL), lower control limit (LCL), and centerline (CL). These lines define the average (CL) and extreme (UCL and LCL) performance of the process when it is behaving as designed (i.e., only random variation is present). Readings outside the UCL or LCL or unnatural patterns occurring within the UCL and LCL indicate that some new source of variation is affecting the process.

Check sheets are useful during data collection. They provide a simple means for recording data by categories and enable the analyst to determine the relative frequency of occurrence of the various categories of the data. Mystery Chemical

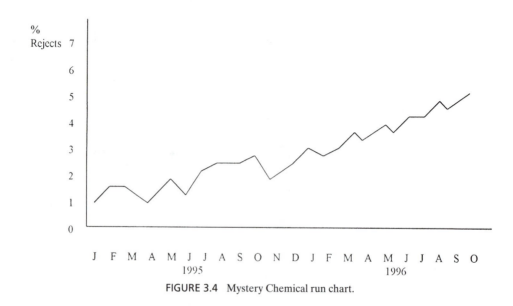

FIGURE 3.4   Mystery Chemical run chart.

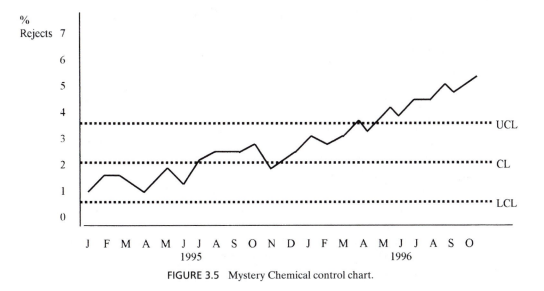

FIGURE 3.5 Mystery Chemical control chart.

may start collecting data about the causes for rejected batches. The check sheet used for this purpose is shown in Figure 3.6.

From the check sheet it is possible to easily determine that the most frequent reason for a defective batch is *poor dispersion. Wrong ingredient present* and *pigment degradation* are the least frequent reasons for a defective batch.

Another way to analyze data is by use of a *Pareto diagram.* Like the check sheet, the Pareto diagram provides the same type of insight into the most and least frequent occurrences. But the Pareto diagram provides a better organization of the

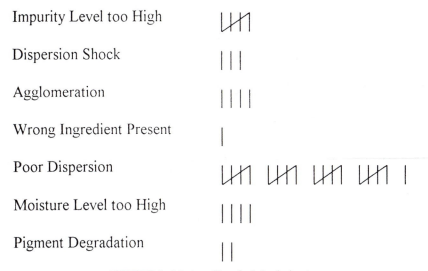

FIGURE 3.6 Mystery Chemical check sheet.

data than does the check sheet and also provides a more polished presentation. Frequently the results from a check sheet are transferred to a Pareto diagram for presentation.

The Pareto diagram sorts the data categories from highest to lowest and also shows the cumulative frequencies. This information is helpful in focusing attention on the highest-priority category. The Pareto diagram for the data in Figure 3.6 is shown in Figure 3.7.

The Pareto diagram clearly shows that Mystery Chemical could reduce the incidence of rejected batches by 52 percent if the company could identify the cause(s) of poor dispersion. Resources directed toward this one reason for rejected batches would likely have the highest potential payoff.

In order to reduce the incidence of rejected batches due to poor dispersion, Mystery Chemical must understand why poor dispersion occurs. *Cause and effect diagrams* are helpful at this stage. Mystery Chemical invited representatives from operations, quality control, process engineering, and development engineering to a meeting to brainstorm potential causes for poor dispersion. They used a cause and effect diagram, shown in Figure 3.8, to organize the ideas generated during the meeting.

At the end of the meeting the development engineer was assigned to investigate the methods, the quality engineer was assigned to investigate materials, the production supervisor was assigned to investigate the workers, and the process engineer was assigned to investigate the machines. The cause and effect diagram facilitated the logical assignment of responsibilities.

At the next team meeting, the quality engineer reported that a defective stack vent on one of the solvent tanks was allowing moisture to seep into the tank. Using

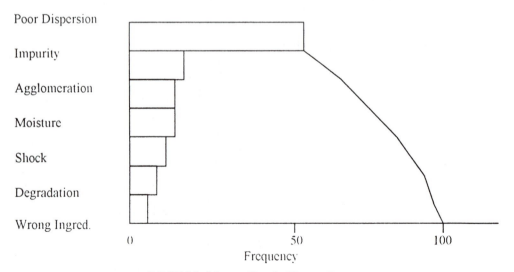

FIGURE 3.7   Mystery Chemical Pareto diagram.

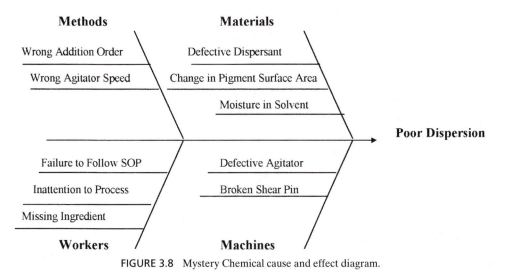

FIGURE 3.8   Mystery Chemical cause and effect diagram.

a *scatter diagram* (Figure 3.9), she demonstrated the results of a series of experiments she conducted to document the relationship between the two variables, moisture content and dispersion quality. The scatter diagram indicates that from low to moderate levels of solvent moisture content, dispersion quality decreases as moisture content increases. This is referred to as a negative correlation between solvent moisture content and dispersion quality.

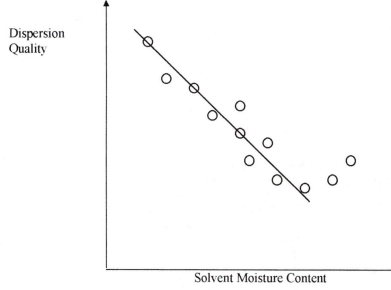

FIGURE 3.9   Mystery Chemical scatter diagram.

The problem cannot be listed as solved until there is appropriate follow-up to assure that the solution implemented had the desired effect. Run charts and process control charts are useful in the follow-up stage.

PARETO DIAGRAM IN ACTION

The Wire Division of a Fortune 500 corporation was experiencing excessive scrap rates in its extruder operation. The Extruder Department consists of six extruders which apply the plastic insulating coating on copper wire. The Quality Department was asked to assist in finding the reasons for the excessive rejects in the Extruder Department. The engineers in the Quality Department began by analyzing the past month's rejects by extruder using a Pareto diagram.

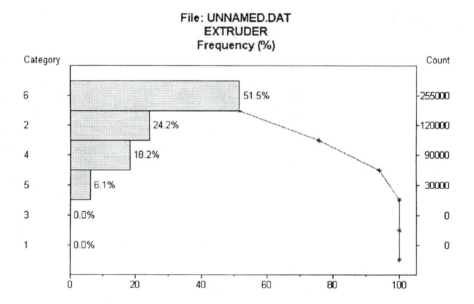

File: UNNAMED.DAT
EXTRUDER
Frequency (%)

Diagram constructed using NWA Quality Analyst™

The Pareto diagram clearly shows that Extruder 6 is producing most (51.5 percent) of the rejects. Another Pareto diagram was constructed for the rejects from Extruder 6. This Pareto diagram clearly indicated that most (80.4 percent) of the rejects from Extruder 6 were due to tangled wire. The quality engineer worked with Process Engineering to determine why Extruder 6 was producing so much tangled wire. The cause was found to be an oversized sheave on the level wind in the take-up section which was creating a loose and overlapping wind on the take-up reel. Once the sheave was replaced with one of the correct size, the problem was solved. Further investigation revealed that the oversized sheave had been installed during the last preventive maintenance check of the machine. The maintenance technician could not find a sheave of the correct size and thought that an oversized sheave "would not hurt anything." The training procedures for maintenance technicians and the instruction sheets for preventive maintenance checks were amended to ensure that the problem did not recur.

File: UNNAMED.DAT
CAUSE
Frequency (%)

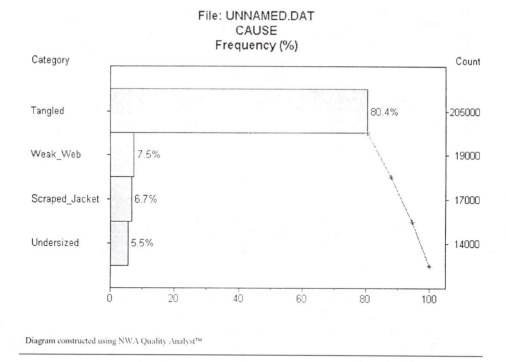

Diagram constructed using NWA Quality Analyst™

THE SEVEN MANAGEMENT TOOLS

The seven management tools are designed to assist in the organization and communication of information. They are particularly useful in the analysis of qualitative information, making it more useful in management planning. The tools are:

Affinity diagram
Tree diagram
Process decision program chart (PDPC)
Matrix diagram
Interrelationship digraph
Prioritization matrix
Activity network diagram

Affinity diagrams are similar in function to cause and effect diagrams in that they are designed to help in the organization of ideas and facts relating to a broad concept into categories. Ideas which have affinities for each other are placed under the same category. For example, ideas generated in a brainstorming session provide more information for planning purposes when they are organized into categories using an affinity diagram. Figure 3.10 shows an affinity diagram developed by the owner of a pizza delivery service who was brainstorming ways that he could differentiate his pizza and delivery service from the competition.

Tree diagrams allow managers to plan the actions necessary to implement the ideas and objectives shown on the affinity diagram. Figure 3.11 shows a partial tree diagram for Roger's Take-Out Pizza.

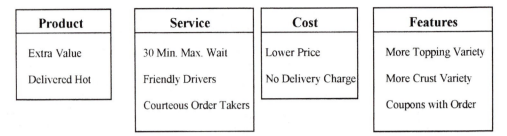

FIGURE 3.10   Affinity diagram for Roger's Take-Out Pizza.

A proactive approach to planning considers the possibility that plans will not work out as expected. The *process decision program chart (PDPC)* provides a framework for developing contingency plans for preventing the unexpected or dealing with it if it does occur. The PDPC begins with the tree diagram. Possible negative outcomes are considered for each branch of the tree diagram, and contingency plans are listed for each as shown in Figure 3.12.

Matrix diagrams enable planners to graphically depict relationships between concepts. Figure 3.13 depicts a portion of a matrix diagram for Roger's Take-Out Pizza. It shows the relationship between the desired objectives and possible actions that could be taken. The strength of the relationship is indicated by the shading of the dot. An objective not having a relationship with at least one action indicates that the action plan is incomplete.

The *interrelationship digraph* graphically depicts causal relationships among the categories from an affinity diagram. Figure 3.14 depicts the interrelationship

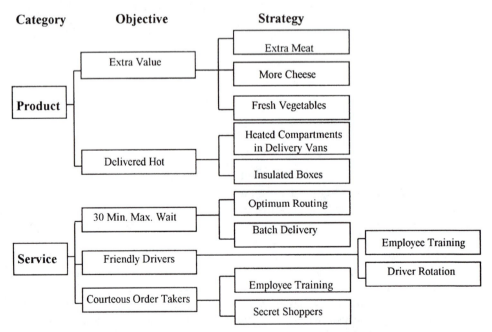

FIGURE 3.11   Partial tree diagram for Roger's Take-Out Pizza.

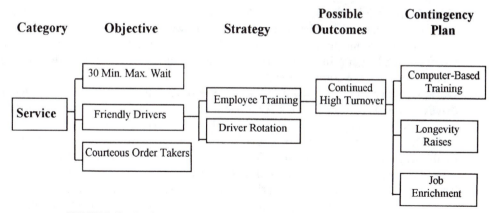

FIGURE 3.12   Partial process decision program chart for Roger's Take-Out Pizza.

Objective \ Action	Improved Employee Training	Improved Kitchen Process	Improved Delivery Process	Improved Controls
30 Min. Max. Wait	●	●	●	◐
Friendly Drivers	●	○	◐	●
Courteous Order Takers	●			●

KEY: ●   Strong relationship

◐   Moderate relationship

○   Weak relationship

FIGURE 3.13   Partial matrix program chart for Roger's Take-Out Pizza.

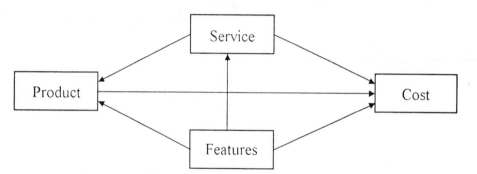

FIGURE 3.14   Interrelationship digraph for Roger's Take-Out Pizza.

digraph produced from the affinity diagram in Figure 3.10. Arrows indicate which categories affect which other categories, that is, which factors are drivers of other categories. From this digraph it is evident that features has the greatest effect on the factors which Roger's Take-Out Pizza believes are most important to differentiating themselves from the competition. Features is a driver of cost, product, and service—i.e., any change in features will impact all the other categories. No other category drives as many other categories. As a result of this analysis, Roger's may decide to focus first on features.

The *prioritization matrix* allows the comparison of both quantitative and qualitative data in the same analysis. Figure 3.15 shows how a prioritization matrix is used to compare Roger's Take-Out Pizza with its leading competitor, X-O's Pizza. The dimensions used in the comparison are the categories from the affinity diagram (Figure 3.10). In developing the matrix, and prior to rating the two companies, Roger's decided on an importance weight for each category. These weights must sum to 1.0. The higher the weight, the more important the category. Then each company is rated on each category using a scale of 1 to 10 (with 10 being the best). Roger's higher total weighted score indicates that, overall, Roger's provides a better "pizza experience" than X-O's, the leading competitor. The positive difference weighted scores for product and service indicate categories where X-O's has a competitive advantage and thus might be fruitful areas for Roger's to examine for improvement.

The seventh management tool is the *activity network diagram,* which is also known as PERT (program evaluation and review technique) or CPM (critical path method). Figure 3.16 is the activity network diagram for the evaluation of installing heated compartments on Roger's Take-Out Pizza's delivery vans.

The activity network diagram is both a project planning and a project control tool. As a project planning tool, it requires that the entire project be broken down into its component activities, that the duration of each activity be forecast, and that the precedence relationship among the activities be defined. The estimated project duration can be determined by the length of the longest path through the network. This is called the critical path because a delay in any activity on this path will delay the entire project.

Category	Weight	Roger's Raw Score	Roger's Wtd. Score	X-O's Raw Score	X-O's Wtd. Score	Difference Wtd. Score
Product	0.30	7	2.10	8	2.40	+0.30
Service	0.25	6	1.50	7	1.75	+0.25
Cost	0.25	8	2.00	6	1.50	−0.50
Features	0.20	9	1.80	7	1.40	−0.40
TOTAL	1.00		7.40		7.05	

FIGURE 3.15 Prioritization matrix for Roger's Take-Out Pizza.

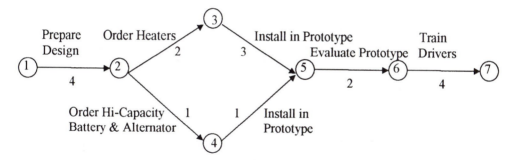

FIGURE 3.16 Activity network for evaluation of heated compartments in delivery vans for Roger's Take-Out Pizza.

The estimated project duration for the evaluation of a prototype installation of a heated compartment on a Roger's Take-Out Pizza delivery van is 15 weeks—the length of the longest path (1-2-3-5-6-7) in the diagram. Any delays in the completion of the activities on this path will delay the project. Since the length of the noncritical path is 12 weeks, a delay of up to 3 weeks in the 2-4 or 4-5 activities can be tolerated without delaying completion of the project.

QUALITY FUNCTION DEPLOYMENT

Quality Function Deployment (QFD) was developed in Japan by Professor Yoji Akao. QFD, also known as the House of Quality (see Figure 3.17), is defined as "a structural method in which customer requirements are translated into appropriate technical requirements for each stage of product development and production. The QFD process is often referred to as listening to the voice of the customer."[7] Quality is defined by the customer. Information about what is important to the customer can be lost in transit from the marketing department, which usually gathers that information from the customer, to the product/service design team. QFD is a systematic way to ensure that the customer's definition of quality is considered during the product/service design process (the first House of Quality) and throughout the production process (the second, third, and fourth Houses of Quality).

QFD is a series of matrices that begins in the "west wing" of the House of Quality with customer requirements. The "second floor" of the House of Quality is a translation of the customer requirements into design requirements. The "main floor" of the house is a matrix showing the correlation of the design requirements with the customer requirements. In the "attic" is a matrix which shows the interrelationship of the design requirements. This matrix is useful in analyzing trade-offs among the design requirements. The "basement" contains the target values for the design requirements. The "east wing" shows a comparison of the product or service under design with its leading competitors.

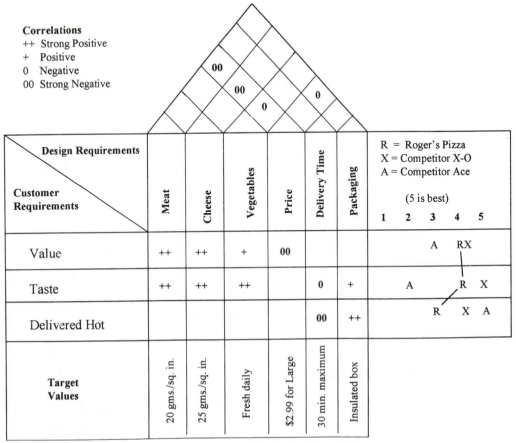

FIGURE 3.17 House of Quality for Roger's Pizza.

The example in Figure 3.17 is a simple first House of Quality for Roger's Take-Out Pizza, which is working on a redesign of its pizza products. The example shows that Roger's Take-Out Pizza customers want value, taste, and pizza delivered hot. Roger's is superior to Ace Pizza on two of the three customer requirements, but ranks equal to or below X-O's Pizza on all three requirements. The purpose of this product redesign project is to make Roger's Take-Out Pizza superior to both competitors on all three customer requirements.

There is a strong positive correlation between the design requirements of meat and cheese and the customer requirement of value. That means that the more meat and cheese on the pizza, the higher the value to the customer. There is a strong negative correlation between the design requirement of price and the customer requirement of value. This means that the higher the price, the lower the value to the customer.

The correlation matrix in the "attic" shows that there is a strong negative correlation between meat and cheese and price. This means that there is a trade-off to be considered. Roger's design team must find a way to provide a meaty, cheesy pizza at a low price.

The correlation matrix in the "basement" shows the target values that the design team has determined must be met to meet the design requirements. These are the specifications for the pizza that will put Roger's ahead of its two competitors.

The second House of Quality applies the same systematic approach to defining component characteristics. The third House of Quality addresses process operations, while the fourth addresses the quality control plan.[8] Use of all four Houses of Quality will help organizations ensure that the products and services they produce match customer requirements.

SUMMARY

Problem solving is a key activity engaged in by quality engineers. This chapter has described the problem-solving process and tools which are effective in dealing with problems and opportunities for improvement. The seven quality tools are simple but powerful tools for understanding processes and analyzing data. The seven management tools are effective aids in the organization and communication of ideas. These tools should be in every quality engineer's tool box.

Quality Function Deployment (QFD) is a tool that is of considerable value to quality engineers as they participate in design teams for new products and services.

DISCUSSION QUESTIONS

1. Discuss the difference between a symptom and a problem.
2. Would you classify excessive employee absenteeism as a symptom or a problem? Discuss.
3. Prepare a flow chart for getting to work in the morning. Discuss areas for improvement revealed by the flow chart.
4. Compare the use of check sheets and Pareto diagrams. Discuss the advantages and disadvantages of each and under which circumstances each would be preferred.
5. Discuss the relationship between the tree diagram and the process decision program chart.
6. Prepare an activity network for the process of purchasing a new car to be paid for by a bank automobile loan. What are the critical activities?
7. What is the House of Quality? What is its purpose?

PROBLEMS

1. You have just received the prints from your first roll of film taken with your new camera. You are disappointed that all the prints are blurry. Use a cause and effect diagram to develop potential causes of the blurry prints.

2. You have collected the following data from customer comment cards at your restaurant. Construct a Pareto diagram to show which of the problems should be investigated first. Show the cumulative frequency line on your diagram.

Comment	Frequency
Dirty dishes	11
Dirty silverware	18
Inattentive service	137
Cold food	23
Wrong order	5
Overpriced	37

3. Use the following data to construct a scatter diagram. Does there appear to be a relationship between hours of overtime and number of rejects?

Hours of Overtime	Number of Rejects
127	33
90	25
95	23
160	40
10	9
80	19
27	14
103	26
48	19
65	31

4. Your boss has asked you to evaluate the reject percentage for the past year on one of the production lines. Use the following data to construct a run chart. Does there appear to be a pattern in the change in reject rate over the year?

Month	Reject (%)
January	1.7
February	1.6
March	2.2
April	2.5
May	2.3
June	3.0
July	2.7
August	3.3
September	3.5
October	3.1
November	3.3
December	3.7

5. Roll a single die 100 times. Use a check sheet to record the frequency with which the numbers 1 through 6 occur. Use the same data to construct a Pareto diagram.

6. Prepare a flow chart of the process you use to prepare a pot of coffee. Do you believe that someone could use your flow chart to prepare coffee that would taste the same as yours? Can you see ways to improve your coffee-making process?

NOTES

1. Evans, J., & W. Lindsay. *The Management and Control of Quality,* 3rd ed. St. Paul, MN: West, 1996, pp. 349–371.

2. Osborn, A. *Applied Imagination,* 3rd ed. New York: Scribner's, 1963.

3. Parnes, S., R. Noller, & A. Biondi (eds.). *Guide to Creative Action.* New York: Scribner's, 1977.

4. Burns, Robert. *To a Mouse,* 1785.

5. Bemowski, K. "The Quality Glossary." *Quality Progress,* vol. 25, February 1992, p. 21.

6. Galloway, D. *Mapping Work Processes.* Milwaukee, WI: ASQC Quality Press, 1994.

7. Bemowski, K. "The Quality Glossary." *Quality Progress,* vol. 25, February 1992, p.26.

8. Sullivan, L. "Quality Function Deployment." *Quality Progress,* vol. 19, no. 6, June 1986, pp. 39–50.

SUGGESTED READINGS

Evans, J., & W. Lindsay. *The Management and Control of Quality* 3rd ed. St. Paul, MN: West, 1996, Chapters 5, 6, and 9, pp. 146–185, 186–226, and 326–391.

Galloway, D. *Mapping Work Processes.* Milwaukee, WI: ASQC Quality Press, 1994.

Grant, E. L., & R. S. Leavenworth. *Statistical Quality Control,* 7th ed. New York: McGraw-Hill, 1996, Chapter 19, pp. 669–689.

Montgomery, D. C. *Introduction to Statistical Quality Control,* 3rd ed. New York: Wiley, 1996, Chapter 4, pp. 129–178.

Walton, M. *The Deming Management Method.* New York: Perigee Books, 1986, Chapter 20, pp. 96–118.

CASE I   SOUR GRAPE ICE CREAM

The Quality Ice Cream Company has recently introduced a new flavor, sour grape. The company has not been able to meet demand for this new product due to quality problems—many batches have been discarded. It has collected a large amount of data but is at a loss about how to use the data. Quality Ice Cream is overwhelmed with numbers. It has asked you to help address the problems. What do you recommend? [Be specific.]

Process Description:

1. Pull ingredients from warehouse.
2. Blend ingredients in mixer.
3. Pump mixture to freeze machine.
4. Run freeze machine until consistency is correct.
5. Extrude ice cream into package.
6. Inspect and test ice cream.
7. Transfer packages to finished good storage.

Reject Log:

	Number of Rejects by Cause				
Date	Ice Crystals	Soupy	Too Stiff	Tastes Bad	Off Color
2/1	1	7	0	0	1
2/2	0	2	0	0	0
2/3	2	4	0	1	0
2/4	1	6	1	0	0
2/5	0	5	0	1	1
2/6	1	4	0	1	0
2/7	0	3	0	1	0
2/8	0	5	0	0	0
2/9	1	2	0	1	0
2/10	2	4	0	1	0

Ice crystals seem to be related to the mixing process. *Soupy* and *too stiff* refer to consistency (*soupy* is viscosity below 5,000 cps (centipoise); *too stiff* is viscosity above 6,000 cps). *Tastes bad* and *off color* seem to be related to raw materials.

One of the production operators believes that the consistency of the ice cream (measured by the ice cream's viscosity) is related to the length of time in the freeze machine. She had collected some data but didn't know what to do with them.

Run Time (min)	Viscosity (cps)	Run Time (min)	Viscosity (cps)
93	5,500	97	5,750
90	5,100	77	3,000
89	4,950	83	4,200
94	5,375	95	5,600
93	5,400	81	4,300

SECTION II

Statistical Quality Control

CHAPTER 4

Statistical Process Control

CHAPTER OBJECTIVES

This chapter introduces the following topics:

- The concept of the control chart
- Control chart signals which indicate the process may be out of control
- How to construct variables control charts (x-bar, range and s-charts)
- How to construct attributes control charts (p, np, c, and u-charts)
- Process capability study

INTRODUCTION

Quality as a concept can be subdivided into quality of design and quality of conformance. Quality of design is determined by the extent to which products and services are designed with the needs and desires of the customers in mind. Quality of conformance is determined by the extent to which the intent of the designer is actually built into the product or service.

Statistical process control (SPC) is concerned with quality of conformance. Organizations that have properly designed their products or services (i.e., quality of design is assured) and that use SPC to assure quality of conformance can answer the question, "How are things going?" very simply and precisely. If things are going very well, it means that all processes are capable and are operating in control. This question is not so easily answered by organizations not using SPC.

SPC AND VARIATION

Statistical Process Control is defined as "the application of statistical techniques to control a process."[1] Walter Shewhart[2] is credited with creating the concept of the control chart and statistical process control during the late 1920s and early 1930s. Shewhart recognized that variation is the enemy of quality. He determined that variation in a process may be partitioned between "common causes" and "assignable causes" (also referred to as "special causes").

Common cause variation is inherent in a process when it is operating as designed. Assignable cause variation is unnatural variation in a process. For example, a thermostat is designed to maintain room temperature within ±2 degrees of the set point. Temperature readings taken at random intervals when the thermostat is operating correctly will vary over the *normal* 4-degree temperature range. This is common cause variation. If the thermostat malfunctions so that it only maintains the temperature within ±4 degrees of the set point, the excessive variation is assignable cause variation.

The primary function of a control chart is to determine which type of variation is present and whether adjustments need to be made to the process. It can be just as damaging to adjust a process which is operating in control (only common cause variation present) as it is to fail to adjust a process which is operating out of control (assignable cause variation present). It is therefore important to be able to determine what type of variation is present in a process.

W. Edwards Deming[3] contended that only management can address common cause variation since it is inherent in the process as designed by management. If, for example, the current machines cannot hold the required tolerance when operating properly, management must decide to upgrade the machines. Workers can address assignable cause variation since it occurs as the result of special causes not naturally inherent in the process. Examples of special causes include dull cutting blades, incorrect machine settings, and misaligned dies.

Control charts by themselves tell us nothing about whether the process, when operating with only common cause variation present (in control), is capable of producing a product which meets specifications for the characteristic being measured. The process capability study, discussed later in this chapter, is designed to enable this determination to be made.

SPC addresses the quality control process of Juran's quality trilogy.[4] The trilogy of quality planning, quality control, and quality improvement is central to Juran's quality philosophy. The quality control process consists of the process for meeting quality goals during operations. SPC is designed to be used as an in-process or "real-time" tool for monitoring a process. SPC, then, can be said to be a tool for preventing the production of defective products by ensuring that the process is both in control and capable.

VARIABLES CONTROL CHARTS

Variables data are those data which can be measured on a continuous scale. Examples include measurements such as height, length, width, wavelength, and pressure. Variables data are plotted on a combination of two charts—usually an x-bar ($\bar{x}$) chart and a range (R) chart. However, an S chart (standard deviation chart) should be used in place of a range chart for large sample sizes ($n > 10$). This is because the range method loses efficiency relative to S^2 as sample size increases. For a sample size of 2, the 2 methods are equivalent. For a sample size of 10, the range method efficiency is only 0.85 relative to S^2.[5]

The x-bar chart plots sample means. It is a measure of between-sample variation and is used to assess the centering and long-term variation of the process. The range chart and the S chart measure the within-sample variation and assess the short-term variation of the process.

Concept of the Control Chart

All control charts discussed in this chapter (x-bar, R, S, p, np, c, and u) operate on the basis of the same basic concept. The differences among the types of control charts revolve around the type of data being plotted and the data's underlying distribution. The concept of the control chart will be illustrated here using the x-bar chart.

The construction of an x-bar chart begins with the collection of a series of samples from a process. The samples consist of two or more observations (sample sizes of 3 to 10 are best[6]) each. The individual observations are averaged for each sample to determine the sample mean ($\bar{x}$). The average of at least 25 to 30 sample means is called the grand mean or x-double bar ($\bar{\bar{x}}$). The underlying distribution for the x-bar chart is the normal distribution; however, Shewhart[7] and Burr[8] demonstrated through simulation that the x-bar chart is robust to nonnormality in the distribution of x-bar. An x-bar chart is shown in Figure 4.1. The centerline (CL) of the x-bar chart is $\bar{\bar{x}}$. The upper control limit (UCL) is set at $\bar{\bar{x}} + 3$ standard deviations (+3 sigma); the lower control limit (LCL) is set at $\bar{\bar{x}} - 3$ standard deviations (−3 sigma).

The 25 to 30 sample means are then plotted on the control chart. If none of the points fall outside the control limits and there are no discernible patterns in the plot, the process is said to be in control (as in Figure 4.1). The chart can then be used to plot subsequent sample means.

Out-of-Control Signals

One point falling outside the control limits indicates the process mean may have shifted from $\bar{\bar{x}}$. This shift is due to some assignable cause which must be identified and corrected. The probability of a point outside the control limits actually coming from the distribution upon which the control chart was developed is very small ($p < 0.0027$). The risk of unnecessarily taking action based upon a point outside the control limits when the process is actually in control is a Type I error. The risk of the control chart failing to produce a signal when the process is actually out of control is a Type II error. The probability of a Type II error must be assessed for each individual sample.

There are other ways that a control chart can signal an out-of-control condition. A run of 7 or 8 points falling on one side of the centerline is an indication that the process mean has shifted. This might be the result of a change in operator or a change in raw material lots. Similarly, a run of 7 or 8 points on a rising or falling trend indicates that the process is out of control. This could be due to gradual tool wear, temperature buildup, or operator fatigue.

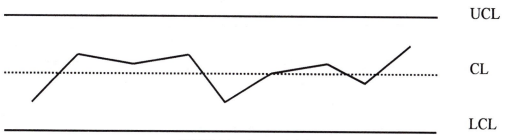

FIGURE 4.1 x-bar control chart.

Points observed to be hugging the centerline are an indication that the control limits are too wide. This can result from a reduction in process variation which has occurred since the limits were calculated. If this is the case, new control limits should be calculated. This can also be a signal that the control limits were miscalculated.

Points observed to be changing on a regular, cyclical basis may be an indication of shift-to-shift variation. This could be the result of differences in the training and experience of the operators or setup technicians from shift to shift.

Figure 4.2 shows examples of out-of-control signals observed in practice and the assignable causes associated with those signals. An excellent discussion of out-of-control signals is contained in Western Electric's *Statistical Quality Control Handbook.*[9]

Constructing Variables Control Charts

The first step in constructing variables control charts is to determine the variable to be measured. Frequently this is the most critical dimension of a product or a dimension which is highly sensitive to changes in the process. The second step is to evaluate the process to ensure that it is being operated as designed. Among the things to look for would be the use of incorrect procedures, off-specification materials, or worn parts. If nonstandard conditions are found, they should be adjusted to design standards.

After the process is brought up to design standards, 25 to 30 samples (k) consisting of 3 to 10 observations (n) are taken. The dimension of interest is measured using a system which is known to be accurate and reliable. The mean ($\bar{x}$) and range (R) are calculated for each sample. These values are used to calculate the grand mean ($\bar{\bar{x}}$) and average range ($\bar{R}$).

$$\bar{x} = \frac{\sum_{i=1}^{n} x_i}{n} \tag{4.1}$$

$$\bar{\bar{x}} = \frac{\sum_{i=1}^{k} \bar{x}_i}{k} \tag{4.2}$$

$$R = x_k(\text{largest}) - x_k(\text{smallest}) \tag{4.3}$$

$$\bar{R} = \frac{\sum_{i=1}^{k} R_i}{k} \tag{4.4}$$

The centerline for the x-bar chart is $\bar{\bar{x}}$. The upper control limit and lower control limit are calculated using Equations (4.5) and (4.6), respectively. The constant A_2 is found in Table 4.1.

$$\text{UCL} = \bar{\bar{x}} + A_2\bar{R} \tag{4.5}$$

$$\text{LCL} = \bar{\bar{x}} - A_2\bar{R} \tag{4.6}$$

a. One point outside the control limit

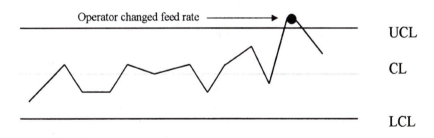

b. Eight points on one side of the centerline

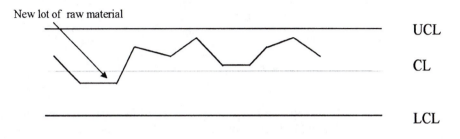

c. Eight points on a rising (or falling) trend

d. Hugging the centerline

FIGURE 4.2   Examples of out-of-control signals.

TABLE 4.1 Factors for Variables Control Charts

n	A_2	D_3	D_4	d_2
2	1.880	0	3.267	1.128
3	1.023	0	2.574	1.693
4	0.729	0	2.282	2.059
5	0.577	0	2.114	2.326
6	0.480	0	2.004	2.534
7	0.419	0.076	1.924	2.704
8	0.373	0.136	1.864	2.847
9	0.337	0.184	1.816	2.970
10	0.308	0.223	1.777	3.078
11	0.285	0.256	1.744	3.173
12	0.266	0.283	1.717	3.258
13	0.249	0.307	1.693	3.336
14	0.235	0.328	1.672	3.407
15	0.223	0.347	1.653	3.472
16	0.212	0.363	1.637	3.532

Adapted from Table 27 of ASTM STP 15D7.

The centerline for the range chart is $\overline{R}$. The UCL and LCL are calculated using Equations (4.7) and (4.8), respectively. The constants D_3 and D_4 are found in Table 4.1.

$$UCL = D_4\overline{R} \qquad (4.7)$$

$$LCL = D_3\overline{R} \qquad (4.8)$$

The range chart is evaluated first. If it is in control, then the x-bar chart can be evaluated. An out-of-control signal on either chart is an indication that the process is out of control.

EXAMPLE 4.1

An analyst collects 4 samples of 3 observations during a production shift. She measures and records the length in centimeters of each part and uses these data to construct x-bar and range charts.

	Observations				
Sample	1	2	3	$\overline{x}$	Range
1	1.003	1.012	1.005	1.0067	0.009
2	1.000	1.010	1.012	1.0073	0.012
3	1.011	1.006	1.008	1.0083	0.005
4	1.005	1.010	1.005	1.0067	0.005

$$\overline{\overline{x}} = 1.00725$$
$$\overline{R} = 0.00775$$

The sample mean ($\overline{x}_1$) for Sample 1 is:

$$\frac{1.003 + 1.012 + 1.005}{3} = 1.0067 \qquad \text{(Equation 4.1)}$$

The range for Sample 1 is:

$$1.012 - 1.003 = 0.009 \qquad \text{(Equation 4.3)}$$

The sample means and ranges for Samples 2 to 4 are calculated similarly.
$\bar{\bar{x}}$ is the mean of the sample means (Equation 4.2), and $\bar{R}$ is the mean of the sample ranges (Equation 4.4).

The control limits of the x-bar and range charts are calculated ($n = 3$):

$$\text{UCL} = \bar{\bar{x}} + A_2\bar{R} = 1.00725 + 1.023(0.00775) = 1.01518 \quad \text{(Equation 4.5)}$$
$$\text{LCL} = \bar{\bar{x}} - A_2\bar{R} = 1.00725 - 1.023(0.00775) = 0.9993 \quad \text{(Equation 4.6)}$$
$$\text{UCL} = D_4\bar{R} = 2.574(0.00775) = 0.01995 \quad \text{(Equation 4.7)}$$
$$\text{LCL} = D_3\bar{R} = 0(0.00775) = 0 \quad \text{(Equation 4.8)}$$

The control charts are constructed, and the 4 sample means and ranges are plotted:

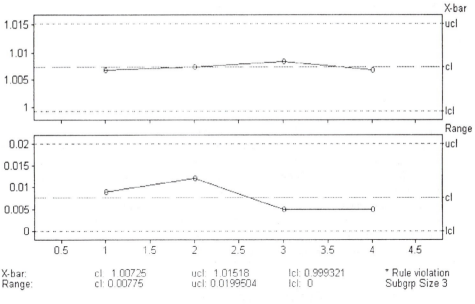

File: UNNAMED.DAT
LENGTH

X-bar:	cl: 1.00725	ucl: 1.01518	lcl: 0.999321	* Rule violation
Range:	cl: 0.00775	ucl: 0.0199504	lcl: 0	Subgrp Size 3

Constructed using NWA Quality Analyst™

INTERPRETING CONTROL CHART PATTERNS IN ACTION

The injection molding division of a major company had recently instituted statistical process control for the molding operation producing plastic housings for personal computers. The process defied all the company's efforts to bring it under statistical control. The control charts showed a cyclical pattern of a brief period of stability, a period of instability, then stability again but at another level.

The plant operated on a 24-hour-a-day basis. The quality engineer began her investigation by interviewing operating personnel on all shifts. When she asked the setup technician

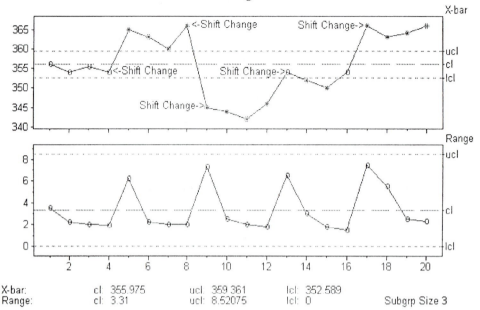

Part 3056B Weight in Grams

Chart constructed using NWA Quality Analyst™

on the evening shift what he thought the biggest problem was, he replied, "The first shift technician doesn't know how to run the process." The technicians on the other shifts had similar comments about the technician on the preceding shift. All three technicians had considerable experience in molding operations. The engineer found that each technician felt that he knew ways to improve the process by making small changes in the setup. None had bothered to share this information with anyone else. The engineer met with the technicians as a group. They studied the process together and produced a standard setup sheet that all agreed was the right way to run the process. Once the standard setup was approved and implemented, the patterns due to this assignable cause disappeared.

A Special Form of the *x*-bar Control Chart for Short Production Runs

Many manufacturing organizations feel that they cannot use variables control charts because their average production run length is too short. Short production runs, which are the norm for job shops, do not lend themselves to the usual *x*-bar chart (and its companion range chart) because short runs sometimes allow for only 2 or 3 samples to be taken during the run. Then the process is set up for the next run and a new pair of charts is needed.

A delta[10] chart (also referred to as a deviation from nominal[11] chart, DNOM[12] chart, Nom-I-Nal[13] chart, or code value[14] chart) often can be used for short-run process variables measurements. The delta chart plots the deviation from a nominal value instead of plotting the measured value directly. Consider a specialty shop that fills bottles with cleaning solution in small lots. The automatic bottle filling equipment can be adjusted to fill 1 pint, 1 quart, and half-gallon sizes of the cleaning solution. A run of a given size might last 1 to 2 hours. If it has been shown that the variance in fill volume does not change with the setting, instead of using the actual fill volume for control charting purposes, the difference from the nominal fill volume can be used. A reading of 1.003 quarts becomes a delta statistic of 0.003 (1.003 − nominal of 1.000). A reading of 1.003 pints also becomes a delta statistic of 0.003. x-bar and range charts can now be created based on the delta statistics rather than the actual measurements. One delta chart (special type of an x-bar chart) can now be used for all three fill volumes.

DELTA CHART IN ACTION

The metals fabrication division of a major corporation uses cutoff saws to produce different-length aluminum housings for multiple-outlet surge protectors. The length of the housings varied from 6 to 14 inches. All lengths were cut from the same aluminum extrusions using the same cutoff saw. To change from one length to another, the operator adjusted a hard stop. The tolerance limits for all lengths of the housing were the same, ±0.020 inch. A process capability study found that the variance in length was constant regardless of the length being cut.

The plant initially tried to use x-bar and range charts to control the process. Because the run lengths were short (<8 hours), plant workers seldom plotted more than 4 or 5 samples before they had to change setups and run a different length using separate control charts. Using a delta chart enabled the plant to use just one set of charts for the process, simplifying the SPC process.

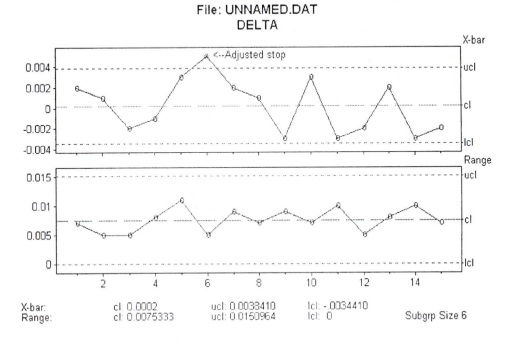

File: UNNAMED.DAT
DELTA

X-bar: cl: 0.0002   ucl: 0.0038410   lcl: -.0034410
Range: cl: 0.0075333   ucl: 0.0150964   lcl: 0   Subgrp Size 6

Chart constructed using NWA Quality Analyst™

ATTRIBUTES CONTROL CHARTS

Variables control charts provide more information about a process than attributes control charts because variables charts show actual measurement data while attributes charts show only count data. But it is often preferable to use attributes control charts instead of variables control charts. Attributes control charts are required when there are multiple possible causes for rejecting a product and the parameter of interest is the proportion of rejected products from the process or the average number of defects per sample or product. Attributes control charts are also required when the test used is a "go–no-go" type of test (e.g., meets specification or fails to meet specification) rather than a continuous measurement (e.g., length, width, weight).

The concept of attributes control charts is the same as for the x-bar chart. However, instead of being based upon the normal distribution (a continuous distribution), attributes control charts are based upon some discrete distribution (e.g., binomial, Poisson). The interpretation of out-of-control signals is the same for both attributes and variables control charts.

Control Charts for Nonconforming Units

The *proportion defective chart* (p-chart) is used to control the proportion of defective product in samples taken from a process. This chart is also referred to as the fraction nonconforming or fraction defective chart. The underlying distribution for the p-chart is the binomial. While the sample size for a p-chart may vary, in practice it is desirable to hold the sample size constant. If the sample size varies, it is necessary to recalculate the control limits for each sample (see Figure 4.3).

The sample size required for a p-chart is usually larger than for a variables control chart. Typically, sample sizes vary from about 30 to more than 100. Duncan[15] provides a complete discussion of the procedure for determining the appropriate sample size based upon the degree of variation in the proportion defective expected in the process.

As in the construction of variables control charts, 25 to 30 samples are from the process after the process has been inspected and determined to be operating as designed. The proportion defective (p) is calculated for each sample by dividing the number of defective units by the sample size. Control limits for the p-chart are calculated as follows, where $k =$ the number of samples and $n =$ the number of observations in each sample. The centerline for the p-chart is $\overline{p}$.

$$\overline{p} = \frac{\sum\limits_{i=1}^{k} p_i}{k} \tag{4.9}$$

$$\text{UCL} = \overline{p} + 3\sqrt{\frac{\overline{p}(1 - \overline{p})}{n}} \tag{4.10}$$

$$LCL = \overline{p} - 3\sqrt{\frac{\overline{p}(1 - \overline{p})}{n}} \qquad (4.11)$$

When the LCL formula yields a value that is negative, the LCL is set to 0.

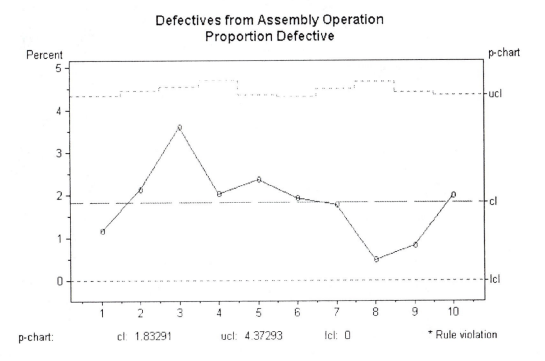

FIGURE 4.3   Example of *p*-chart with variable sample size.

EXAMPLE 4.2

An analyst collects 4 samples of 200 observations during a production shift. The number of defective units in each sample is determined and recorded. A proportion defective chart (*p*-chart) is constructed.

Sample	No. Defective	*p*
1	5	0.025
2	3	0.015
3	7	0.035
4	2	0.010

$$\overline{p} = \frac{0.025 + 0.015 + 0.035 + 0.010}{4} = 0.02125 \qquad \text{or } 2.125\% \quad \text{(Equation 4.9)}$$

The control limits for the p-chart are calculated:

$$UCL = \bar{p} + 3\sqrt{\frac{\bar{p}(1 - \bar{p})}{n}} = 0.02125 + 3\sqrt{\frac{0.02125(1 - 0.02125)}{200}}$$

$$= 0.051843 \quad \text{or } 5.1843\%$$

(Equation 4.10)

$$LCL = \bar{p} - 3\sqrt{\frac{\bar{p}(1 - \bar{p})}{n}} = 0.02125 - 3\sqrt{\frac{0.02125(1 - 0.02125)}{200}}$$

$$= -0.0093$$

(Equation 4.11)

Since LCL < 0, set equal to 0.

The control chart is constructed, and the data points are plotted.

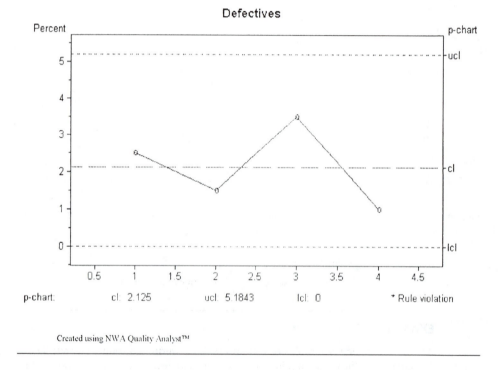

Created using NWA Quality Analyst™

The *number defective chart* (np-chart) is an alternative chart that may be substituted for the p-chart. The underlying distribution for the np-chart is the binomial. In the case of the np-chart, the sample size must be constant. Rather than calculating the proportion of defective items in a sample for plotting on a p-chart, the np-chart allows the actual number of defective units to be plotted directly. This eliminates the need for one calculation (p), thereby decreasing the probability of an error. The np-chart also is somewhat easier for production operators to understand. No power is lost by using the np-chart instead of the p-chart.

As in the construction of the p-chart, 25 to 30 samples are taken from the process after the process has been inspected and determined to be operating as designed. The number of defective units (np) is recorded for each sample. For calculation of the control limits, $\bar{p}$ must also be calculated for these 25 to 30 samples.

Control limits for the *np*-chart are calculated as follows, where k = the number of samples. The centerline for the *np*-chart is $n\bar{p}$.

$$n\bar{p} = \frac{\sum_{i=1}^{k} np_i}{k} \tag{4.12}$$

$$\text{UCL} = n\bar{p} + 3\sqrt{n\bar{p}(1 - \bar{p})} \tag{4.13}$$

$$\text{LCL} = n\bar{p} - 3\sqrt{n\bar{p}(1 - \bar{p})} \tag{4.14}$$

When the LCL formula yields a value that is negative, the LCL is set to 0.

EXAMPLE 4.3

Using the same data from Example 4.2, an *np*-chart is constructed.

$$n\bar{p} = \frac{\sum_{i=1}^{k} np_i}{k} = \frac{5 + 3 + 7 + 2}{4} = 4.25 \qquad \text{(Equation 4.12)}$$

$$\text{UCL} = n\bar{p} + 3\sqrt{n\bar{p}(1 - \bar{p})} = 4.25 + 3\sqrt{4.25(1 - 0.02125)} = 10.3686 \quad \text{(Equation 4.13)}$$

$$\text{LCL} = n\bar{p} - 3\sqrt{n\bar{p}(1 - \bar{p})} = 4.25 - 3\sqrt{4.25(1 - 0.02125)} = -1.87 \quad \text{(Equation 4.14)}$$

Since LCL <0, set equal to 0.

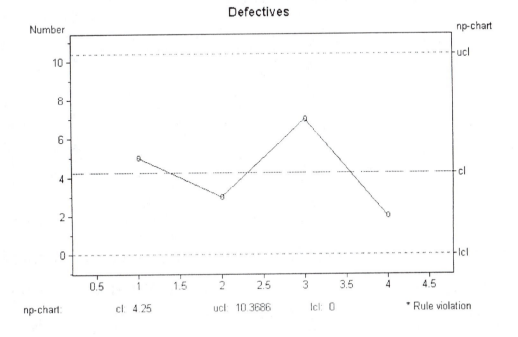

Created using NWA Quality Analyst™

Control Charts for Nonconformities (Defects)

The *c-chart* is used to control the average number of defects per inspection unit in samples of fixed size. The inspection unit may be one item or multiple items. The underlying distribution for the c-chart is the Poisson. Initial data are collected in the same way as for the previously discussed control charts. For each sample the number of defects (c) is recorded. The centerline for the c-chart is $\bar{c}$, and the control limits for the c-chart are calculated as follows:

$$\bar{c} = \frac{\text{total defects}}{\text{no. of samples}} \tag{4.15}$$

$$UCL = \bar{c} + 3\sqrt{\bar{c}} \tag{4.16}$$

$$LCL = \bar{c} - 3\sqrt{\bar{c}} \tag{4.17}$$

When the LCL formula yields a value that is negative, the LCL is set to 0.

EXAMPLE 4.4

An analyst takes 5 samples of 100 jelly beans from a production line over a shift. The number of minor defects in each sample is recorded.

Sample No.	No. of Defects
1	4
2	7
3	2
4	8
5	6

A c-chart is constructed:

$$\bar{c} = \frac{4 + 7 + 2 + 8 + 6}{5} = 5.4 \qquad \text{(Equation 4.15)}$$

$$UCL = \bar{c} + 3\sqrt{\bar{c}} = 5.4 + 3\sqrt{5.4} = 12.3714 \qquad \text{(Equation 4.16)}$$

$$LCL = \bar{c} - 3\sqrt{\bar{c}} = 5.4 - 3\sqrt{5.4} = -1.5714 \qquad \text{(Equation 4.17)}$$

Since LCL < 0, set equal to 0.

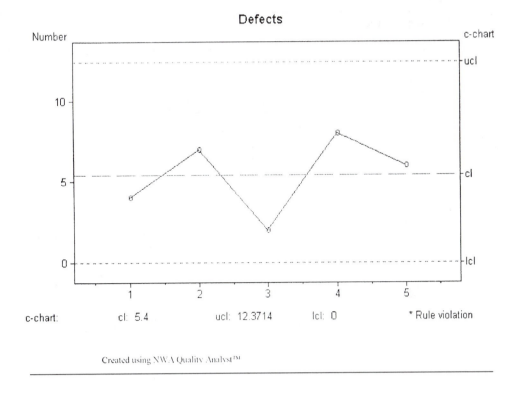

The *u-chart* is used to control the average number of defects per sample when the sample size varies and the inspection unit is 1 unit. The underlying distribution for the *u*-chart is the Poisson. Initial data are collected in the same way as for the previously discussed control charts. For each sample the number of defects (u) is recorded. Control limits for the *u*-chart are calculated as follows, where $k =$ the number of samples and $n =$ the number of observations in each sample. The center-line for the *u*-chart is $\bar{u}$.

$$\bar{u} = \frac{\sum_{i-1}^{k} u_i}{k} \tag{4.18}$$

$$\text{UCL} = \bar{u} + 3\sqrt{\frac{\bar{u}}{n}} \tag{4.19}$$

$$\text{LCL} = \bar{u} - 3\sqrt{\frac{\bar{u}}{n}} \tag{4.20}$$

When the LCL formula yields a value that is negative, the LCL is set to 0.

EXAMPLE 4.5

An analyst examines 5 plywood sheets taken at random times during a production shift and records the number of defects in each sheet.

Sample No.	No. of Defects
1	1
2	4
3	5
4	3
5	6

A u-chart is constructed:

$$\bar{u} = \frac{1 + 4 + 5 + 3 + 6}{5} = 3.8 \qquad \text{(Equation 4.18)}$$

$$UCL = \bar{u} + 3\sqrt{\frac{\bar{u}}{n}} = 3.8 + 3\sqrt{\frac{3.8}{1}} = 9.64808 \qquad \text{(Equation 4.19)}$$

$$LCL = \bar{u} - 3\sqrt{\frac{\bar{u}}{n}} = 3.8 - 3\sqrt{\frac{3.8}{1}} = -2.048 \qquad \text{(Equation 4.20)}$$

Since LCL < 0, set equal to 0.

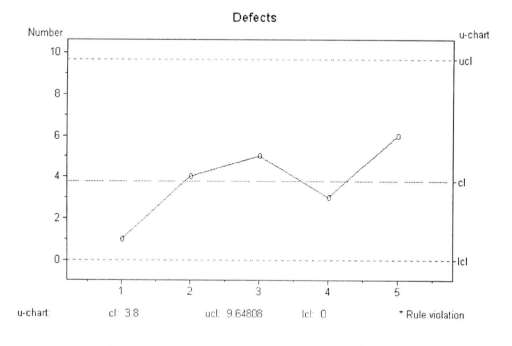

Defects

u-chart: cl: 3.8   ucl: 9.64808   lcl: 0   * Rule violation

Created using NWA Quality Analyst™

Other control charts exist for a variety of specialized situations. These are thoroughly discussed in the books contained in the Suggested Readings at the end of this chapter.

PROCESS CAPABILITY

Thus far we have concerned ourselves with assessing whether the process is in control (i.e., predictable). Another important question is whether the in-control process is capable of meeting the specifications for the item being produced. This is determined through process capability study.

Process capability is defined as "a statistical measure of the inherent process variability for a given characteristic. The most widely accepted formula for process capability is 6σ."[16] The process capability index is defined as "the value of the tolerance specified for the characteristic divided by the process capability. There are several types of process capability indexes, including the widely used C_{pk} and C_p."[17] A process capability index only has meaning when calculated from data collected while the process is in control.

When using attributes control charts for defective units, the measure of process capability is $\bar{p}$—the average proportion defective produced by the process when it is operating in control. Therefore, $\bar{p} = 0.0023$ would indicate that on average 99.77 percent of the product produced by this process when it is operating in control is acceptable (0.0023×100 percent $= 0.23$ percent defective).

When using variables control charts, the appropriate measure of process capability is C_p when the process average is centered on the nominal value (centerline or target value) of the specification, or C_{pk} when the process average is off-center relative to the nominal value (centerline or target value) of the specification. These two situations are illustrated in Figure 4.4.

C_p compares the spread of the specification (upper specification limit $-$ lower specification limit) to the process capability as measured by 6σ. In order for the calculated value of C_p to have any meaning, the data used to calculate the process capability must have been taken when the process was operating in control.

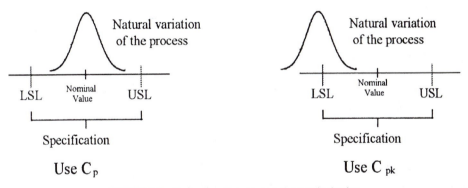

FIGURE 4.4 Centering of process on the nominal value.

The sigma (σ) used to calculate the process capability is not the same as the sigma used to calculate the "3-sigma control limits" on the x-bar chart. The control limits are calculated using an estimate of $\sigma_{\bar{x}}$, the standard deviation of the sample means. Process capability is calculated using an estimate of σ_x, the standard deviation of the individual measurements. These two "sigmas" are related, as shown in Equation (4.21):

$$\sigma_{\bar{x}} = \frac{\sigma_x}{\sqrt{n}} \tag{4.21}$$

It can be seen from the equation that σ_x is larger than $\sigma_{\bar{x}}$. In practice, σ_x is often estimated from the range using Equation (4.22), where d_2 is a constant obtained from Table 4.1 on page 58.

$$\hat{\sigma}_x = \frac{\overline{R}}{d_2} \tag{4.22}$$

WHERE DO THE FACTORS IN TABLE 4.1 COME FROM?

Some of the mystery surrounding the factors in Table 4.1 can now be unraveled. The UCL of the x-bar chart is defined as:

$$UCL = \bar{\bar{x}} + 3\sigma_{\bar{x}}$$

σ_x can be estimated by using Equation (4.22):

$$\hat{\sigma}_x = \frac{\overline{R}}{d_2}$$

$\sigma_{\bar{x}}$ can be estimated by using Equation (4.21):

$$\sigma_{\bar{x}} = \frac{\sigma_x}{\sqrt{n}}$$

So the equations for calculating the UCL:

$$UCL = \bar{\bar{x}} + 3\frac{\hat{\sigma}_x}{\sqrt{n}}$$

and

$$UCL = \bar{\bar{x}} + A_2\overline{R} \tag{Equation 4.5}$$

where

$$A_2 = \frac{3}{d_2\sqrt{n}}$$

are equivalent.

See Duncan[18] for a more detailed discussion.

When the process mean is centered on the nominal value of the specification, C_p may be used as the process capability index. C_p is calculated using Equation (4.23), where USL and LSL are the upper and lower specification limits, respectively.

$$C_p = \frac{\text{USL} - \text{LSL}}{6\sigma_x} \tag{4.23}$$

A value of C_p that is greater than or equal to 1.33 is usually used as the indicator that the process is capable. Note that a value of 1.00 for C_p indicates that the specification range and the $6\sigma_x$ range are exactly the same. In such a case, 0.0023 (or 0.23 percent) of the output from the process when it is operating in control would be expected to fail to meet specifications.

When the process mean is not centered on the nominal value of the specification, C_{pk} may be used instead of C_p as the process capability index. C_{pk} is calculated using Equation (4.24):

$$C_{pk} = \min(C_{pl}, C_{pu}) \tag{4.24}$$

where

$$C_{pl} = \frac{\mu - \text{LSL}}{3\sigma_x} \tag{4.25}$$

and

$$C_{pu} = \frac{\text{USL} - \mu}{3\sigma_x} \tag{4.26}$$

As is the case with C_p, a value of C_{pk} that is greater than or equal to 1.33 is usually used as the indicator that the process is capable. Note that when the process mean is centered on the nominal value of the specification, $C_p = C_{pk}$.

Huntsville Memorial Hospital

SPC IN THE SERVICE INDUSTRY

SPC is not just for the manufacturing industry. Service organizations also use SPC effectively. One example is Huntsville Memorial Hospital. The hospital measures patient satisfaction using patient surveys. Staff members record each month's survey data on x-bar and s control charts—one set for each of the 8 dimensions of service quality that they measure.

The control charts enable the hospital to differentiate between random variation and assignable cause variation in patient satisfaction scores. This helps to

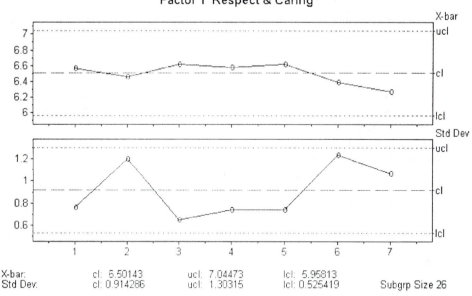

Control Charts
Factor 1 Respect & Caring

| X-bar: | cl: 6.50143 | ucl: 7.04473 | lcl: 5.95813 | |
| Std Dev: | cl: 0.914286 | ucl: 1.30315 | lcl: 0.525419 | Subgrp Size 26 |

Created using NWA Quality Analyst™

ensure that appropriate action is taken to identify assignable causes and that inappropriate action is not taken as a result of common cause variation.

CHAPTER SUMMARY

SPC is designed to be used as an in-process or real-time tool for monitoring a process. SPC, then, is a tool for preventing the production of defective products by ensuring that the process is both in control and capable. Control charts (see example on following page) are used to determine whether a process is in control. Process capability study is used to determine whether a process is capable. SPC is not just for manufacturing industries. Service organizations can also use SPC effectively.

DISCUSSION QUESTIONS

1. Discuss the difference between assignable cause variation and common cause variation.
2. How is it possible for a process to be in control and yet be producing a large percentage of nonconforming product?
3. Discuss the difference between a Type I error and a Type II error.
4. What does the term *out of control* mean?
5. How does a control chart signal that the process being monitored is out of control?

Selecting the Proper Basic Control Chart(s)

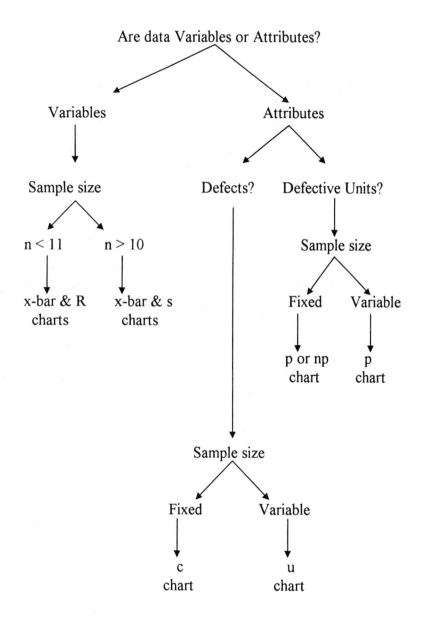

6. When is it preferable to use an attributes control chart instead of a variables control chart?

7. What is the difference between the p-chart and the np-chart?

8. What are the circumstances which require the use of C_{pk} rather than C_p as a measure of process capability?

9. How does a delta chart differ from an x-bar chart? Under what conditions should a delta chart be used instead of an x-bar chart?

PROBLEMS

1. Samples consisting of 6 observations have been taken from a process. Use the following data to construct x-bar and range charts using 3-sigma control limits. Does the process appear to be in control?

Sample No.	$\bar{x}$, Inches	Range, Inches
1	27.2	1.5
2	28.1	1.2
3	28.0	1.3
4	27.6	1.0
5	27.5	1.1

2. The specification for the product in Problem 1 is 27.5 ± 1.0 inch. Calculate C_{pk} for the process. Is the process capable?

3. In all, 10 samples of 200 observations each were taken from a stamping machine. The samples were inspected, and the number of defective units in each sample was recorded.

   (a) Use the following data to construct a proportion defective chart. Does the process appear to be in control?

   (b) Use the following data to construct a number defective chart. Does the process appear to be in control?

Sample No.	No. of Defective Units in Sample
1	12
2	9
3	11
4	3
5	0
6	5
7	9
8	7
9	11
10	8

4. An inspector takes samples of 20 painted panels from a painting line at random intervals. She records the number of minor defects in each sample. Use the following data to construct a c-chart. Does the process appear to be in control?

Sample No.	No. of Minor Defects in Sample
1	2
2	0
3	0
4	3
5	1
6	2
7	2
8	1
9	0
10	3

5. A drilling process produces two similar products in short runs. Product A has a 1-inch hole drilled in the center. Product B has a ¾-inch hole drilled in the center. The quality engineer has determined that the variances for the 2 hole diameters are equal. Construct a delta chart and range chart for the data provided.

Sample No.	Observation 1	Observation 2	Observation 3
1	1.001	1.003	1.001
2	1.000	1.002	1.002
3	1.003	1.002	1.001
4	0.753	0.753	0.752
5	0.751	0.753	0.752
6	0.752	0.751	0.750

6. One automobile each hour is selected at random for inspection of its paint finish. The finish may have as many as 5 minor defects and is still considered to be acceptable. The inspector records the number of defects in each automobile inspected. Use the following data to create a u-chart. Does the process appear to be in control?

Sample No.	No. of Minor Defects in Sample
1	2
2	2
3	4
4	3
5	12
6	1
7	0
8	0
9	2
10	3

NOTES

1. Bemowski, K. "The Quality Glossary." *Quality Progress,* vol. 25, February 1992, p. 28.

2. Shewhart, W. *Economic Control of Quality of Manufactured Product.* New York: Van Nostrand, 1931.

3. Deming, W. E. *The New Economics.* Cambridge, MA: MIT Center for Advanced Engineering Study, 1993, p. 35.

4. Juran, J. "The Quality Trilogy." *Quality Progress,* vol. 19, August 1986, pp. 19–24. Reprinted in Sower V., J. Motwani, & M. Savoie, *Classic Readings in Operations Management.* Ft. Worth, TX: Dryden, 1995, pp. 277–287.

5. Montgomery, D. C. *Statistical Quality Control,* 3rd ed. New York: Wiley, 1996, pp. 184–185.

6. Evans, J., & W. Lindsay. *The Management and Control of Quality,* 3rd ed. St. Paul, MN: West, 1996, p. 643.

7. Shewart.

8. Burr, I. "The Effect of Non-Normality on Constants for X-bar and R Charts." *Industrial Quality Control,* vol. 23, no. 9, March 1967, pp. 563–568.

9. Western Electric. *Statistical Quality Control Handbook.* Indianapolis: Western Electric Co., 1956.

10. Sower, V., J. Motwani, & M. Savoie. "Delta Charts for Short Run Statistical Process Control." *International Journal of Quality & Reliability Management,* vol. 11, no. 6, 1994, pp. 50–56.

11. Montgomery, D. C. *Statistical Quality Control,* 3rd ed. New York: Wiley, 1996, p. 314.

12. Farnum, N. R. "Control Charts for Short Runs: Nonconstant Process and Measurement Error." *Journal of Quality Technology,* July 1992, pp. 138–144.

13. Bothe, D. R. "SPC for Short Production Runs." *Quality,* December 1988, pp. 58–59.

14. Pyzdek, T. "Process Control for Short and Small Runs." *Quality Progress,* April 1993, pp. 51–60.

15. Duncan, A. *Quality Control and Industrial Statistics,* 5th ed. Homewood, IL: Irwin, 1986, pp. 451–454.

16. Bemowski, p. 26.

17. Ibid.

18. Duncan, p. 503.

SUGGESTED READINGS

Control Charts

Duncan, A. *Quality Control and Industrial Statistics,* 5th ed. Homewood, IL: Irwin, 1986, Chapters 18–23, pp. 417–556.

Evans, J., & W. Lindsay. *The Management and Control of Quality,* 3rd ed. St. Paul, MN: West, 1996, Chapters 15 and 16, pp. 638–734.

Montgomery, D. *Introduction to Statistical Quality Control,* 3rd ed. Wiley, New York, 1996, Chapters 4–9, pp. 129–474.

Shewhart, W. "Excerpts from Economic Control of Manufactured Product" (1931) and "Excerpts from Statistical Method from the Viewpoint of Quality Control" (1939). Reprinted in Sower V., J. Motwani, & M. Savoie. *Classic Readings in Operations Management,* Ft. Worth, TX: Dryden, 1995, pp. 191–230.

Process Capability

Evans, J., & W. Lindsay. *The Management and Control of Quality,* 3d ed. St. Paul, MN: West, 1996, pp. 590–604 and 615–618.

Montgomery, D. *Introduction to Statistical Quality Control,* 3rd ed. New York: Wiley, 1996, Chapter 9, pp. 430–474.

CHAPTER 5

Acceptance Sampling

CHAPTER OBJECTIVES

This chapter introduces the following topics:

- Fundamentals of sampling theory
- Sampling types
- Acceptance sampling plans

INTRODUCTION

It often is impossible to inspect every unit of interest to determine the quality of a lot. A lot is "a defined quantity of product accumulated under conditions that are considered uniform for sampling purposes."[1] Acceptance sampling is an approach to sampling a lot to determine whether the lot should be accepted or rejected (sometimes referred to as lot sentencing). Acceptance sampling is not designed to enable an inspector to estimate the quality of the lot.

Acceptance sampling is by design an "end-of-line" inspection process. It is not a substitute for process control; however, acceptance sampling does have its place in the quality system.[2]

WHEN ACCEPTANCE SAMPLING IS APPROPRIATE

There are a number of reasons why 100 percent inspection is often not practical. Montgomery[3] lists six situations in which acceptance sampling is likely to be useful:

1. When testing is destructive
2. When the cost of 100 percent inspection is extremely high
3. When 100 percent inspection is not technologically feasible or would require so much calendar time that production scheduling would be seriously impacted
4. When there are so many items to be inspected and the inspection error rate is sufficiently high that 100 percent inspection might cause a higher percentage of defective units to be passed than would occur with the use of a sampling plan

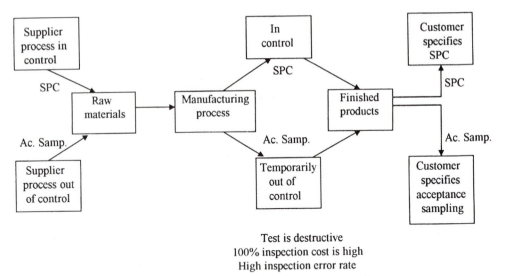

Test is destructive
100% inspection cost is high
High inspection error rate

FIGURE 5.1   Integration of SPC and acceptance sampling.

5. When the vendor has an excellent quality history, and some reduction in inspection from 100 percent is desired, but the vendor's process capability is sufficiently low as to make no inspection an unsatisfactory alternative

6. When there are potentially serious product liability risks, and although the vendor's process is satisfactory, a program for continuously monitoring the product is necessary

Acceptance sampling is condemned by some in the quality field. Deming criticized acceptance sampling plans as techniques that "guarantee that some customers will get defective product."[4] Most, however, concede that acceptance sampling has a legitimate and useful role to play in a quality system. Sower, Motwani, and Savoie[5] provide a model (Figure 5.1) that shows an approach for the appropriate integration of acceptance sampling and statistical process control in a quality system.

Acceptance sampling assumes that the upstream process is not in statistical control and that the proportion of defective product produced by that process can vary widely without warning.[6] Gitlow, Oppenheim, and Oppenheim[7] show that acceptance sampling is invalid for stable processes. As illustrated in Figure 5.1, there are frequent situations where the upstream process is not known to be in a state of statistical control. Therein lies the usefulness of acceptance sampling.

FUNDAMENTALS OF SAMPLING THEORY

In acceptance sampling a decision about a population is made based upon the results of an inspection of a sample taken from that lot. As Figure 5.2 illustrates, the population is the universe of all possible individuals (for a lot of incoming parts, the population is all the individual parts that constitute the lot), and a sample is a subset of that population. In order for a statistically valid decision to be made, the sample must be selected from the population using some random process.

Population

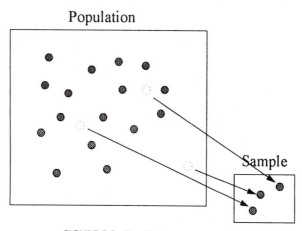

FIGURE 5.2   Population versus sample.

The term *statistically valid* (as in "this is a statistically valid sampling plan") does not mean that the decision dictated by the results of the sampling inspection will always be the correct decision. *Statistically valid* in this context means the probabilities of making the wrong decision can be assessed (calculated). This cannot be done for a statistically *invalid* sampling plan.

Two types of errors (or wrong decisions) can result from sampling inspection. We can incorrectly reject a lot which should be accepted, or we can incorrectly accept a lot which should be rejected. The former is referred to as a Type I or α error; the latter is referred to as a Type II or β error. The risk of making a Type I error is referred to as the *producer's risk;* the risk of making a Type II error is referred to as the *consumer's risk.*

Types of Sampling Plans

A single-sampling plan (where the accept/reject decision is based upon the results of a single sample) is defined by two parameters: the sample size (n) and the acceptance number (c). A sample of size n is randomly selected from a lot of size N. The lot is accepted if the number of defective units in the sample is c or smaller.

Each sampling plan has an operating characteristic (OC) curve associated with it which is uniquely defined by n and c. The OC curve can be used to estimate the probability of making either a Type I or a Type II error. Figure 5.3 shows the general form of an OC curve. The vertical axis shows the probability of accepting the lot. The horizontal axis shows the true fraction of defective items in the lot. From the OC curve in Figure 5.3 we can estimate the probability of, for example, accepting a lot (using this sampling plan) which has a true fraction defective (p) of 0.025. The probability of accepting (P_{ac}) this lot is approximately 0.50. If a lot which contains 0.025 fraction defective is considered to be a rejectable lot, then there is a 0.50 probability (consumer's risk) of accepting this lot. If a lot which contains 0.015 fraction defective is considered to be an acceptable lot, we can estimate the probability of rejecting this lot (producer's risk) as approximately 0.15 ($1 - 0.85$).

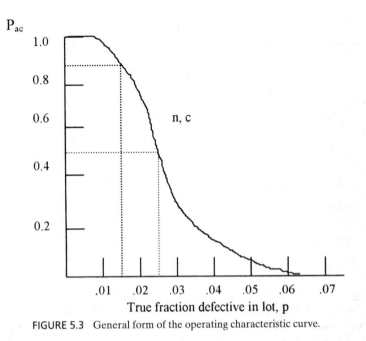

FIGURE 5.3   General form of the operating characteristic curve.

Figure 5.4 shows the ideal operating characteristic curve for a situation where a lot containing a fraction defective of 0.02 or less is considered to be acceptable and greater than 0.02 is considered to be unacceptable. This sampling plan has 0 producer's and 0 consumer's risk. All lots with a fraction defective of 0.02 or less will be accepted with a $P_{ac} = 1.00$. Lots with a fraction defective greater than 0.02 will be rejected with a $P_{ac} = 0$.

The OC curve of a sampling plan can be made to more closely resemble the idealized form by changing the sample size, n, or the acceptance number, c. By increasing the sample size and keeping the acceptance number proportional to n, the OC curve becomes steeper, indicating that the sampling plan is more discriminating. Decreasing the acceptance number while holding n constant has the same effect—the shape of the OC curve becomes more like the ideal.

Sampling plans are often selected based upon the acceptable quality level (AQL). The AQL is the highest proportion defective that is considered acceptable as a long-run average for the process. The AQL focuses on producer's risk. The selection of a sampling plan can also be made on the basis of the lot tolerance percent defective (LTPD). The LTPD is the highest proportion defective that is considered acceptable for a given lot. The LTPD focuses on consumer's risk.

When used for inspecting outgoing lots, acceptance sampling plans are often used in conjunction with 100 percent screening of rejected lots where defective items are replaced with acceptable ones. This is known as rectifying inspection. The average outgoing quality (AOQ) is defined as "the expected average quality level of outgoing product for a given value of incoming product quality."[8] For a process with

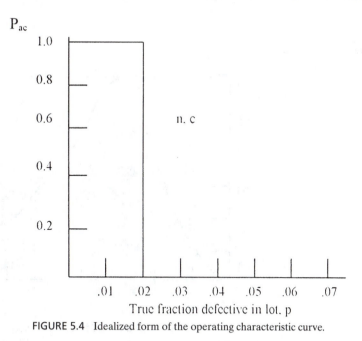

FIGURE 5.4   Idealized form of the operating characteristic curve.

an incoming long-run average fraction defective, p, the AOQ for an acceptance sampling plan with rectifying inspection can be computed as

$$\text{AOQ} = P_{\text{ac}} \times p\left(\frac{N - n}{N}\right) \tag{5.1}$$

If N is large relative to n, Equation (5.2) provides a reasonable approximation to Equation (5.1).

$$\text{AOQ} = P_{\text{ac}}p \tag{5.2}$$

The AOQ changes as the incoming average fraction defective changes. As Figure 5.5 indicates, when lots contain a very low average fraction defective, p, the average fraction defective of outgoing lots is low. Most lots pass without the need for rectifying inspection. As p increases for incoming lots, those lots which pass contain a higher fraction defective resulting in a higher p for outgoing lots. As p increases further, more lots are rejected and are subject to 100 percent rectifying inspection. The p for lots after rectifying inspection is theoretically 0 (assuming no errors in the 100 percent inspection process).

The highest point on the AOQ curve represents the average outgoing quality limit (AOQL). The AOQL represents the highest possible average fraction defective in the outgoing lots resulting from the acceptance sampling plan with rectifying inspection.

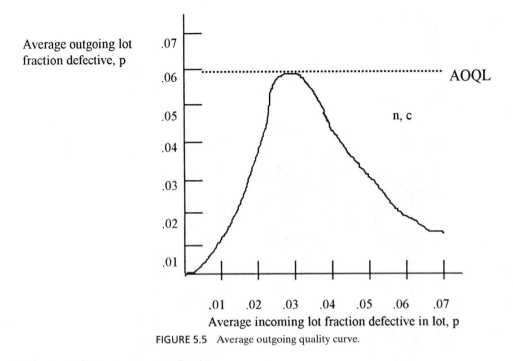

FIGURE 5.5   Average outgoing quality curve.

GENERAL METHODS OF SAMPLING

Several methods of sampling are applicable to acceptance sampling plans. These include:

Simple random sampling
Stratified random sampling
Systematic sampling
Cluster sampling

There are advantages and disadvantages to each method.

Simple random sampling is the most common method of sampling. This method is defined as "a commonly used sampling technique in which sample units are selected in such a manner that all combinations of *n* units under consideration have an equal chance of being selected as the sample."[9] Random sampling frequently utilizes a list of random numbers to determine which units are selected as part of the sample. Figure 5.6 demonstrates one approach to simple random sampling. A pallet load of boxes which constitutes a lot is to be evaluated using acceptance sampling. For a sampling plan which calls for the random selection of 8 boxes for inspection, each box is assigned a sequential number. Using the table of 2-digit random numbers in the figure and starting in column 1, a worker would select 8 boxes (numbers 9, 15, 4, 12, 29, 11, 24, and 7) for inspection. (*Note:* The numbers 67, 56, 89, 91, 59, 83, and 69 are ignored since they are outside the range of the sequence of box numbers.)

Stratified random sampling is used when simple random sampling might produce a sample that would not be representative of the lot. Such a case exists when

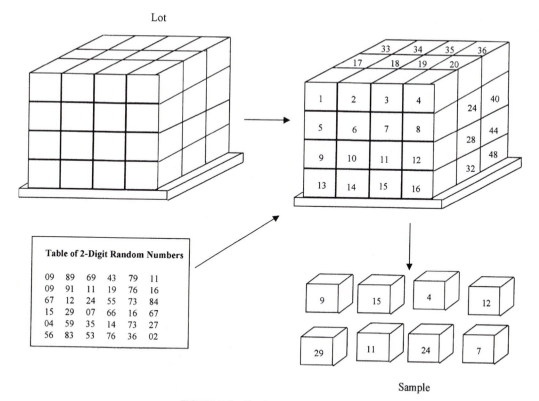

FIGURE 5.6   Simple random sampling.

lots are composed of the output of several processes. In order to properly represent the lot, the sample should consist of random samples from each process in the proportion that each composes the lot.

Consider a lot composed of 1,000 parts produced on two machines, A and B. Machine A produces twice as many parts per hour as Machine B. Therefore the lot to be sampled consists of approximately 67 percent Machine A parts and 33 percent Machine B parts. The sampling plan calls for 80 parts to be selected for inspection. Using stratified random sampling, an inspector would take 53 parts (80 × 0.67) at random from the portion of the lot produced by Machine A and 27 parts (80 × 0.33) at random from the portion of the lot produced by Machine B.

Systematic sampling involves selecting parts for inspection according to a set schedule or plan. An example of systematic sampling would be selecting every *n*th part for inspection from a continuous process. An advantage of systematic sampling is its simplicity. A disadvantage is that it may mask some types of periodic variation in the process.

Cluster sampling involves identifying a typical subgroup (cluster) in the population and taking a random sample from the subgroup to represent the population.[10] Consider the example used in Figure 5.6. If each box on the pallet contained 100 parts, and a sample of 80 was to be selected for inspection, the 8 randomly selected boxes could be considered clusters and 10 parts could be randomly selected from each box.

SAMPLING TYPES

Four main sampling types are used with acceptance sampling plans:

Single sampling
Double sampling
Multiple sampling
Sequential sampling

Under *single sampling,* one sample is taken at random from the lot under consideration and the decision to accept or reject the lot is based upon the results of the inspection of the single sample.

Under *double sampling,* a sample smaller than that used for single sampling is taken from the lot for inspection. The results of the inspection may result in one of three decisions:

Accept the lot.
Reject the lot.
Resample the lot.

If the inspection results do not indicate a clear-cut accept or reject decision, a second sample is taken at random from the lot for inspection. The decision to accept or reject the lot is based upon the result of the inspection of the cumulative sample (i.e., the first and second samples combined). Under *multiple sampling,* the procedure is the same as for double sampling "except that the number of successive samples required to reach a decision might be more than two."[11]

Sequential sampling is a version of multiple sampling whereby units are selected from the lot one at a time. After each unit is inspected, a decision is made to accept the lot, reject the lot, or select another unit for inspection.

SAMPLING PLANS

Three types of sampling plans will be discussed in this section:

Sampling inspection by attributes (ANSI/ASQC Z1.4-1981)
Sampling inspection by variables (ANSI/ASQC Z1.9-1980)
Dodge-Romig

Attributes and variables sampling plans focus on the acceptable quality level and the producer's risk. Dodge-Romig sampling plans focus on the lot tolerance percent defective and the consumer's risk.

Sampling Inspection by Attributes

The most widely accepted plan for sampling inspection by attributes is MIL-STD-105E or its civilian equivalent, ANSI/ASQC Z1.4-1981.[12] There are 7 inspection levels in the Z1.4 systems: 4 special inspection levels (S-1, S-2, S-3, S-4) for use when small sample sizes are required and 3 general inspection levels (I, II, III). Usually the general inspection levels are used. The combination of inspection level and lot size is used to determine the specific sampling plan to use (see Figure 5.7). For

Lot or batch size			Special inspection levels				General inspection levels		
			S-1	S-2	S-3	S-4	I	II	III
2	to	8	A	A	A	A	A	A	B
9	to	15	A	A	A	A	A	B	C
16	to	25	A	A	B	B	B	C	D
26	to	50	A	B	B	C	C	D	E
51	to	90	B	B	C	C	C	E	F
91	to	150	B	B	C	D	D	F	G
151	to	280	B	C	D	E	E	G	H
281	to	500	B	C	D	E	F	H	J
501	to	1200	C	C	E	F	G	J	K
1201	to	3200	C	D	E	G	H	K	L
3201	to	10000	C	D	F	G	J	L	M
10001	to	35000	C	D	F	H	K	M	N
35001	to	150000	D	E	G	J	L	N	P
150001	to	500000	D	E	G	J	M	P	Q
500001	and	over	D	E	H	K	N	Q	R

FIGURE 5.7   Sample size code letters. (Copyright 1981, American Society for Quality Control, used with permission.)

example, using Figure 5.7, if the lot size is 200 and general inspection level II is to be used, sampling plan code letter G (Figure 5.8) is selected.

The sampling type (single, double, or multiple) must be selected as well as the AQL to be used. For example, using Figure 5.8, if single sampling and a 2.5 percent AQL is used, a sample of size 32 must be taken from the lot. If 2 or fewer nonconformities are found, the lot is accepted. If 3 or more nonconformities are found, the lot is rejected.

Integral to the effectiveness of this sampling plan is the employment of the switching rules. These are summarized in Figure 5.9 taken from the ANSI/ASQC Z1.4-1981 standard. Sampling starts with normal inspection (general inspection level II). When 2 out of 5 consecutive lots are not accepted, a switch is made to tightened inspection (general inspection level III). Normal inspection may resume when 5 consecutive lots are accepted under tightened inspection. Should 10 consecutive lots remain on tightened inspection (i.e., no 5 consecutive lots are accepted in the first 10 lots inspected under tightened inspection), sampling under Z1.4 should be discontinued.

A switch is often made from normal to reduced inspection (general inspection level I) when 10 consecutive lots are accepted under normal inspection, production is steady, and the switch is approved by the responsible authority. This enables the lot sentence to be determined using a smaller sample size.

Sampling Inspection by Variables

MIL-STD-414 and its civilian equivalent ANSI/ASQC Z1.9-1980 are standards for sampling inspection by variables. These plans "apply to a single quality characteristic which can be measured on a continuous scale, and for which the quality is expressed in terms of percent nonconforming."[13] The plans "assume that measurements of the quality characteristic are independent, identically distributed normal random variables."[14]

Acceptable Quality Levels (normal inspection)

Type of sampling plan	Cumulative sample size	Less than 0.40 (Ac Re)	0.40 (Ac Re)	0.65 (Ac Re)	1.0 (Ac Re)	1.5 (Ac Re)	2.5 (Ac Re)	4.0 (Ac Re)	6.5 (Ac Re)	10 (Ac Re)	✗ (Ac Re)	15 (Ac Re)	✗ (Ac Re)	25 (Ac Re)	✗ (Ac Re)	40 (Ac Re)	Higher than 40 (Ac Re)	Cumulative sample size
Single	32	▽	0 1	Use	Use	1 2	2 3	3 4	5 6	7 8	8 9	10 11	12 13	14 15	18 19	21 22	△	32
Double	20	▽	*	Letter	Letter	0 2	0 3	1 4	2 5	3 7		5 9		7 11	9 14	11 16	▽	20
	40					1 2	3 4	4 5	6 7	8 9		12 13		18 19	23 24	26 27		40
Multiple	8	▽	*	F	J	# 2	# 2	# 3	# 4	0 4	0 4	0 5	0 6	1 7	1 8	2 9	△	8
	16					# 2	0 3	0 3	1 5	1 6	2 7	3 8	3 9	4 10	6 12	7 14		16
	24					0 2	0 3	1 4	2 6	3 8	4 9	6 10	7 12	8 13	11 17	13 19		24
	32					0 3	1 4	2 5	3 7	5 10	6 11	8 13	10 15	12 17	16 22	19 25		32
	40					1 3	2 4	3 6	5 8	7 11	9 12	11 15	14 17	17 20	22 25	25 29		40
	48					1 3	3 5	4 6	7 9	10 12	12 14	14 17	18 20	21 23	27 29	31 33		48
	56					2 3	4 5	6 7	9 10	13 14	14 15	18 19	21 22	25 26	32 33	37 38		56
Tightened header →		Less than 0.65	0.65	1.0	1.5	2.5	4.0	6.5	10	✗	15	✗	25	✗	40	✗	Higher than 40	

Acceptable Quality Levels (tightened inspection)

△ = Use next preceding sample size code letter for which acceptance and rejection numbers are available.

▽ = Use next subsequent sample size code letter for which acceptance and rejection numbers are available.

Ac = Acceptance number.

Re = Rejection number.

* = Use single sampling plan above (or alternatively use letter K).

= Acceptance not permitted at this sample size.

FIGURE 5.8 Sampling plans for sample size code letter: G. (Copyright 1981, American Society for Quality Control, used with permission.)

G

PLANS

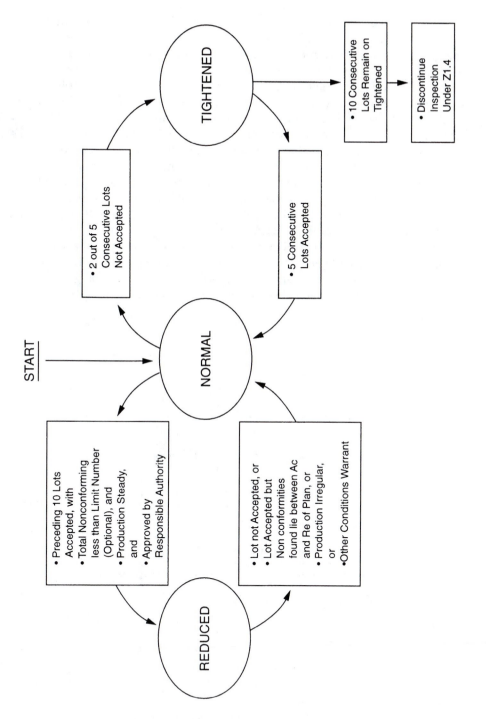

FIGURE 5.9 Switching rules for ANSI Z1.4 system. (Copyright 1981, American Society for Quality Control, used with permission.)

87

Variables data provide more information than do attributes data. Attributes data simply define the units under test as *conforming* (acceptable) or *nonconforming* (not acceptable). Variables data provide actual measurement data for the quality characteristic under consideration, thus providing information such as how close are the observations to the specification limit—information that is not available using attributes data.

While there are some differences between MIL-STD-414 and ANSI/ASQC Z1.9-1980, the general procedures for using these plans are the same. These procedures generally follow the plan for using MIL-STD-105E and ANSI/ASQC Z1.4-1981. The switching rules (for switching to/from normal, tightened, and reduced inspection) are essentially identical to those for MIL-STD-414 and ANSI/ASQC Z1.9-1980.

There are 5 inspection levels in the Z1.9 system, 2 special inspection levels (I and II in MIL-STD-414; S3 and S4 in ANSI/ASQC Z1.9) and 3 general inspection levels (III, IV, and V in MIL-STD-414; I, II, and III in ANSI/ASQC Z1.9). Usually the general inspection levels are used. As with sampling inspection by attributes, the combination of inspection level and lot size is used to determine the specific sampling plan to use (see Figure 5.10). For example, using Figure 5.10, if the lot size is 200, and the specification is 1-sided (single specification limit), and general inspection level II is used, then sample size code letter G (Figure 5.11) is selected.

Lot Size		Inspection Levels				
		Special S3	S4	General I	II	III
2 to	8	B	B	B	B	C
9 to	15	B	B	B	B	D
16 to	25	B	B	B	C	E
26 to	50	B	B	C	D	F
51 to	90	B	B	D	E	G
91 to	150	B	C	E	F	H
151 to	280	B	D	F	G	I
281 to	400	C	E	G	H	J
401 to	500	C	E	G	I	J
501 to	1,200	D	F	H	J	K
1,201 to	3,200	E	G	I	K	L
3,201 to	10,000	F	H	J	L	M
10,001 to	35,000	G	I	K	M	N
35,001 to	150,000	H	J	L	N	P
150,001 to	500,000	H	K	M	P	P
500,001 and	over	H	K	N	P	P

[1]Sample size code letters given in body of table are applicable when the indicated inspection levels are to be used.

[2]The theory governing inspection by variables depends on the properties of the normal distribution and, therefore, this method of inspection is only applicable when there is reason to believe that the frequency of distribution is normal.

FIGURE 5.10 Sample size code letters. (Copyright 1980, American Society for Quality Control, used with permission.)

Acceptable Quality Levels (normal inspection)

Sample size code letter	Sample size	T (k)	.10 (k)	.15 (k)	.25 (k)	.40 (k)	.65 (k)	1.00 (k)	1.50 (k)	2.50 (k)	4.00 (k)	6.50 (k)	10.00 (k)
B	3	↓	↓	↓	↓	↓	↓	↓	↓	1.12	.958	.765	.566
C	4	↓	↓	↓	↓	↓	↓	1.45	1.34	1.17	1.01	.814	.617
D	5	↓	↓	↓	↓	↓	1.65	1.53	1.40	1.24	1.07	.874	.675
E	7	↓	↓	↓	2.00	1.88	1.75	1.62	1.50	1.33	1.15	.955	.755
F	10	↓	↓	2.24	2.11	1.98	1.84	1.72	1.58	1.41	1.23	1.03	.828
G	15	2.53	2.42	2.32	2.20	2.06	1.91	1.79	1.65	1.47	1.30	1.09	.886
H	20	2.58	2.47	2.36	2.24	2.11	1.96	1.82	1.69	1.51	1.33	1.12	.917
I	25	2.61	2.50	2.40	2.26	2.14	1.98	1.85	1.72	1.53	1.35	1.14	.936
J	35	2.65	2.54	2.45	2.31	2.18	2.03	1.89	1.76	1.57	1.39	1.18	.969
K	50	2.71	2.60	2.50	2.35	2.22	2.08	1.93	1.80	1.61	1.42	1.21	1.00
L	75	2.77	2.66	2.55	2.41	2.27	2.12	1.98	1.84	1.65	1.46	1.24	1.03
M	100	2.80	2.69	2.58	2.43	2.29	2.14	2.00	1.86	1.67	1.48	1.26	1.05
N	150	2.84	2.73	2.61	2.47	2.33	2.18	2.03	1.89	1.70	1.51	1.29	1.07
P	200	2.85	2.73	2.62	2.47	2.33	2.18	2.04	1.89	1.70	1.51	1.29	1.07
		.10	.15	.25	.40	.65	1.00	1.50	2.50	4.00	6.50	10.00	

Acceptable Quality Levels (tightened inspection)

All AQL values are in percent nonconforming. *T* denotes plan used exclusively on tightened inspection and provides symbol for identification of appropriate OC curve.

↓ Use first sampling plan below arrow; that is, both sample size as well as *k* value. When sample size equals or exceeds lot size, every item in the lot must be inspected.

FIGURE 5.11 Master table for normal and tightened inspection for plans based on variability unknown (Single Specification Limit—Form 1). Standard Deviation Method

Sample size code letter G specifies a sample of size 15 be randomly selected from the lot. Note that this is less than half the size of the sample required for the same lot size under sampling inspection by attributes. Sampling inspection by variables provides roughly the same discriminating ability (OC curve) using a smaller sample size than sampling inspection by attributes. If the AQL selected is 2.5 percent, the k value (acceptability constant) to be used is 1.47. Example 5.1 illus-

A lot containing 50 bottles of a pressurized solution is presented for inspection. The specification for this product requires that the pressure in each bottle not exceed 50 psi (single specification limit). Normal inspection is to be used (IV in MIL-STD-414; II in ANSI/ASQC Z1.9) with an AQL of 2.5 percent. Using Figures 5.10 and 5.11, a sample of size 5 is required and the k value (acceptability constant) to be used is 1.24. The calculations, using Form 1, are:

Sample size $(n) = 5$

AQL = 2.5%

Acceptability constant $(k) = 1.24$

The samples are randomly selected and tested, and the following results are obtained:

Sample No.	Pressure, psi	Pressure Squared
1	49.5	2,450.25
2	49.2	2,420.64
3	49.2	2,420.64
4	49.4	2,440.36
5	49.1	2,410.81
Sum of measurements =	246.4	
Sum of squared measurements =		12,142.70

Correction factor $[CF = (\Sigma x)^2/n] = 12{,}142.59$

Corrected sum of squares $[SS = \Sigma x^2 - CF] = 12{,}142.70 - 12{,}142.59 = 0.11$

Variance $[V = SS/(n-1)] = 0.11/4 = 0.028$

Estimated lot standard deviation $[s = \sqrt{V}] = \sqrt{0.028} = 0.167$

Sample mean $[\overline{X} = \Sigma x/n] = 49.28$

Specification limit $[U] = 50.00$

$(U - \overline{X})/s = 4.31$

Compare $(U - \overline{X})/s$ with k: 4.31 > 1.24

Accept the lot since $(U - \overline{X})/s$ is greater than k.

EXAMPLE 5.1 Example of sampling inspection by variables calculations.

trates the calculations required to determine the disposition of a lot using this sampling plan.

Dodge-Romig Sampling Plans

Dodge-Romig sampling plans are designed for use with rectifying inspection where rejected lots are subjected to 100 percent inspection. There are Dodge-Romig tables for desired AOQL levels. These tables show the sample size, n, (based upon the lot size) and the acceptance number, c, for the specified AOQL. The tables also show the resulting LTPD, where the probability of acceptance, P_{ac}, on the OC curve is equal to 0.10 (see Figure 5.12).

Using the partial table in Figure 5.12, we see that the sample size for a lot of size 300 taken from a process whose process average proportion defective is 0.75 percent would be 26. The acceptance number would be 1 (accept with 0 or 1 nonconforming units, reject with 2 or more). The probability of accepting a lot with 14.6 percent nonconforming would be 0.10. This means that the probability of rejecting incoming lots as bad as 14.6 percent defective is 0.90 (1.00–0.10).

There also are Dodge-Romig tables for desired LTPD levels. These tables show the sample size, n, (based upon the lot size) and the acceptance number, c, for the specified LTPD. The tables also show the resulting AOQL for each plan (see Figure 5.13).

Using the partial table in Figure 5.13, we see that the sample size for a lot of size 300 taken from a process whose process average proportion defective is 0.45 percent would be 165. The acceptance number would be 0 (accept with 0 nonconforming units, reject with 1 or more). The AOQL associated with this sampling plan (assuming rectifying inspection) would be 0.10 percent.

Single-Sampling Plans for AOQL = 3.0%

| | Process Average | | | | | | | | | | | | | | |
| | 0-0.06% | | | 0.07-0.60% | | | 0.61-1.20% | | | 1.21-1.80% | | | 1.81-2.40% | | |
Lot Size	n	c	LTPD %	n	c	LTPD %	n	c	LTPD %	n	c	LTPD %	n	c	LTPD %
11-50	10	0	19.0	10	0	19.0	10	0	19.0	10	0	19.0	10	0	19.0
51-100	11	0	18.0	11	0	18.0	11	0	18.0	11	0	18.0	11	0	18.0
101-200	12	0	17.0	12	0	17.0	12	0	17.0	25	1	15.1	24	1	15.1
201-300	12	0	17.0	12	0	17.0	26	1	14.6	26	1	14.6	26	1	14.6
301-400	12	0	17.1	12	0	17.1	26	1	14.7	26	1	14.7	41	2	12.7

FIGURE 5.12   Extract from Dodge-Romig AOQL table.[15]

Single-Sampling Plans for LTPD = 1.0%

| Lot Size | Process Average | | | | | | | | | | | | | |
| | 0 | | | 0.01-0.10% | | | 0.11-0.20% | | | 0.31-0.40% | | | 0.41-0.50% | | |
	n	c	AOQL %	n	c	AOQL %	n	c	AOQL %	n	c	AOQL %	n	c	AOQL %
1-120	All	0	0	All	0	0	All	0	0	All	0	0	All	0	0
121-150	120	0	0.06	120	0	0.06	120	0	0.06	120	0	0.06	120	0	0.06
151-200	140	0	0.08	140	0	0.08	140	0	0.08	140	0	0.08	140	0	0.08
201-300	165	0	0.10	165	0	0.10	165	0	0.10	165	0	0.10	165	0	0.10
301-400	175	0	0.12	175	0	0.12	175	0	0.12	175	0	0.12	175	0	0.12

FIGURE 5.13.   Extract from Dodge-Romig LTPD table.[16]

SUMMARY

Inspection of 100 percent of the units that make up the lots is often not practical. Acceptance sampling provides a means for making the decision to either accept or reject the lot based upon the inspection of a sample taken from that lot. There is an appropriate place for acceptance sampling even within a statistical process control environment. It is important to understand the theory of sampling in order to properly utilize sampling plans. There are sampling plans which focus on the AQL (producer's risk) and others which focus on the LTPD (consumer's risk). Each type of sampling plan has its appropriate place within the quality system.

DISCUSSION QUESTIONS

1. Discuss the integration of acceptance sampling with statistical process control in a quality system.
2. Why is it important that a sample taken from a lot be random?
3. What is meant by the term *statistically valid?*
4. Discuss the information to be obtained from the OC curve for a particular sampling plan.
5. How can a quality engineer make the OC curve closer to the ideal shape?
6. Discuss the significance of the difference between AQL and LTPD.
7. What method of sampling would be most appropriate when the population consists of two categories of members in unequal numbers?
8. Under what circumstances is cluster sampling appropriate?
9. What are switching rules and why are they important?

PROBLEMS

1. Supplier A ships materials to your company in lots of 200 units. Your company uses an ANSI Z1.4 acceptance sampling plan (general inspection levels) to inspect incoming lots of material. Supplier A has been on tightened inspection, but the last 5 consecutive lots have been accepted. What sample size code letter should be used for the next lot?

2. Using the OC curve in Figure 5.3, what is the probability of accepting a lot whose true fraction defective is 0.40?

3. Use the first two digits in the first column of the random number table in Appendix A to select 5 sample boxes from the lot depicted in Figure 5.5. Which 5 boxes would be selected?

4. There are 600 female and 400 male students enrolled in basic mathematics courses at State University. The chair of the Mathematics Department wants to select a stratified random sample of 50 students to participate in a survey. How many male and how many female students should be in the sample of 50?

5. A company is using sampling plan code letter G of ANSI/ASQC Z1.4 to inspect an incoming lot of material. The company is using normal inspection, single sampling, and an AQL of 2.5 percent. Using Figure 5.8 in the text, determine how many units from the lot should be inspected. What disposition should be made of the lot if 1 defective unit is found in the sample? If 4 defective units are found in the sample?

NOTES

1. Bemowski, K. "The Quality Glossary." *Quality Progress,* vol. 25, no. 2, February 1992, p. 25.

2. Sower, V. E., J. Motwani, & M. Savoie. "Are Acceptance Sampling and Statistical Process Control Complementary or Incompatible?" *Quality Progress,* vol. 26, no. 9, September 1993, pp. 85–89.

3. Montgomery, D. C. *Introduction to Statistical Quality Control,* 3rd ed. New York: Wiley, New York, 1996, p. 608.

4. Deming, W. E. *Out of the Crisis.* Cambridge, MA: Massachusetts Institute of Technology, 1986.

5. Sower et al., p. 86.

6. Ibid.

7. Gitlow, H., A. Oppenheim, & R. Oppenheim. *Quality Management,* 2nd ed. Burr Ridge, IL: Irwin, 1995, pp. 439–442.

8. Bemowski, K., p. 20.

9. Ibid., p. 27.

10. See paragraph 7.2, page 4, of ANSI/ASQC Z1.4-1981.

11. ANSI/ASQC Z1.4-1981, p. 6.

12. Montgomery, p. 636.

13. ANSI/ASQC Z1.9-1980, p. vi.

14. Ibid., p. vi.

15. Dodge, H., & H. Romig. *Sampling Inspection Tables, Single and Double Sampling,* 2nd ed. New York: Wiley, 1959.

16. Ibid.

SUGGESTED READINGS

ANSI/ASQC Z1.4-1981

ANSI/ASQC Z1.9-1980

Dodge, H. F., & H. G. Romig. *Sampling Inspection Tables, Single and Double Sampling,* 2nd ed. New York: Wiley, 1959.

Duncan, A. J. *Quality Control and Industrial Statistics,* 5th ed. Homewood, IL: Irwin, 1986, Chapters 7–17, pp. 161–414.

Evans, J. R., & W. M. Lindsay. *The Management and Control of Quality,* 3rd ed. Minneapolis: West, 1996, Chapter 14, pp. 572–584 and 604–613.

Grant, E. L., & R. S. Leavenworth. *Statistical Quality Control,* 7th ed. New York: McGraw-Hill, 1996, Chapters 11–15, pp. 425–601.

MIL-STD-105.

MIL-STD-414.

MIL-STD-1235.

Montgomery, D. C. *Introduction to Statistical Quality Control,* 3rd ed. New York: Wiley, 1996, Chapters 13 and 14, pp. 605–677.

CHAPTER 6

Experimental Design

CHAPTER OBJECTIVES

This chapter introduces the following topics:

- Basic concepts and definitions of experimental design
- Characteristics of experimental design
- Examples of the different types and methodologies of experimental design and the pros and cons associated with each
- One-way and two-way analysis of variance (ANOVA)
- Taguchi methods, including the three elements of quality engineering, loss function, orthogonal arrays and linear graphs, and robustness

INTRODUCTION

Experiments can be performed by anyone wishing to answer a question. We all perform experiments of one kind or another. When we take a different route home from work, we are experimenting to see if there is a significant difference in the amount of time it takes to get home the new way versus the amount of time when we take the old way. An experiment is a test performed to discover something about a particular process or system. Like all things, the better the design of the test or experiment, the better chance of finding out the desired information.

Experimental design is defined as "a formal plan that details the specifics for conducting an experiment, such as which responses, factors, levels, blocks, treatments, and tools are to be used."[1] Designed experiments are important tools for optimizing processes, identifying interactions among process variables, and reducing variation in processes.

BASIC CONCEPTS AND DEFINITIONS

In design of experiments the experimenter changes the inputs to a process in a systematic way and evaluates resulting changes in the outputs. The inputs are called the independent variables (X-variables), and the outputs are called the dependent variables (Y-variables). A *dependent variable* is the variable of primary interest in an experiment. *Independent variables* are those we believe will affect the measurements obtained on the dependent variable for a given experiment. It is possible for several independent variables to be under investigation simultaneously.

In an experimental investigation, each independent variable that is assumed to influence the dependent variable of interest is called a *factor*. The various logical categories or intensities of the factors being investigated are referred to as *levels* or *treatments*. In a given experiment, several independent variables, or factors, might be under investigation simultaneously. A specific combination of factor levels imposed on a single unit of experimental material is called a *treatment combination*.

Three basic concepts of experimental design are replication, randomization, and local control.[2] When 2 identical experimental units receive the same treatment or treatment combination and yield different responses or measurements, the difference between a value obtained through statistical analysis of a sample and the actual value based on the population as a whole is defined as *error*. Error arises due to random forces and due to other variables which contribute to variation, but which are not singled out for investigation (i.e., not included as factors in the experiment). When two or more identical experimental units are subjected to the same treatment, the experiment is said to be replicated. *Replication* is necessary in an experiment in order to provide a measure of experimental error.

Randomization is a requirement for the statistical methods used to analyze the results of designed experiments and also minimizes the effect of procedural bias. Randomization is achieved through the use of random numbers to determine the order of experimental trials and to assign the order for specific inputs.

Local control refers to the use of *blocks*. Blocks are a "subdivision of the experiment space into relatively homogeneous experimental units between which the experimental error can be expected to be smaller than would be expected should a similar number of units be randomly located within the experimental space."[3] An example of the use of blocking would be the testing of fertilizers by applying the different treatments to test plots within a small block of the field. The external variables (e.g., amount of sunlight, basic soil fertility, drainage) within the block would be expected to vary less than over the entire field. This provides for "a more homogeneous experiment subspace."[4]

Blocking is used as an alternative to a completely randomized experiment. Consider a case of testing the hardness of material used in a metal stamping process. The experimenter has been provided several different stamping tools—i.e., different designs, materials, weights, etc. He or she wants to determine which of various stamping tools will provide the best impact on the metal plates being stamped. In a completely randomized design, each tool would be used to stamp randomized pieces of stamping material and the results compared. While this sounds okay, a closer examination could reveal that random variations in the stamping material could introduce a bias to the experiment that may skew the test results. In order to minimize this bias, a randomized block design is used. In this case, a number of pieces of stamping material are randomly selected. All tools are tested at random points on each piece of material. By using this method, we have minimized the potential bias from variations in the stamping material and thus have a more robust data set for comparing the various stamping tools.

EXPERIMENTAL DESIGN CHARACTERISTICS

There are 4 basic design characteristics in experimental design:

1. Balance
2. Replication
3. Efficiency
4. Fit

Balance refers to having an equal number of observations, n, in each cell. For example, if we are studying three groups—men, women, and children—and we want to ensure that we have balanced treatment in the experiment, we would make sure that each group would have the same number of subjects, say 50 men, 50 women, and 50 children. Balance is important because it facilitates the use of more multiple comparison procedures. It can also prevent certain forms of bias from affecting the experimental results. If, for example, we were to include 200 men, 50 women, and 50 children, the overall study would be biased toward the results obtained for the group of men and, therefore, would provide an inaccurate portrayal of the overall dynamics of the situation. An *orthogonal design* provides both horizontal and vertical balancing.

Replication, discussed in the previous section, refers to the repetition of the basic experiment. Replication is necessary "to increase the precision of the estimates of the effects."[5]

Efficiency has to do with how focused or precise is the experimental design. For example, in a higher-order factorial design, we may perform a partial factorial (i.e., look at a specific set of variables while ignoring others) because we are interested in the reaction of specific components of the interaction. This would be more efficient than a full k-factorial design, which would take into account all factors, thus including specific factors that are not of interest for this particular experiment. The upside to this approach is that experiments are easier to run and the variables (factors) are those in which we are interested. The downside is that we may miss a relation that we did not expect since only those factors previously identified as pertinent are being evaluated.

Fit refers to how well the experimental design fits the actual population. Fit is usually calculated using error, which measures the difference between what our experimental analysis tells us the outcome should be and what the actual outcome is using the entire population.

TYPES OF DESIGN

There are various types of experimental designs. When there are several factors of interest in an experiment, a factorial design should be used. In a *full-factorial design* or experiment, all possible combinations of the levels of the factors are investigated in each complete trial of the experiment. Thus if there are two factors, A and B, with j levels of factor A and k levels of factor B, then each replicate contains all jk possible combinations.

Single-Factor Design

When a single factor is of interest a *one-factor* or *single-factor design* is appropriate. The single-factor design is appropriate when we desire information on the relationship between a single input factor and the output factor in the experiment. A single-factor design saves time and effort since it focuses on a single item rather than all possible combinations of many factors; yet it may result in a suboptimal solution for the same reason. A full-factorial design is best used when we are concerned about the effects of the interactions of the multiple factors because single-factor experiments cannot assess these interaction effects. As well, a full-factorial design is best used when the need for a complete data set outweighs the potential cost savings of a smaller, more focused experiment.

An example of a single-factor experiment would be the analysis of the effect of input concentration of a chlorinator on bacterial counts in a stream of water. Three levels of chlorination are to be evaluated, and the trials are to be replicated three times. Using the random number table in Appendix A results in the following sequence of trials:

Trial	Chlorination Level
1	1
2	2
3	1
4	1
5	2
6	3
7	2
8	3
9	3

Clorination levels: 1—0.2%
                     2—0.4%
                     3—0.6%

EXAMPLE 6.1

An engineer is interested in finding the values of temperature and time that maximize yield. Suppose we fix temperature at 160°F (the current operating level) and perform 5 runs at different levels of time. The results of this series of runs are shown in the table below.

Run Time (hr)	Yield (%)
0.5	42
1.0	50
1.5	62
2.0	70
2.5	66

This experiment indicates that maximum yield is achieved at approximately 2.0 hours of reaction time. To optimize temperature, the engineer fixes time at 2.0 hours (the apparent optimum) and performs 5 runs at different temperatures.

Temperature (°F)	Yield (%)
140	36
150	44
160	76
170	62
180	31

Based on the data from the second experiment, maximum yield occurs at 160°F.

Therefore, we would conclude that running the process at 160°F and 2.0 hours is the best set of operating conditions, resulting in a yield around 73 percent $[(70 + 76)/2]$.

The downside of one-factor design is that it fails to detect the interactions between the two factors (in this case time and temperature). For the example above, a full-factor analysis indicates that optimal yield is really around 95 percent at a temperature between 180°F and 190°F and a time around 0.5 hour.

One-Factor-at-a-Time Design

When multiple factors are to be considered, a simplistic approach is to vary one factor at a time and hold the other factors constant. This is a very inefficient experimental design, and unless all possible combinations are run, it does not allow for the estimation of inter-action effects among the variables. Using the one-factor-at-a-time approach to evaluate 3 levels of 3 factors would result in the need to run 3^3, or 27, trials (without replications). The following table shows the testing of 7 of the 27 combinations. The results would provide no ability to assess possible interaction effects among the variables.

Run	X_1	X_2	X_3
1	1	1	1
2	2	1	1
3	3	1	1
4	3	2	1
5	3	3	1
6	3	3	2
7	3	3	3

This problem increases as the number of factors and levels increases. To evaluate 3 levels of 10 factors would require 3^{10}, or 59,049, trials.

Full-Factorial Design

A full factorial design involves testing all possible combinations of the factors in an experiment at a number of levels. A full-factorial design allows for the estimation of

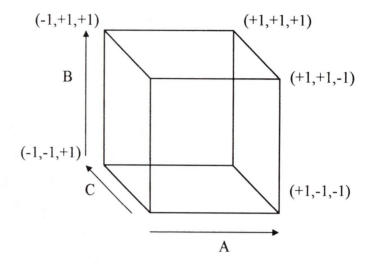

Run	A	B	C	A × B	A × C	B × C	A × B × C
1	−1	−1	−1	+1	+1	+1	−1
2	+1	−1	−1	−1	−1	+1	+1
3	−1	+1	−1	−1	+1	−1	+1
4	+1	+1	−1	+1	−1	−1	−1
5	−1	−1	+1	+1	−1	−1	+1
6	+1	−1	+1	−1	+1	−1	−1
7	−1	+1	+1	−1	−1	+1	−1
8	+1	+1	+1	+1	+1	+1	+1

FIGURE 6.1 2^3 full-factorial design.

all main effects and all interaction effects. The difficulty is that this design requires a considerable investment of time and resources. This becomes of increasing importance as the number of factors increases. A full-factorial design for 2 levels of 3 factors (k) is shown in Figure 6.1.

Fractional-Factorial Design

A fractional-factorial design involves testing an orthogonal subset of all possible combinations of the factors. A fractional-factorial design allows for the estimation of all main effects and selected interaction effects. The sacrifice in information obtained is balanced by the reduced resource requirements compared with a full-factorial design. A 2^{3-1} fractional factorial design for the example in Figure 6.1 is shown in Figure 6.2.

Run	A	B	C	A×B	A×C	B×C	A×B×C
2	+1	−1	−1	−1	−1	+1	+1
3	−1	+1	−1	−1	+1	−1	+1
5	−1	−1	+1	+1	−1	−1	+1
8	+1	+1	+1	+1	+1	+1	+1

FIGURE 6.2 2^{3-1} fractional-factorial design.

ANALYSIS OF RESULTS

As discussed earlier, design of experiments is used to study the product or process. Once we have the data from the experiment, however, they must be analyzed. Analysis of variance (ANOVA) is used to interpret the experimental data. For example, a researcher is often concerned with knowing if two or more groups differ on a specific factor (dependent variable). While the groups may occur naturally, more often than not the researcher creates the groups. Either way, the researcher can use a fixed-effects linear model to test for differences.

EXAMPLE 6.2   ONE-WAY ANALYSIS OF VARIANCE

Suppose we conduct a survey concerning the attitudes of Silicon Valley executives toward national economic policy. For our example, 16 firms were examined, 4 each in each of the following categories: small, medium, large, and very large. Determine if attitudes are different given the size of the corporation.

The 16 executives are questioned and the results tabulated. The higher the score, the more favorable the attitude toward economic policy. Assume the population means of the 4 company size groups are:

Small	50
Medium	55
Large	60
Very large	65

and the population variance for each group is 10. Since the means are population means, we can conclude that the means are different without a hypothesis test and, therefore, that the attitudes are different among the 4 groups.

With equal numbers in each group, a grand mean (u_{grand}) can be calculated by taking the average of the group means:

$$u_{grand} = (u_s + u_m + u_1 + u_{vl})/p = (50 + 55 + 60 + 65)/4 = 230/4 = 57.5$$

An effect is defined as the difference between a group mean and a grand mean. Furthermore, each group effect is represented by the difference between the group mean and the grand mean. For example, the effect for the smallest company is obtained by subtracting the grand mean from the group mean for the small companies.

$$\text{Group effect (small)} = u_s - u_{grand} = 50 - 57.5 = -7.5$$

Each effect can be interpreted as either adding to or reducing an attitude score, depending on the sign of the effect and the particular group. The above calculation, therefore, would be interpreted as meaning that being in a small company reduces an executive's attitude score by an average of 7.5 units.

In the real world, we rarely have full population data. Most of our experiments will use samples, not populations. We also need to keep in mind that inherent in all studies are components of error. Sample statistics and assumptions allow the researcher to test hypotheses about the parameters in a given model. To perform an analysis of variance using sample data, we make four basic assumptions:

1. The samples are random.
2. The populations are normal.
3. Variances in the populations are equal.
4. The samples are independent of each other.

The components of the model are estimated using least squares calculations on the sample data.

EXAMPLE 6.3

Suppose instead of the population used in Example 6.2, we conduct a survey of business manager's attitudes toward national economic policy. Once again, we are interested in determining if corporate size has an effect on attitude. We design our experiment to sample 4 executives from 4 different size companies in similar types of business. The higher the score, the more favorable the manager's attitude toward national economic policy. The data from the survey are shown below.

Sample	Small	Medium	Large	Very Large
1	37	36	43	76
2	22	45	75	66
3	22	47	66	43
4	25	23	46	62
$n=$	4	4	4	4

The null hypothesis for the test is that the population means are equal:

$$H_0 = \mu_s = \mu_m = \mu_l = \mu_{vl}$$

To test this hypothesis, we use analysis of variance. The linear model for a one-way ANOVA is

$$Y_{ij} = \mu + \alpha_j + e_{ij}$$

where Y_{ij} represents the ith attitude score of an executive in the jth group.

The estimates of the model parameters based upon the collected data can replace the model parameters, resulting in the following equation:

$$Y_{ij} = Y_G + (Y_j - Y_G) + (Y_{ij} - Y_j)$$

where
$$Y_{ij} = \text{attitude score}$$
$$Y_g = \text{grand mean}$$
$$(Y_j - Y_G) = \text{effect of membership in the } j\text{th group}$$
$$(Y_{ij} - Y_j) = \text{individual error}$$

Solving this equation can reproduce any score in the above table.

Total variance can be broken down into 2 components: between-group variation and within-group variation. We use the sum of squares to represent the partitioned variation. By calculating the sum of squares and the appropriate degrees of freedom for each component of variation, the null hypothesis can be tested using the F distribution (see Appendix C). It is common to see the sum of squares (SS) presented in an ANOVA table that gives all the pertinent data to test the null hypothesis by calculating the proper test statistic.

EXAMPLE 6.4   ANALYSIS OF VARIANCE TABLE

Continuing with the data from Example 6.3, we can create the following ANOVA table:

Company Size	Sum Y_{ij}	(Sum Y_{ij})²	Sum Y_{ij}^2
Small	106	11,236	
Medium	151	22,801	
Large	230	52,900	
Very large	247	61,009	
Totals	734	147,946	38,792

Grand mean = sum of all the scores/N = 734/16 = 45.875

Sum of squared group totals/n = 147,946/4 = 36,986.50

Correction term (CT) = grand total squared/total sample size = $734^2/16$ = 33,672.25

Sum of squares total = sum of squared observations − CT = 38,792 − 33,672.25 = 5,119.75

Sum of squares between = sum of squared group totals/n − CT = 36,986.50 − 33,672.25
$$= 3,314.25$$

Sum of squares within = SS total − SS between = 5,119.75 − 3,314.25 = 1,805.50

Source of Variation	SS	Degree of Freedom	MS (Mean of Squares)	F
Between (B) groups	3,314.25	$(p-1) = 3$	$\text{SS}_B/(p-1) = 1,104.75$	
Within (W) groups	1,805.50	$p(n-1) = 12$	$\text{SS}_W/[p(n-1)] = 150.46$	$\text{MS}_B/\text{MS}_W = 7.34$
Total	5,119.75	$N-1 = 15$		

The above table provides all the necessary data to test the null hypothesis using the F distribution.

If we choose a level of significance, α, of 0.01, we can then calculate the F statistic for

$$\alpha = 0.01 \qquad (3,12) \text{ degrees of freedom}$$
$$\text{Critical } F = 5.95$$

The test statistic from the ANOVA table above is 7.34.

Since the test statistic is greater than the critical value $(7.34 > 5.95)$, we can conclude that the population means are not all the same and therefore we can reject the null hypothesis.

In the previous discussion, we dealt with a situation in which the dependent variable is maintained at the same level across the different groups. The problem with this approach is the inability to replicate the results. The patterns observed in a particular experiment may be the result of another relevant variable that was held constant in the experiment.

The two-way ANOVA provides one solution to this problem by allowing the effect of an independent variable to be averaged over levels of another relevant variable. Classification variables in a two-way ANOVA are called factors, and the categories within the factors are referred to as levels of a factor. There are two classification variables and one dependent variable of interest in this design.

The model for the two-way ANOVA is similar to the one-way ANOVA model with the exception of an added effect term for each factor (the main effect) and an effect term for the combined effects of both factors (the interaction effect). The linear model is

$$Y_{ijk} + \mu + \alpha_l + \beta_j + \gamma_{ij} + e_{ijk}$$
$$i = 1, 2, \ldots, r$$
$$j = 1, 2, \ldots, c$$
$$k = 1, 2, \ldots, m$$

where Y_{ijk} = the kth attitude score for Level i of factor A and Level j of factor B
μ = grand mean
α_i = effect of the ith group
β_j = effect of the jth group
γ_{ij} = combined effect for the ijth cell
e_{ijk} = difference between μ and Y_{ijk}

EXAMPLE 6.5   TWO-WAY ANALYSIS OF VARIANCE

The results of our initial analysis of executive attitudes toward national policy showed that company size had a significant influence on executive attitude. In studying the data, however, we realize that the age of the executives being polled may be a factor in their attitude as well. We now want to analyze the data for the effects of executive age, company size, and any combinations of the two factors. We have summarized our data in the table that follows.

Age Group (Factor A)	Company Size (Factor B)			
a1 25–39 years	Small (b1)	Medium (b2)	Large (b3)*	Row Means
	42	50	49	
	46	46	52	$Y1 = 45.0$
	44	42	34	
Sums	**132**	**138**	**135**	
Cell Means	44	46	45	
a2 40–65 years	36	50	62	
	38	36	60	$Y2 = 46.33$
	31	49	55	
Sums	**105**	**135**	**177**	
Cell Means	35	45	59	
Column Means	39.5	45.5	52.0	

* To simplify the example, we have combined the large and extra-large factors into a single factor.

The first step is to add up scores in each cell to obtain cell totals, which are shown in the sums rows in the above table.

Step 2 is to square each score in the entire table and sum the values:

$$42^2 + 46^2 + 44^2 +$$
$$36^2 + 38^2 + 31^2 +$$
$$50^2 + 46^2 + 42^2 +$$
$$50^2 + 36^2 + 49^2 +$$
$$49^2 + 52^2 + 34^2 +$$
$$62^2 + 60^2 + 55^2 = 38,824$$

In Step 3, we add up all the cell totals:

$$132 + 138 + 135 + 105 + 135 + 177 = 822$$

In Step 4, we square the total of all the cells and divide by N (the total number of scores in the table). This is the correction term (CT):

$$CT = (822)^2/18 = 37,538$$

In Step 5, we calculate the total sum of squares (SS_T)

$$SS_T = 38,824 - 37,538 = 1,286$$

In Step 6, we compute the effects of factor B. First, add the column sums together:

$$132 + 105 = 237$$
$$138 + 135 = 273$$
$$135 + 177 = 312$$

Now square each value and divide by the total number of observations in a column:

$$237^2/6 = 9,361.50$$
$$273^2/6 = 12,421.50$$
$$312^2/6 = 16,224.00$$

Then add them together:

$$9,361.50 + 12,421.50 + 16,224 = 38,007.00$$

Now subtract the correction term from this value:

$$38,007 - 37,538 = 469 = SS_B$$

In Step 7, we compute the effects of factor A. Add the row sums together:

$$132 + 138 + 135 = 405$$
$$105 + 135 + 177 = 417$$

Square each value and divide by the total number of observations in a row:

$$405^2/9 = 18,225$$
$$417^2/9 = 19,321$$

Now add the sums together:

$$18,225 + 19,321 = 37,546$$

Subtract the correction term from this value:

$$37,546 - 37,538 = 8 = SS_A$$

In Step 8, we compute the interactive effects of factors A and B. First, square each cell sum and divide by the cell size:

$$132^2/3 = 5,808$$
$$138^2/3 = 6,348$$
$$135^2/3 = 6,075$$
$$105^2/3 = 3,675$$
$$135^2/3 = 6,075$$
$$177^2/3 = 10,443$$

Next, add the squared values together:

$$5,808 + 6,348 + 6,075 + 3,675 + 6,075 + 10,443 = 38,424$$

Now subtract CT, SS_B, and SS_A from this value:

$$38,424 - 37,538 - 469 - 8 = 409 = SS_{A \times B}$$

In Step 9, we compute the sum of squares within each factor. Subtract SS_A, SS_B, and $SS_{A \times B}$ from SS_T:

$$SS_W = SS_T - SS_A - SS_B - SS_{A \times B}$$
$$SS_W = 1,286 - 8 - 469 - 409 = 400$$

Now we have all the data necessary to construct the ANOVA table.

Source of Variation	SS	Degrees of Freedom	MS	F
A	8	$r-1=1$	$SS_A/(r-1)=8$	$MS_A/MS_W=0.24$
B	469	$c-1=2$	$SS_B/(c-1)=234.50$	$MS_B/MS_W=7.04$
$A \times B$	409	$(r-1)(c-1)=2$	$SS_{A \times B}/[(r-1)(c-1)]=204.50$	$MS_{A \times B}/MS_W=6.13$
Within groups	400	$rc(n-1)=12$	$SS_W/[rc(n-1)]=33.33$	
Total	1,286	$rcn-1=17$		

State hypotheses and test statistics:

$$F_A = 0.24 \qquad H_0\text{: } \alpha_i = 0 \text{ for all } i$$
$$F_B = 7.04 \qquad H_0\text{: } \beta_j = 0 \text{ for all } j$$
$$F_{A \times B} = 6.13 \qquad H_0\text{: } \delta_{ij} = 0 \text{ for all } i \text{ and } j$$

Find the critical F factor from the table in Appendix C.

$$\text{Significance level} = 1 - \alpha$$
$$(r-1)(c-1), rc(n-1) \text{ degrees of freedom}$$

If the test statistic F factor is greater than the critical F factor, we reject the null hypothesis. Setting the alpha value at 0.05, we can create the following table:

Source of Variation	Calculated F	Critical F
A	0.24	4.75
B	7.04	3.89
$A \times B$	6.13	3.59

We can therefore conclude that the B main effects and the interaction effects are statistically significant. This means that the mean attitude scores are not the same for executives across all company sizes. The difference in mean attitude scores between executives in the 2 age groups is not the same for all 3 company sizes.

TAGUCHI ROBUSTNESS CONCEPTS

In the early 1980s Professor Genichi Taguchi introduced his approach to using experimental design for:

1. Designing products or processes so that they are robust to environmental conditions
2. Designing and developing products so that they are robust to component variation
3. Minimizing variation around a target

Taguchi refers to these 3 activities as quality engineering. They flow in order from system design to tolerance design. System design occurs in the initial or idea phase of product or process development. Parameter design is the middle component of the 3 where the system is "fine-tuned" to ensure that it consistently functions as intended. Tolerance design determines the acceptable variations around the nominal settings determined in parameter design.

Taguchi took assumptions from engineering knowledge and used them to reduce the size of experiments, thereby speeding up the experimental process. One of the areas he looked at involved random noise and its effect on variability. He used the orthogonal array, which had previously been used to reduce experimental bias, as a design tool for determining the influence of each variable under study on both the mean result and the variation from that result. Before Taguchi's adaptations, traditional design of experiments (DOE) had been performed using a full-factorial approach. As discussed earlier, while comprehensive, this approach was tedious and time consuming.

Unlike traditional DOE which attempted to remove the root causes of variation, Taguchi focused on minimizing the effect of the causes of variation. By inserting a second orthogonal array into the experiment, Taguchi added the capability of determining those combinations of controllable factors that minimize the effect of the sources of experimentation variability. He defined this ability as *robustness*. In other words, the product or process performs consistently on target and is relatively insensitive to factors that are difficult to control.

The purpose of experimentation using Taguchi's methods is to identify the key factors that have the greatest contribution to variation and to ascertain those settings or values that result in the least variability. In the field of quality, Dr. Taguchi is recognized for three major contributions:

1. The (Taguchi) loss function
2. Orthogonal arrays and linear graphs
3. Robustness

Taguchi developed a mathematical model in which loss (in terms of profitability) is a quadratic function of the deviation of the quality of interest from its target value (see Figure 6.3). The farther away from the target value, the greater the loss. Traditional DOE, while using mathematical equations, did not focus on the profitability and loss functions of the experiment. With Taguchi's model, management decisions can be made on the true worth of quality improvement efforts using factual rather than anecdotal analysis of the data.

As discussed earlier, Dr. Taguchi adapted orthogonal arrays for designing and analyzing experimental data. Orthogonal arrays were originally developed to control experimental error. Taguchi methods use orthogonal arrays to measure the effect of a factor on the average result, and also to determine the variation from the mean. The primary advantage of orthogonal arrays is the relationship among the factors under investigation. For each level of any one factor, all levels of the other factors occur an equal number of times. This constitutes a balanced experiment and permits the effect of one factor under study to be separable from the effects of other factors. The result is that the findings of the experiment are reproducible. This compares with full-factor analysis, in which the effect of each and every variable on each and every other variable must be determined (adding significantly to the time of the

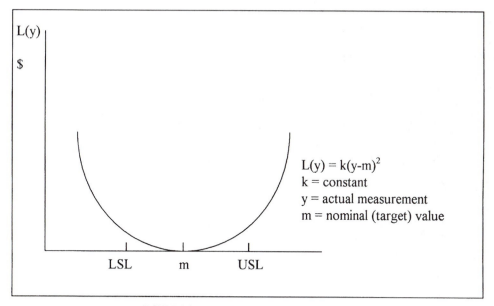

$$L(y) = k(y-m)^2$$
k = constant
y = actual measurement
m = nominal (target) value

FIGURE 6.3   Taguchi's quadratic loss function.

experiment), and single-factor analysis, in which factors not of interest are eliminated, thus jeopardizing the reproducibility of the study.

To enhance the flexibility of the arrays, Dr. Taguchi used linear graphs to represent them. By using these graphs, the experimenter can effectively study the interactions between experimental factors as well as the effects of the individual factors (main effects) themselves. Linear graphs make this possible by providing a logical scheme for assigning interactions to the orthogonal array without confounding the effects of the interactions with the effects of the individual factors being studied.

As shown in Figure 6.4, there are 2 linear graphs for the L_8 array. If all interactions of interest involve a common factor, graph ii (on the right) would be the most appropriate. If the design requires the study of 3 interactions involving the same 3 factors ($A \times B$, $B \times C$, and $A \times C$), graph i (on the left) should be selected. For 2 interactions with a common factor, either graph can be used.

The graphs are constructed of interconnecting dots, with each dot representing a column within the array in which a factor (main effect) can be assigned. The connecting line represents the interaction between the two dots (factors) at each end of the line segment. The number accompanying the line segment represents the column within the array to which the interaction should be assigned.

The third major contribution by Dr. Taguchi deals with the concept of robustness. Earlier we defined robustness as the ability of the product or process to perform consistently on target and to be relatively insensitive to factors that are difficult to control. Note that robustness deals with both product and process. From a product standpoint, we can further define robustness as "the ability of the product to perform consistently as designed with minimal effect from changes in uncontrollable operating influences."[6] From the standpoint of process, we define robustness

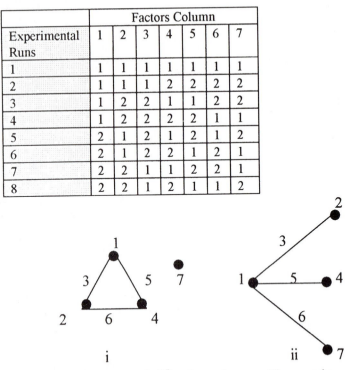

	Factors Column						
Experimental Runs	1	2	3	4	5	6	7
1	1	1	1	1	1	1	1
2	1	1	1	2	2	2	2
3	1	2	2	1	1	2	2
4	1	2	2	2	2	1	1
5	2	1	2	1	2	1	2
6	2	1	2	2	1	2	1
7	2	2	1	1	2	2	1
8	2	2	1	2	1	1	2

FIGURE 6.4 Example of an L_8 (2^7) orthogonal array and linear graphs.
(*Source:* The American Supplier Institute, Dearborn, Michigan.)

as "the ability of the process to produce consistently good product with minimal effect from changes in uncontrollable manufacturing influences."[7]

These definitions differ from traditional experimentation in that they recognize that we cannot always control some of the things that create variation within the process or the product. Edwards Deming referred to this as random variation and recognized its existence in all processes. Similar to Deming's view, Dr. Taguchi's approach is to identify and control those factors that are significant causes of variation and to do so in a way that minimizes the effect of those variables that cannot be controlled or that are not practical to control.

SUMMARY

This chapter has provided a brief overview of experimental design. It has looked at reasons why experimental design is important, the different types and methodologies associated with experimental design, and the advantages and disadvantages of each. The final section of the chapter discussed the contributions of Genichi Taguchi to the field of experimental design. Dr. Taguchi's methods provide us with a way to increase the validity and reproducibility of our experiments, while minimizing the time and cost associated with them.

DISCUSSION QUESTIONS

1. Discuss what is meant by factor, level, and treatment.
2. What is meant by the term *replication?* What role does it play in DOE?
3. Define and discuss the term *blocking.*
4. What are the advantages and disadvantages of full-factorial design over 1-factor-at-a-time experimentation?
5. How is variance broken down in ANOVA?
6. How does Taguchi's concept of the effect of variation differ from the traditional view?
7. What is meant by the term *orthogonal array?*
8. Define and discuss Taguchi's concept of robustness.

PROBLEMS

1. A new cutting lathe has been in operation for 10 weeks. The cutting tool for this lathe lasts an average of 24 hours with a standard deviation of 1.2 hours. A review of the quality logs for the department indicates the following data for the 5 other cutting lathes in the department:

Cutting Lathe	Average Life of Cutting Tools (Hours)
1	20
2	21
3	16
4	24
5	22
x-bar	20.6

Assuming a 95 percent confidence level, is the life of the cutting tools on the new machine significantly different from the life of the cutting tools used on the other 5 machines?

2. Recently people in the United States were surveyed about their attitudes toward smoking. We are interested in determining if geographic location has an effect on attitude. We design our experiment to have 5 samples consisting of individuals from each of 4 geographic areas of the country. Each individual was asked to rate his or her opposition to smoking in public places on a scale from 1 to 10. The higher the score, the more opposed the group's attitude was to smoking. The data from the survey are shown below.

Sample	South	West	North	East
1	6	9	7	4
2	7	8	6	7
3	6	9	6	6
4	9	7	7	5
5	5	8	7	6

Determine if attitudes are different given the different geographic location of the respondents.

3. Assuming that the respondents in samples 1, 3, and 5 in Problem 2 are all female and the respondents in samples 2 and 4 are all male, analyze the data for the effects of sex, geographic location, and any combinations of the two factors.

NOTES

1. Fisher, R. A. *Statistical Methods for Research Workers,* 13th ed. Edinburgh: Oliver & Boyd, 1958.
2. Bemowski, K. "The Quality Glossary." *Quality Progress,* February 1992, p. 23.
3. ASQC Statistics Division. *Glossary & Tables for Statistical Quality Control.* Milwaukee, WI: ASQC Quality Press, p. 62.
4. Ibid., pp. 62–63.
5. Ibid., p. 64.
6. Peace, G. S. *Taguchi Methods: A Hands-On Approach.* Reading, MA: Addison-Wesley, 1993, p. 5
7. Ibid.

SUGGESTED READINGS

Berenson, M. L., & D. M. Levine. *Basic Business Statistics.* Englewood Cliffs, NJ: Prentice-Hall, 1992, pp. 493–532.

Davis, D., & R. M. Cosenza. *Business Research for Decision Making.* Boston: Kent Publishing Company, 1985, pp. 365–381.

Ealey, L. A. *Quality by Design.* Dearborn, MI: ASI Press, 1988, pp. 102–108.

Frigon, N. L., & D. Mathews. *Practical Guide to Experimental Design.* New York: Wiley, 1997.

Hamburg, M. *Statistical Analysis for Decision Making,* 3rd ed. New York: HBJ, 1983, pp. 327–346.

Montgomery, D. C. *Design and Analysis of Experiments,* 3rd ed. New York: Wiley, 1991.

Peace, Glen Stuart. *Taguchi Methods: A Hands-On Approach.* Reading, MA: Addison-Wesley, 1993.

Taguchi, G. *Introduction to Quality Engineering.* Asian Productivity Organization, White Plains, NY: UNIPUB, 1986.

Taguchi, G., and S. Konishi. *Orthogonal Arrays and Linear Graphs.* Dearborn, MI: American Supplier Institute, 1987.

CASE II   WESTOVER WIRE WINDING, INC.

As a new graduate, you feel good about your first week as a management trainee at Westover Wire Winding, Inc. You have been given an office area to yourself equipped with the latest personal computer but no secretary. You have not yet developed any technical knowledge about the manufacturing process, but you have toured the entire facility and have met many people in various areas of the operation. Westover is a medium-sized manufacturer of wire windings used in transformer manufacturing. These windings are produced in Westover's manufacturing plant which uses a process-type layout. Bill, the Production Control Manager, described the windings as being of standardized design. Your plant tour followed the manufacturing sequence for the windings: drawing, extrusion, winding, inspection, and packaging. After inspection, good product is packaged and sent to Finished Product Storage; defective product is stored separately until it can be reworked. You sketched the layout (Figure A) after your plant tour so that you could find your way around the plant.

This morning, Maria Espania, Westover's General Manager and your boss, stopped by your office and asked you to attend the staff meeting to be held at 1:00 PM today. "Let's get started with the business at hand," Maria said, opening the meeting. "You all have met <your name>, our new management trainee. <Your name> studied quality management during the last year of his/her university studies, so I feel she/he is competent to help us with a problem we have been discussing for a long time without resolution. I'm sure that each of you on my staff will give <your name> your full cooperation."

You are a little surprised and apprehensive to hear that you are about to receive a high-profile important assignment so early in your career. However, you are confident in your own ability and in the education you received in operations management.

Westover Wire Winding, Inc.

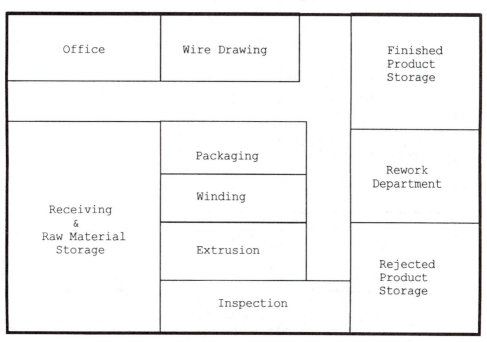

FIGURE A   Plant layout.

Maria continues, "Joe Wilson, our Operations Manager, has experienced an increasing problem with rejected product found during the manufacturing operation."

"Yeah, I'm not sure where to begin," said Joe, "but we know you covered quality control in your studies. Rejects in the Winding Department have been killing us the past 2 months. Nobody in operations has any idea why. I would like you to take a look at the situation and make recommendations about how we can find out what is going on. I know that you haven't been here long enough to become a 'technical expert' in our processes, so I don't expect you to make technical recommendations— just see if you can point us in the right direction."

After the meeting your first stop was the production floor. Your discussions with the production supervisors in the Winding Department indicated they had no real grasp of what the problem(s) was or what to do to correct it. They did give you a more detailed tour of the winding operation and a copy of the Winding Department layout (Figure B). There were 3 machines that wound wire onto plastic cores to produce the primary and secondary transformer windings. After inspection by quality control (QC), these windings then went to the Packaging Department. Packaging personnel inspect their own work and make corrections on the spot to any packaging defects they find. The problem is, too many windings are found to be defective by QC and require reworking before they can be sent to Packaging.

Your next stop was the Quality Control Department where you obtained the records for the past month's Winding Department rejects (Figure C). You then retired to your office area to decide how to approach this project.

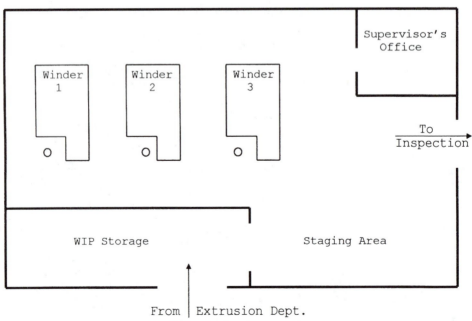

FIGURE B Winding department layout.

Westover Wire Winding, Inc.

January Transformer Reject Log—Winding Process

Date	No. Inspected	Winder No.	Bad Wind	Twisted Wire	Broken Leads	Abraded Wire	Wrong Core	Wrong Wire	Failed El. Test
1	100	1	1	0	4	1	0	0	1
	100	2	2	1	0	0	1	5	0
	100	3	0	0	0	5	0	0	3
2	100	1	0	1	3	0	0	0	0
	100	2	3	1	0	0	2	3	0
	100	3	0	0	1	6	0	0	0
3	100	1	1	0	0	2	0	0	0
	100	2	0	0	0	0	0	3	0
	100	3	0	0	1	4	0	0	3
4	100	1	0	0	3	0	0	0	0
	100	2	0	0	0	0	0	2	0
	100	3	0	0	0	3	1	0	3
5	100	1	0	1	5	0	0	0	0
	100	2	0	0	0	0	0	2	1
	100	3	0	0	0	3	0	0	2
8	100	1	0	0	2	0	0	0	0
	100	2	0	0	0	0	0	1	0
	100	3	0	0	0	3	0	0	3
9	100	1	0	1	2	0	0	0	0
	100	2	0	0	0	0	0	1	0
	100	3	0	0	0	3	0	0	4
10	100	1	0	0	5	0	0	0	0
	100	2	1	0	0	0	1	0	0
	100	3	0	0	0	5	0	0	4
11	100	1	0	0	4	0	0	0	0
	100	2	0	0	0	0	0	0	0
	100	3	0	0	0	4	0	0	4
12	100	1	0	0	3	0	1	0	0
	100	2	1	0	1	0	0	0	0
	100	3	0	0	0	5	0	0	4
15	100	1	0	0	2	0	0	1	0
	100	2	0	0	0	0	0	1	0
	100	3	0	0	0	3	0	0	3
16	100	1	0	0	6	0	0	0	0
	100	2	0	0	0	0	0	0	0
	100	3	0	0	0	3	0	0	3
17	100	1	0	1	1	0	0	0	0
	100	2	0	0	0	0	0	0	1
	100	3	0	0	0	3	0	0	3
18	100	1	1	0	2	0	0	0	0
	100	2	0	0	0	0	0	1	0
	100	3	0	0	0	4	0	0	1
19	100	1	0	0	2	0	0	0	0
	100	2	0	0	0	0	0	0	0
	100	3	0	0	0	3	0	0	1

FIGURE C

Westover Wire Winding, Inc.

January Transformer Reject Log—Winding Process

Date	No. Inspected	Winder No.	Bad Wind	Twisted Wire	Broken Leads	Abraded Wire	Wrong Core	Wrong Wire	Failed El. Test
22	100	1	0	1	4	0	0	0	0
	100	2	0	0	0	0	0	0	0
	100	3	0	0	0	3	0	1	2
23	100	1	0	0	4	0	0	0	0
	100	2	0	0	0	0	0	0	1
	100	3	0	0	0	4	0	0	3
24	100	1	0	0	2	0	0	1	0
	100	2	0	1	0	0	0	0	0
	100	3	0	0	0	4	0	0	3
25	100	1	0	0	3	0	0	0	0
	100	2	0	0	0	1	0	0	0
	100	3	0	0	0	2	0	0	4
26	100	1	0	0	1	0	0	0	0
	100	2	0	1	0	1	0	0	0
	100	3	0	0	0	2	0	0	3
29	100	1	0	0	2	0	0	0	0
	100	2	0	0	1	0	0	0	0
	100	3	0	0	0	2	0	0	3
30	100	1	0	0	2	0	0	0	0
	100	2	0	0	0	0	1	0	0
	100	3	0	0	0	2	0	0	3

FIGURE C (*continued*)

Note: Your recommendations *with justification* should be presented in the first page of a report to Maria. Your detailed analysis should be contained in the subsequent pages of that report so that she can understand how you arrived at your recommendations. Any charts, graphs, computer printouts, etc., you used should be included in the report.

SECTION III

Product/Service Design and Testing

CHAPTER 7

Metrology, Inspection, and Testing

CHAPTER OBJECTIVES

This chapter introduces the following topics:

- Fundamentals of metrology
- Gauge repeatability and reproducibility
- Nondestructive testing concepts

INTRODUCTION

When technicians use a gauge to take a measurement, the value they obtain really consists of 2 components: (1) the actual value of the dimension being measured and (2) errors relating to the ability of the gauging system to measure that dimension. Unless the second component is assessed, it is impossible to determine how well the reported measurement reflects the true value of the dimension. *Metrology* is the science of measurement.[1] The focus of metrology and this chapter is how to minimize the contribution of the second factor to the total reported measurement value—that is, how to ensure that the reported value really reflects the true value.

METROLOGY

The measurement value determined by use of a gauge or instrument can be considered to be a function of four terms:

$$MV = f(TV + Ac + Rep + Rpr)$$

where

MV = measured value
TV = true value
Ac = gauge accuracy
Rep = gauge repeatability
Rpr = gauge reproducibility.

Gauge accuracy is the ability of the gauge to provide a measurement that is free of bias. The accuracy of a gauge is addressed through calibration. *Gauge repeatability* is the ability of a single operator to obtain the same measurement value multiple times using the same measuring device on the same part. *Gauge reproducibility* is the ability of separate operators to obtain the same measurement value using the same gauge on the same part. Reproducibility and repeatability together are referred to as *precision*. The precision of a gauging system is addressed through gauge repeatability and reproducibility (gauge R & R) studies. The relationship of accuracy and precision is shown in Figure 7.1. The goal is to have a measurement system that is both accurate and precise.

Types of Gauges

Measurement instruments come in all shapes, sizes, and types to measure everything from chemical properties (e.g., pH) to electrical parameters (e.g., volts). The focus of this section will be on instruments designed to enable the measurement of physical dimensions.

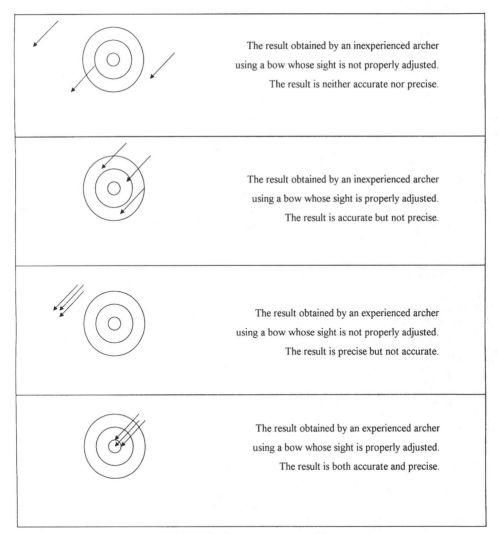

FIGURE 7.1 Accuracy versus precision.

Variable gauges are adjustable gauges used to measure part dimensions. Variable gauges include line-graduated gauges, such as rulers and vernier calipers, dial gauges, digital gauges, and optical gauges. Figure 7.2 illustrates three types of variable gauges: vernier calipers, dial calipers, and digital calipers. All three of these calipers can be used to measure inside and outside dimensions as well as depth dimensions.

Figure 7.3 illustrates a simple optical gauge. The calibrations on the reticule of this portable instrument enable measurement of linear dimensions. More complex optical gauges magnify the part to be measured and project the profile on a screen for measurement.

Fixed gauges are designed to measure a particular dimension and are not adjustable. Examples include go–no-go gauges, feeler gauges, ring gauges, and plug gauges. Feeler gauges are thin metal strips or wires used to measure gap dimensions. Ring gauges are used to measure outside diameters, while plug gauges measure inside diameters. Both ring and plug gauges are forms of go–no-go gauges.

Automated Gauging and Inspection

The preceding gauge types are normally considered to be manual inspection gauges. The digital gauges can, however, be adapted to partial automation by adding a data collection device. Figure 7.4 shows a digital caliper used with a data collection device which is capable of sophisticated analysis of the data on-site. Additional analysis can be performed by downloading the data from the data collection device to a personal computer.

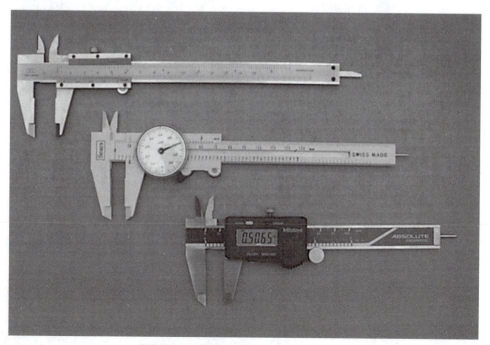

FIGURE 7.2   Vernier, dial, and digital calipers.

FIGURE 7.3 Optical gauge.

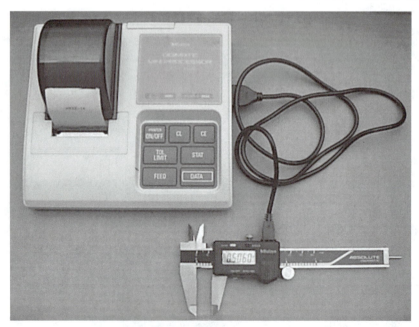

FIGURE 7.4 Digital caliper with automated data collection.

Fully automated on-line gauging and inspection can be accomplished using a variety of sensors linked to data collection and display units. Examples of sensors used for dimensional measurement include linear potentiometers and pixel cameras (vision systems). Coordinate measuring machines (CMM) are fully automated measurement systems designed for off-line dimensional measurement.

ACCURACY AND PRECISION

The *accuracy* of a gauge is "the closeness of agreement between an observed value and an accepted reference value."[2] The accuracy of a gauge is determined by calibration. Use of an instrument whose calibration is unknown results in measurement data which are of questionable validity. Decisions based upon questionable data can be no more valid than the data upon which they are based.

One means of calibrating dimensional gauges is by the use of *gauge blocks*. Gauge blocks are a type of fixed gauge. They are especially machined to close tolerances, and their accuracy can be traced to reference standards at the National Institute of Standards and Technology (NIST). Traceability of a gauge's accuracy through working standards to NIST reference standards is an important aspect of ensuring the accuracy of a measurement system.

Calibration records should be maintained in the laboratory and on the instrument, and recalibration schedules should be established and adhered to. An example of a calibration label which would be affixed to a gauge is shown in Figure 7.5. Gauges with labels showing they are overdue for calibration should be taken out of service until the calibration is performed.

Repeatability and reproducibility (R & R) studies are designed experiments to evaluate the precision of a measurement system. The measurement system should be properly calibrated prior to the gauge R & R study. The following process for conducting a gauge R & R study is based on the procedure established by the ASQ Automotive Division.[3]

1. Verify that the gauge to be studied is properly calibrated.
2. Select at least 2 (*m*) operators and at least 10 (*n*) parts to be measured. Identify each part with a number which is not visible to the operator.

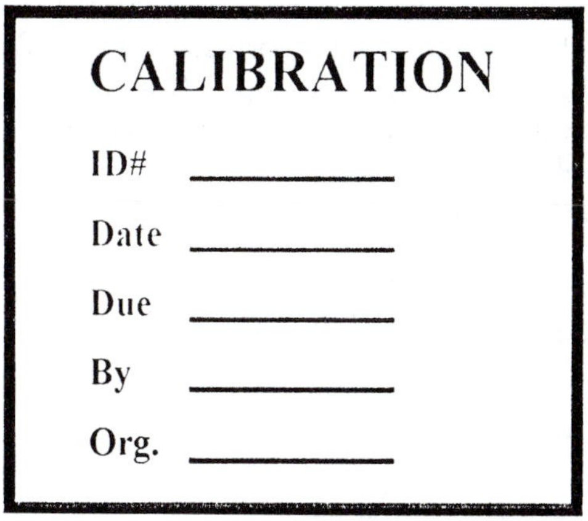

CALIBRATION

ID# _____

Date _____

Due _____

By _____

Org. _____

FIGURE 7.5   Gauge calibration label.

3. Present the parts to the operator for measurement in random sequence and record each measurement (M). Repeat this process until each part has been measured at least 2 (r) times.

4. Compute the average measurement ($\bar{x}_i$) for each operator (i) where M_{ijk} represents operator i's kth measurement on part j:

$$\bar{x}_i = \frac{\left(\sum\limits_j \sum\limits_k M_{ijk} \right)}{nr} \tag{7.1}$$

5. Compute the difference between the largest and smallest average ($\bar{x}_D$):

$$\bar{x}_D = \max(\bar{x}_i) - \min(\bar{x}_i) \tag{7.2}$$

6. Compute the range (R_{ij}) for each part (j) and each operator (i):

$$R_{ij} = \max(M_{ijk}) - \min(M_{ijk}) \tag{7.3}$$

7. Compute the average range ($\bar{R}_i$) for each operator (i):

$$\bar{R}_i = \frac{\sum\limits_j R_{ij}}{n} \tag{7.4}$$

8. Compute the overall range ($\bar{\bar{R}}$):

$$\bar{\bar{R}} = \frac{\sum\limits_i \bar{R}_i}{m} \tag{7.5}$$

9. Compute the control limit on the individual ranges (R_{ij}). The constant D_4 may be found in Table 4.1 in Chapter 4 using the number of trials (r) for n.

$$\text{Control limit} = D_4\bar{\bar{R}} \tag{7.6}$$

Compare each range with the control limit. Any range which exceeds the control limit should be investigated for some assignable cause. Typical assignable causes include measurements which have been recorded incorrectly, digits which have been reversed, and ranges which have been incorrectly calculated. If the assignable cause can be identified and is correctable, make the correction and redo the calculations beginning with Step 4. If no assignable cause can be found, eliminate the values beyond the control limit and redo the calculations beginning with Step 4.

10. Compute the equipment variation (EV):

$$\text{EV} = K_1\bar{\bar{R}} \tag{7.7}$$

where K_1 is a constant based on the number of trials (r).

Trials (r)	2	3	4
K_1	4.56	3.05	2.50

11. Compute the operator variation (OV):

$$OV = \sqrt{(K_2 x_D)^2 - (EV^2/nr)} \qquad (7.8)$$

where K_2 is a constant based on the number of operators (m).

Operators (m)	2	3	4
K_2	3.65	2.70	2.30

Note: If a negative value results from EV^2/nr being larger than $(K_2 x_D)^2$, set the OV equal to 0.[4]

12. Compute the overall gauge repeatability and reproducibility (RR):

$$RR = \sqrt{(EV)^2 + (OV)^2} \qquad (7.9)$$

The operator variation, equipment variation, and overall gauge repeatability and reproducibility are usually reported as a percentage of the total allowed tolerance range. The smaller the OV, EV, and RR variations as a percentage of the total tolerance, the more precise the gauging system. A rule of thumb is that an RR that is less than 10 percent of the tolerance range is acceptable; an RR that is 10–20 percent of the tolerance range may be acceptable under certain circumstances; an RR that is greater than 30 percent of the tolerance range is not acceptable.[5]

An example of the gauge R & R calculations using a spreadsheet is shown in Figure 7.6. In this example, 3 (m) operators are used with each operator measuring 10 (n) parts 2 (r) times. The average measurement ($\overline{x}_i$) for each operator (i) is shown below the first trial columns. The range (R_{ij}) for each part (j) is shown in the "Range" column for each operator (i). The EV, OV, and RR are reported in absolute terms and as a percentage of the total tolerance.

"The tendency to accept whatever figure is presented . . . is very dangerous."[6] Prior to using any measurement system it is important that the gauge is properly calibrated and that a gauge R & R study is performed. Otherwise it is impossible to determine whether systematic bias exists in the reported value or how much of the variation in reported values is due to variation in the parts being measured and how much is due to variation in the measurement system itself.

NONDESTRUCTIVE TESTING

Testing is defined as "appraising characteristics of supplies, components, and so forth, that involves the application of established scientific and laboratory methods mostly functional."[7] "Nondestructive testing (NDT) is the name given to procedures and techniques which allow a product to be inspected for internal defects, or microscopic defects on the surface, and those defects identified without the product being destroyed."[8] This section briefly illustrates some of the more common types of nondestructive testing procedures.

One type of NDT is surface finish measurement. The symbol used to specify surface finish specifications on an engineering drawing is $\sqrt{}$. The most common

Part #	Operator 1			Operator 2			Operator 3		
	1	2	Range	1	2	Range	1	2	Range
1	0.71	0.69	0.02	0.56	0.57	0.01	0.52	0.54	0.02
2	0.98	1.00	0.02	1.03	0.96	0.07	1.04	1.01	0.03
3	0.77	0.77	0.00	0.76	0.76	0.00	0.81	0.81	0.00
4	0.86	0.94	0.08	0.82	0.78	0.04	0.82	0.82	0.00
5	0.51	0.51	0.00	0.42	0.42	0.00	0.46	0.49	0.03
6	0.71	0.59	0.12	1.00	1.04	0.04	1.04	1.00	0.04
7	0.96	0.96	0.00	0.94	0.91	0.03	0.97	0.95	0.02
8	0.86	0.86	0.00	0.72	0.74	0.02	0.78	0.78	0.00
9	0.96	0.96	0.00	0.97	0.94	0.03	0.84	0.81	0.03
10	0.64	0.72	0.08	0.56	0.52	0.04	1.01	1.01	0.00
Average =	0.7980		0.0320	0.7710		0.0280	0.8255		0.0170

XD=	0.0545
Avg Rbarbar=	0.0257
D4=	3.267
Control Limit=	0.08385

Percent of Tolerance

EV=	0.11704	Lower Tolerance=	0.49	23.4%
OV=	0.1448	Upper Tolerance=	0.99	29.0%
RR=	0.18619			37.2%

Enter your tolerances here.

FIGURE 7.6   Spreadsheet template for gauge R & R study.

instrument used to measure surface finish is a profilometer. A modern profilometer may be either a contact type (using a stylus) or a noncontact type.

Another type of NDT is hardness testing. Common hardness tests (Rockwell, Brinell, Vickers) measure the penetration of a probe into the surface under test. The Scleroscope hardness test measures hardness by the height of the rebound of a diamond-tipped hammer after it strikes the surface under test.

NDT of welds and castings can be accomplished by a variety of NDT means. In X-ray and gamma-ray inspection, defects such as cracks, holes, or inclusions show up clearly on a film image called a radiograph. Ultrasonic inspection looks for the same types of defects using sound waves instead of radiography.

Microscopic surface defects can be located using dye penetrant inspection. A dye is spread on the surface under test and wiped off. After spraying the surface with a developer, surface defects such as cracks show up clearly under white light or ultraviolet light depending on the type of dye used.

NDT is an important and growing area of testing. With NDT, parts can be inspected for critical defects without incurring the time and cost associated with destructive tests. NDT also offers the prospect of 100 percent inspection, which is infeasible with destructive tests.

SUMMARY

A measured value is subject to bias error due to lack of calibration of the instrument being used. It is also subject to precision error due to poor gauge repeatability and reproducibility. It is important that gauges be calibrated and the measurement system subjected to a gauge R & R study before use. Otherwise it is impossible to determine whether the measurement system is accurate and precise or a "rubber ruler."

This chapter provided a brief introduction to the types of gauges and an introduction to nondestructive testing. There are entire books on these topics—some of which are listed in the Notes and Suggested Readings sections—which are available for more thorough study.

DISCUSSION QUESTIONS

1. Why might there be a difference between the value determined by the use of a gauge and the true value of the dimension?
2. What is the difference between precision and accuracy?
3. What is the difference between a fixed gauge and a variable gauge?
4. What calibration information should be included on the calibration label?
5. Discuss the purpose of conducting a gauge R & R study.
6. List four different types of nondestructive tests and discuss their usefulness.

PROBLEMS

1. A quality engineer is conducting a gauge R & R study of a new measurement system. He has had 2 operators measure 10 parts 2 times and has recorded the following data:

   $$\bar{x}_D = 0.060$$
   $$\bar{\bar{R}} = 0.018 \qquad \text{(None of the individual ranges exceed the control limit.)}$$

   Calculate the EV, OV, and RR.

   If the specification is 0.750 ± 0.250, would the gauging system be considered to be acceptable? Would your answer change if the part being measured was a component of an emergency fire suppression system whose functioning depended on this part being within tolerance?

2. A gauge R & R study has been conducted on a measuring system. In the study, 3 operators measured 5 parts 3 times. The tolerance for the parts is 0.750 ± 0.150.

   $$\bar{x}_D = 0.060$$
   $$\bar{\bar{R}} = 0.018 \qquad \text{(None of the individual ranges exceed the control limit.)}$$

   Calculate EV, OV, and RR in absolute terms and as a percentage of tolerance.

3. A gauge R & R study has determined the following:

   $$EV = 15.0\% \text{ of tolerance}$$
   $$OV = 32.0\% \text{ of tolerance}$$

   Calculate RR. Would this gauging system be considered acceptable? What action would you recommend to improve RR?

NOTES

1. Evans, J. R., & W. M. Lindsay. *The Management and Control of Quality,* 3rd ed. St. Paul, MN: West, 1996, p. 584.

2. ASQC Statistics Division. *Glossary & Tables for Statistical Quality Control.* Milwaukee, WI: ASQC Quality Press, 1983, p. 1.

3. *ASQC Automotive Division Statistical Process Control Manual.* Milwaukee, WI: ASQC Quality Press, 1986.

4. *Measurement Systems Analysis, Reference Manual.* Southfield, MI: Automotive Industry Action Group, 1995, p. 58.

5. Evans & Lindsay, p. 588.

6. Traver, R. W. "Measuring Equipment Repeatability—The Rubber Ruler." *1962 ASQC Annual Convention Transactions.* Milwaukee, WI: ASQC, 1962, p. 25.

7. Griffith, G. *Quality Technician's Handbook.* New York: Wiley, 1986, p. 148.

8. Kennedy, C. W., & D. E. Andrews. *Inspection and Gaging,* 5th ed. New York: Industrial Press, 1977, p. 524.

SUGGESTED READINGS

ANSI/ASQC M1-1996, American National Standard for Calibration Systems.

ASQC Automotive Division Statistical Process Control Manual. Milwaukee, WI: ASQC Quality Press, 1986.

Barrentine, L. B. *Concepts for R&R Studies.* Milwaukee, WI: ASQC Quality Press, 1991.

Duncan, A. J. *Quality Control and Industrial Statistics,* 5th ed. Homewood, IL: Irwin, 1986, Chapter 31, pp. 784–788.

Evans, J. R., & W. M. Lindsay. *The Management and Control of Quality,* 3rd ed. St. Paul, MN: West, 1996, Chapter 14, pp. 572–584 and 604–613.

Farago, F. T. *Handbook of Dimensional Measurement,* 3rd ed. New York: Industrial Press, 1994.

Grant, E. L., & R. S. Leavenworth. *Statistical Quality Control,* 7th ed. New York: McGraw-Hill, 1996, Chapter 8, pp. 302–309.

Griffith, G. *Quality Technician's Handbook.* New York: Wiley, 1986, Chapters 4, 5, and 13, pp. 142–304 and 448–478.

ISO 10012-1-1992, Quality Assurance Requirements for Measuring Equipment—Part 1: Metrological Confirmation System for Measuring Equipment.

ISO 5725-1,2,3-1994, Accuracy (Trueness and Precision) of Measurement Methods and Results.

Kolarik, W. J. *Creating Quality.* New York: McGraw-Hill, 1995, Chapter 18, pp. 402–406.

Montgomery, D. C. *Introduction to Statistical Quality Control,* 3rd ed. New York: Wiley, 1996, Chapter 9, pp. 455–460.

Morris, A. S. *Measurement and Calibration for Quality Assurance.* Englewood Cliffs, NJ: Prentice-Hall, 1991.

Pennella, C. R. *Managing the Metrology System.* Milwaukee, WI: ASQC Quality Press, 1992.

Suntag, C. *Inspection and Inspection Management.* Milwaukee, WI: ASQC Quality Press, 1993.

CHAPTER 8

Reliability Engineering

CHAPTER OBJECTIVES

This chapter introduces the following topics:

- Definition and dimensions of reliability
- Types of reliability systems
- Reliability life concepts (i.e., bathtub curve)
- Mean time between failure
- Risk assessment tools and risk prevention
- Product traceability and recall procedures

INTRODUCTION

In Chapter 2 we introduced the statistical concepts of reliability and redundancy, and how to determine statistically the probability density function and Mean Time Between Failure (MTBF). In this chapter we will apply the statistical concepts to real-world applications.

Reliability is defined as "the probability of a product performing without failure a specified function under given conditions for a specified period of time."[1] Note that in this definition, probability is used to quantify reliability.

There are three dimensions of reliability: as a probability, as a definition of failure, and as prescribed operating conditions.[2] These three dimensions are defined further in Table 8.1.

TABLE 8.1   Dimensions of Reliability

---

1. As a probability:
    - Frequency of successful uses out of a certain number of attempts
    - Likelihood of an item lasting a given amount of time
2. Definition of failure:
    - A situation in which an item does not perform as intended
3. Prescribed operating conditions:
    - How the product should be used
    - "Normal operating conditions"

Reliability as a probability can be defined in two ways. The first is the probability that a system will perform on a given trial. Another way to state this is the frequency of successful performances of a system in a given number of attempts. An example of this definition would be the probability that a fire extinguisher would perform on a given attempt to use it. This probability could be determined through repeated trials to determine the frequency of successful uses as a percentage of attempts.

The second definition of reliability as a probability is the probability that an item will last for a given length of time in use. This can be illustrated by the example of a light bulb. Most bulbs are rated for a given life. This can be determined by life-testing to failure a large number of bulbs and determining the average useful life. These data can be used to determine the probability the light bulb will last for a specified number of hours.

Definition of a failure may seem to be straightforward. In the case of the light bulb it is—the bulb fails when it no longer produces light. This definition is not so clear in other systems. Consider an automobile tire. Short of catastrophic failure (i.e., blowout), at what point is the tread considered to be depleted—that is, at what point is the tire considered to have failed or used up its useful life?

Prescribed operating conditions must be specified. There are specially designed light bulbs for outdoor use that can achieve equivalent useful lives exposed to the weather as indoor bulbs do in a more sheltered operating environment. Therefore, when discussing reliability of a system, the standard operating conditions for which the system was designed must be specified.

TYPES OF RELIABILITY SYSTEMS

System reliability is usually defined as the product of the individual reliabilities of the *n* parts or subsystems within a serial system.

$$P_s = P_1 \times P_2 \times P_3 \times \ldots P_n \tag{8.1}$$

EXAMPLE 8.1

A manufacturing system consists of 4 subsystems with the following reliabilities:

$P_1 = 0.970$
$P_2 = 0.997$
$P_3 = 0.985$
$P_4 = 0.990$

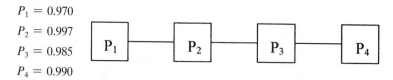

What is the overall reliability of the system?

Recognizing that system reliability is the product of the individual reliabilities of the subsystems, we use Equation (8.1) as follows:

$$P_s = P_1 \times P_2 \times P_3 \times P_4$$
$$P_s = 0.970 \times 0.997 \times 0.985 \times 0.990$$
$$P_s = 0.943$$

While the assumption of system reliability equaling the product of the reliabilities of the subsystems is only true for serial systems, the formula serves two basic purposes. First, it highlights the effect of increased serial system complexity on overall system reliability. As the number of parts or subsystems increases in a serial system, system reliability decreases dramatically. Second, the formula is often a convenient approximation that can be refined as information becomes available on the interrelationships of parts.

Note that in Example 8.1 the reliability of the system is much lower than the reliabilities of individual components. This is because the components are in *serial,* thus requiring all components to work if the system is to work. To increase the reliability of the system, we can use *parallel redundancy.* Parallel redundancy means that we add additional components or system to the existing system. The extra components or system increases the overall reliability since if the primary system or component fails, the backup or redundant system can take over and the system will not fail.

To offset the decrease in system reliability noted above, systems may be designed with *redundancy.* "Redundancy is the existence of more than one element for accomplishing a given task, where all elements must fail before there is an overall failure to the system." [3]

In parallel redundancy two or more subsystems operate at the same time to accomplish the task, and any single subsystem is capable of handling the job by itself in case of failure of the other subsystems. When parallel redundancy is used, the overall reliability of the system is calculated using the following equation:

$$P_s = P_m + P_b(1 - P_m) \tag{8.2}$$

where
$$P_s = \text{reliability of the system}$$
$$P_m = \text{reliability of the main subassembly}$$
$$P_b = \text{reliability of the backup subassembly}$$
$$(1 - P_m) = \text{probability that the main subassembly will fail}$$

EXAMPLE 8.2

Management desires to increase the overall reliability of the system in Example 8.1.

   a. Add a parallel component to each component of the system with the same reliability of the primary system. What does that do to the overall reliability of the system?

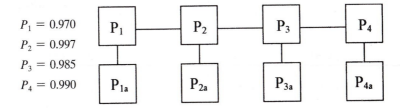

$$P_1 = 0.970$$
$$P_2 = 0.997$$
$$P_3 = 0.985$$
$$P_4 = 0.990$$

$$P_s = P_m + P_b(1 - P_m)$$
$$P_s = [0.970 + 0.970(1 - 0.970)] \times [0.997 + 0.997(1 - 0.997)] \times$$
$$[0.985 + 0.985(1 - 0.985)] \times [0.990 + 0.990(1 - 0.990)]$$
$$P_s = 0.9991 \times 0.9999 \times 0.9998 \times 0.9999 = 0.9987$$

b. Add a parallel system to the existing system with the same component reliabilities. What does that do to the overall reliability of the system?

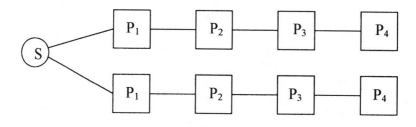

$$P_{\text{main system}} = P_1 \times P_2 \times P_3 \times P_4$$
$$P_s = 0.970 \times 0.997 \times 0.985 \times 0.990 = 0.943$$
$$P_{\text{backup system}} = P_1 \times P_2 \times P_3 \times P_4$$
$$P_b = 0.970 \times 0.997 \times 0.985 \times 0.990 = 0.943$$
$$P_{\text{system}} = P_{\text{main system}} + P_{\text{backup system}}(1 - P_{\text{main system}})$$
$$P_{\text{system}} = 0.943 + 0.943(1 - 0.943) = 0.9968$$

Note that in this case we assumed the reliability of the switch was 1. In the real world, however, switches can and do fail to work when called upon. In such a case, the redundant component does not have an opportunity to function when the main component fails—therefore the system fails. If we assign a probability to the switch, the reliability of the system then is calculated as follows:

$$P_{\text{system}} = P_{\text{main system}} + \left[P_{\text{backup system}}(1 - P_{\text{main system}}) \right] \times P_{\text{switch}} \qquad (8.3)$$

EXAMPLE 8.3

Using the same reliabilities in Example 8.2b above, calculate the reliability of the system with a switch reliability of 0.99 (99 percent).

$$P_{\text{system}} = P_{\text{main system}} + \left[P_{\text{backup system}}(1 - P_{\text{main system}}) \right] \times P_{\text{switch}}$$
$$P_{\text{system}} = 0.943 + 0.943(1 - 0.943) \times 0.99 = 0.9962$$

RELIABILITY LIFE CHARACTERISTIC CONCEPTS (E.G., BATHTUB CURVE)

If we were to run a piece of equipment to failure, repair it, and repeat the process over and over again, recording the failure time for each run, we would have a set of data that would indicate the failure rate for that piece of equipment. *Failure rate* is defined as the number of failures per set unit of time. When we plot failure rate against time, we often see a pattern of failure known as a *bathtub curve* (for additional discussion see "The Exponential Distribution" in Chapter 2).

EXAMPLE 8.4

The data in the table below were collected for a telephone switch. Plot the failure rate versus time for the switch.

Time of Failure (weeks)			
0.1	1.1	4.0	8.2
0.2	1.2	4.1	8.4
0.2	1.4	4.2	8.5
0.3	1.6	4.6	8.7
0.4	2.0	5.5	8.8
0.5	2.2	5.9	9.0
0.6	2.4	5.9	9.1
0.6	2.6	6.0	9.2
0.7	2.8	6.1	9.2
0.8	2.8	6.2	9.3
0.8	2.9	6.5	9.5
0.8	3.1	7.2	9.7
0.9	3.1	7.5	9.8
0.9	3.1	7.7	9.8
0.9	3.1	7.9	9.9
1.0	3.2	8.0	9.9

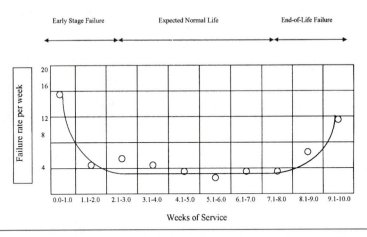

As you can see from Example 8.4, the curve that results resembles a bathtub (see Chapter 2, Equation (2.19), for a discussion of probability density function). There are 3 distinct patterns in the curve:

1. *Early-stage failure.* This phase is characterized by high failure rates early in the life cycle of the switch. These failures are usually the result of design, manufacture, or use errors and are usually correctable given a good quality program.

2. *Expected normal life of the product.* At this stage, we see a pattern of constant and relatively low failure rate. Failures in this stage usually result from design

limitations, changes in the environment, and damage caused by day-to-day use or maintenance. Training in the proper use and maintenance of the equipment can minimize accidents. To reduce the failure rate in this stage, however, would generally require a redesign of the product.

3. *End-of-life failure.* This kind of failure occurs when the product exceeds its intended normal life expectancy. Most products are designed for a set operating life. However, just as variations in manufacture cause some units to fail early, these same variations will allow some units to operate beyond their rated life expectancy. Failures at this stage are mostly the result of the daily wear and stress on equipment. Examples are metal fatigue, worn gears, and brittle or broken parts. Many companies believe in running equipment *to failure*. However, they fail to recognize the different degrees of failure. By continuing to operate equipment with worn or damaged parts, an organization runs the risk of producing out-of-specification product as well as causing a catastrophic failure. Developing a preventative maintenance program will allow controlled replacement of old or worn equipment before a catastrophic failure can occur.

MEAN TIME BETWEEN FAILURE

Mean time between failure (MTBF) is defined as "the average length of time between failures of a product or component."[4] In analyzing failure rate data, it often turns out that the MTBF for both product and equipment can be modeled by a negative exponential distribution (see Figure 8.1). When the failure rate distribution matches the pattern in Figure 8.1, the exponential distribution can be used to determine various probabilities of interest:

- The probability of failure before some specified time, T, is equal to the area under the curve between the time the product was put into service (usually 0) and T.
- Reliability has been defined as the probability that a product will last at least until time T. Reliability is equal to the area under the curve beyond T.

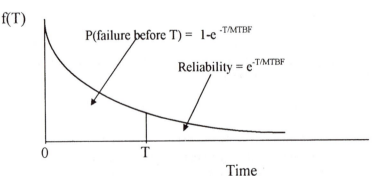

FIGURE 8.1 Negative exponential distribution.

Note that as the specified length of service increases, the area under the curve to the right of that point decreases. In other words, as length of service increases, reliability decreases. When we perform this calculation of failure time for non-repairable products—a light bulb, for example—we usually refer to mean time to failure (MTTF), since additional failures are not possible.

To determine the value for the area under the curve to the right of a given point, T, we use a table of exponential values (see Table 8.2). The table provides us values of $e^{-T/\text{MTBF}}$ for known values of T and MTBF.

The exponential distribution is completely described by the distribution mean, which is the mean time between failures. If we allow T to represent the time in service, we can then determine the probability that failure will not occur before time T using the following equation:

$$P(\text{no failure before } T) = e^{-T/\text{MTBF}} \qquad (8.4)$$

where
$$e = \text{natural logarithm}, 2.7183\ldots$$
$$T = \text{time in service before failure}$$
$$\text{MTBF} = \text{mean time between failures}$$

Since the total area under the curve is 1, then the probability that there will be failure before time T is

$$P(\text{failure before } T) = 1 - P(\text{no failure before } T) = 1 - e^{-T/\text{MTBF}}$$

EXAMPLE 8.5

A computer power supply has an MTBF of 10,000 hours. What is the probability that there will be no failure in this power supply before 15,000 hours?

a. Using Table 8.2, we see that

$$T/\text{MTBF} = 15,000/10,000 = 1.5$$

Finding the value of $T/\text{MTBF} = 1.5$ in Table 8.2, we read the probability of no failure before 15,000 hours $= 0.2231$.

b. Using Equation (8.4), we get

$$P(\text{no failure before } T) = e^{-T/\text{MTBF}} = e^{-15,000/10,000} = 0.2231$$

TABLE 8.2   Values of $e^{-T/\text{MTBF}}$

T/MTBF	$e^{-T/\text{MTBF}}$	T/MTBF	$e^{-T/\text{MTBF}}$
0.10	0.9048	3.50	0.0302
0.50	0.6065	4.00	0.0183
1.00	0.3679	4.50	0.0111
1.50	0.2231	5.00	0.0067
2.00	0.1353	5.50	0.0041
2.50	0.0821	6.00	0.0025
3.00	0.0498	6.50	0.0015

MODELING PRODUCT LIFE WITH THE NORMAL DISTRIBUTION

A process that is in statistical control and that consists of basic items such as ball bearings will rarely experience the early failure trends shown in the exponential distribution. Rather, failures will cluster around a *failure point.* In cases such as this, the central limit theorem applies, and the normal distribution can be used to calculate the expected product life.

Using the standard normal distribution table, we can calculate the area under the curve from negative infinity to some point z. z is a standardized value computed using the following equation (see Chapter 2 for further discussion of z scores):

$$z = (T - \text{mean wear-out time})/\text{standard deviation of wear-out time} \quad (8.5)$$

In order to work with the normal distribution, you need to know the mean of the distribution and its standard deviation. To obtain a probability that the service life will not exceed some time T, use T to compute a z-value and then use the table in Appendix B to calculate the area under the curve to the left of z. To determine the probability that service life will exceed some time T, compute the z-value, find the area under the curve from the table, and then subtract that value from 1.

The time value, T, for a given probability can also be determined. Find the probability of interest in the table in Appendix B. If the exact probability is not in the table, find the nearest probability to the left in the table, i.e., the closest smaller value. Use the corresponding z-value in the above formula and solve for T.

EXAMPLE 8.6

The mean life of a circuit array under normal-use conditions can be modeled using a normal distribution with a mean of 6 months and a standard deviation of 1 month.

Determine each of the following:

1. The probability that a circuit array will wear out before 7 months of service
2. The probability that an array will wear out after 7 months of service
3. The service life that will provide a wear-out probability of 10 percent

Solution:

1. Compute z and use it to obtain the probability directly from the table in Appendix B.

$$z = (7 - 6)/1 = 1.00$$

$$\text{Thus, } P(T < 7) = 0.84132$$

2. Subtract the probability $P(T < 7)$, determined above from 1.

$$P(T > 7) = 1.00 - 0.8413 = 0.1587$$

3. Turn to the normal table and find the value of z that corresponds to an area under the curve of 0.10.

$$z = -1.28 = (t - 6)/1$$

Solving for T, we find $T = 4.72$ months.

RISK ASSESSMENT TOOLS AND RISK PREVENTION

FMEA stands for Failure Mode and Effect Analysis. In FMEA, a product is examined at the system and/or subsystem levels for all possible ways in which a failure may occur. For each potential failure, an estimate is made of its effect on the total system. The seriousness of the effect is also analyzed. A review is made of the corrective action being planned to minimize the probability and effect of any future failure. The failure "mode" is the symptom of the failure, which is distinct from the cause of failure. FMEA can be expanded to include such matters as safety, effect on downtime, access, repair planning, and design changes.

There are 5 basic steps to constructing a FMEA table:

1. Determine how the component can fail.
2. Determine possible cause(s) of failure.
3. Determine the effect on the product or system within which it operates (e.g., safety, downtime, repair requirements, tools required, etc.).
4. Determine the corrective action required.
5. Note any additional comments.

Figure 8.2 shows an incomplete FMEA on a personal computer monitor.

FTA refers to Fault Tree Analysis. FTA is a tool used to identify possible causes for potential operating hazards or undesired events. The starting point in FTA is a list of potential hazards or undesired events generated from historical data of accidents and/or near misses. Each hazard on the list becomes a failure mode requiring analysis. The possible direct causes of the hazard or event are then analyzed and the origins of these causes determined. Finally, methods or actions for avoiding these causes are formulated and analyzed. There are 4 basic steps to constructing a fault tree:

1. Define the flaws giving rise to the functional defects.
2. Identify the possible root causes and their direct and indirect effects.
3. Quantify, as best you can, the event's probability.
4. Determine which fault of a particular kind is most likely to occur and when (time dependency).

An example of FTA is given in Figure 8.3. The tree is composed of branches connected to two different types of nodes:

AND nodes, denoted by the symbol

OR nodes, denoted by the symbol

An AND node is used when all events must occur in order for the event above the node to occur. An OR node is used when at least one of the events must occur in order for the event above the node to occur.

Component Name	Failure Mode	Cause of failure	Effect of failure on system	Correction of Problem	Comments
Electrical plug Part No. EP-1	Loose wiring	Use, vibration, handling	Will not conduct current	Molded plug and wire	Uncorrected, could cause fire
	Damaged contacts	User bends/breaks prongs when plugging or unplugging	Will not conduct current. May conduct current but fail to ground resulting in fire hazard, severe shock or death	Heavy-duty prongs and protective molding	Clear warning on packaging to use 3-prong grounded outlet
CRT picture tube	Bad pixels	Excessive heat, dropping, bumping, shipping	Degrades picture	Improve shipping packaging to prevent damage	Depending on severity may not be noticeable to user
	Cracked	Excessive heat, bumping, dropping, shipping	No picture	Ensure material quality. Improve shipping packaging to prevent damage	
Cabling to CPU	Broken, frayed	Fatigue, heat, carelessness,	Will not conduct signal. May cause shock or damage CPU.	Use wiring suitable for long life in anticipated environment	Danger warning on instructions
	Internal short circuit	Heat, brittle insulation	May cause electrical shock, damage CPU or monitor	Use wiring suitable for long life in anticipated environment	

FIGURE 8.2 Partial FMEA on personal computer monitor.

PRODUCT TRACEABILITY SYSTEMS AND RECALL PROCEDURES

Product traceability systems provide the ability to identify and track a part or product back to its point of origin. Product/material traceability is discussed in Chapter 9. In this chapter, traceability is discussed relative to reliability. Traceability is important in reliability because it simplifies investigation of product failure and minimizes the effort required by product recalls.

While there are instances where complete traceability is required (e.g., pharmaceuticals and aircraft), most commercial products limit traceability to safety-oriented qualities and to those components which are decisive in achieving overall

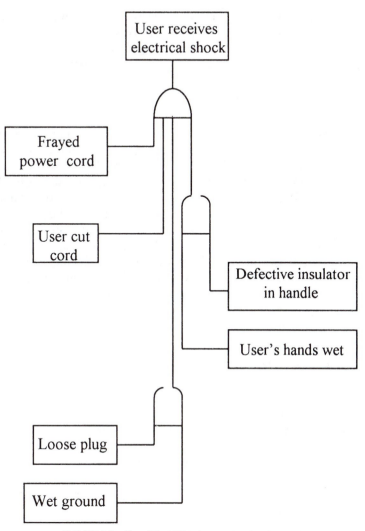

FIGURE 8.3   Simplified FTA for an electric trimmer.

fitness for use. Traceability is usually accomplished with part serial numbers (for unique identification) or with batch numbers, where specific identification is either unwarranted or not possible (e.g., drug batches).

Utilizing traceability can significantly limit the size of a recall by allowing a company to recall only those batch or item numbers under investigation. The general procedure for recalls is to maintain a sample from each batch produced and, when information regarding nonperformance is received, to test the sample to see if the failure can be repeated. If the failure is repeated, a recall should be implemented immediately. If the failure cannot be repeated on the sample, effort should be made to obtain the product that failed and to perform a detailed failure analysis on the failed item.

With today's business climate, however, many companies have chosen to recall the product at the first sign of problems. This is done to minimize potential liability and can often result in positive marketing exposure (e.g., the Tylenol poisoning). For further discussion of product/lot traceability, see Chapter 9.

SUMMARY

This chapter has addressed the issue of reliability engineering. Reliability is defined as the probability of a product performing without failure a specified function under given conditions for a specified period of time. The three dimensions of the definition of reliability were discussed as well as ways of calculating the reliability of a process or piece of equipment. In addition, the causes of product and equipment failure and the patterns associated with their failure rates were examined. Equations were shown for calculating failure rates in the two most commonly applicable distributions: the exponential and the standardized normal distribution.

Risk assessment and prevention tools and techniques were discussed including failure mode and effect analysis (FMEA) and fault tree analysis (FTA). Finally, product traceability and recall procedures were discussed.

DISCUSSION QUESTIONS

1. Discuss the two approaches to using probability to define the reliability of a product.
2. Discuss the importance of specifying standard operating conditions.
3. Discuss approaches to defining the failure of road striping paint which is exposed to heavy traffic.
4. Is it always more effective to provide backups for all components than to provide a parallel system?
5. What is the effect of switch reliability on a system?
6. What is meant by the bathtub curve?
7. What is the difference between MTBF and MTTF?
8. When might a normal distribution be a better model for failure rates than an exponential distribution?
9. Discuss the use of FMEA.
10. Discuss the use of FTA.
11. How would product traceability facilitate a product recall?

PROBLEMS

1. An assembly line consists of 4 subsystems with the following reliabilities:

$P_1 = 0.998$

$P_2 = 0.997$

$P_3 = 0.988$

$P_4 = 0.990$

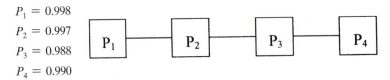

What is the overall reliability of the system?

2. In order to increase the safety of its fleet, Safety-First Airlines (SFA) wants to install a redundant system to ensure against instrument malfunction. The original system consists of 5 components, with reliabilities of 0.995, 0.995, 0.999, 0.998, and 0.980. The airline has the choice of adding a backup to each component (with the same reliabilities as the originals) which will activate automatically if that component fails, or adding a completely separate system with the same components as the original system. This separate system is activated via an automatic switch with a reliability of 0.995. Which system would you recommend SFA install in its planes?

3. Never-Fail Nightlights wants parents to be assured of the integrity of its products. As such, Never-Fail requested Rest-Assured Labs to test its newest nightlight—the Everglo—to determine its life expectancy. The lab determined that the distribution of the life expectancy is exponential, with an average life of 5 years. What is the probability that one of the Everglo units will last:

   (a) Less than 5 years

   (b) More than 30 months

   (c) At least 10 years

4. Under normal-use conditions, the mean life of a heating coil can be modeled using a normal distribution with a mean of 20 months and a standard deviation of 2 months. Determine each of the following:

   (a) The probability that a heating coil will wear out before 15 months of service

   (b) The probability that a heating coil will wear out after 10 months of service

   (c) The service life that will provide a wear-out probability of 10 percent

NOTES

1. *Reliability of Military Electronic Equipment.* Report by the Advisory Group on Reliability of Electronic Equipment, Office of the Assistant Secretary of Defense (R&D), June 1957.

2. Stevenson, W. J. *Production/Operations Management,* 5th ed. Chicago: Irwin, 1996, p. 166.

3. Juran, J. M., & F. M. Gryna. *Quality Planning and Analysis,* 2nd ed. New York: McGraw-Hill, 1980, p. 209.

4. Stevenson, p. 169.

SUGGESTED READINGS

Evans, J. R., & W. M. Lindsay. *The Management and Control of Quality,* 3rd ed. New York: West Publishing, 1996, Chapter 17, pp. 735–767.

Juran, J. M., & F. M. Gryna. *Quality Planning and Analysis,* 2nd ed. New York: McGraw-Hill, 1980, pp. 167–189 and 203–217.

Kenet, R., & S. Zacks. *Modern Industrial Statistics: The Design and Control of Quality and Reliability.* Pacific Grove, CA: Duxbury Press, 1998.

Sinha, M. N., & W. O. Willborn. *The Management of Quality Assurance.* New York: Wiley, 1985, pp. 187–210.

Stevenson, W. J. *Production/Operations Management,* 5th ed. Chicago: Irwin, 1996, pp. 165–179.

SECTION IV

Quality Management

CHAPTER 9

Product, Process, and Materials Control

CHAPTER OBJECTIVES

This chapter introduces the following topics:

- Work instructions
- Classification of quality characteristics and defects
- Identification of materials and status
- Lot traceability
- Materials segregation practices
- Materials review board criteria and procedures

INTRODUCTION

Work instructions are important in ensuring that everyone understands how to perform an operation properly. They minimize variation in the system by standardizing operations, and they also provide a basis for auditing an operation.

Characteristics and defects may be classified according to a number of schemes. One reason for such classifications is to segregate characteristics and defects according to their importance. This allows appropriate focus to be provided to each characteristic and defect.

Identification of materials and status (e.g., awaiting inspection, accepted for use) is important to assuring the quality of manufactured products. Properly identified materials are more likely to be used only where and as intended.

Lot traceability is the ability to match a particular lot of material to a particular lot of product. While there are a number of internal reasons for ensuring lot traceability, there are also many instances where traceability is required by customers or regulatory bodies.

Materials segregation practices ensure that lots of materials which are not approved for use are safeguarded in a separate area from approved materials.

WORK INSTRUCTIONS

Work instructions, in their base form, are nothing more than written instructions on how to perform a particular job or function. They contain the basics of how the work associated with an operation is to be performed and how the performance of that job will be measured. Quality audit systems, including ISO 9000, rely heavily upon work instructions as the standard by which to judge the completeness and quality of an operation. For example, ANSI/ASQC Q1-1986[1] defines a quality system audit as "a documented activity performed to verify, by examination and evaluations of objective evidence, that applicable elements of the quality system are appropriate and have been developed, *documented,* and effectively implemented in accordance and in conjunction with specified requirements." ANSI/ASQC Q9000-1-1994[2] states that:

> Documentation is important for quality improvement. When procedures are documented, deployed, and implemented, it is possible to determine with confidence how things are done currently and to measure current performance. Then reliable evidence of the effect of a change is enhanced. Moreover, documented standard operating procedures are essential for maintaining the gains from quality-improvement efforts.

Shigeo Shingo includes work instructions under the planning function. To link the planning function to the control and execution functions, management must "compile standard work process manuals and standard operations manuals."[3] According to Shingo, defects may occur during the execution stage where[4]:

- Standards devised in the planning stage are flawed.
- Control or execution is not carried out in accordance with standards set during the planning stage because those standards were imperfect or improperly understood.
- Standards established by plans are observed, but deviations from permissible tolerances occur.
- Standards set by the planning function are correctly understood, but inadvertent mistakes occur.

Clearly defined work instructions used as the basis for training and evaluation can reduce confusion among employees, increase morale by clearly stating job requirements and methods of evaluation, and reduce variation in the system. Since reducing variation is a key aspect of quality improvement, improvement in work instructions and greater attention to their consistent application can be important contributors to a quality improvement program.

CLASSIFICATION OF QUALITY CHARACTERISTICS AND DEFECTS

Some quality characteristics are "serious," that is, of critical importance to the fitness for use of the product or service. Most have a relatively minor effect on fitness for use. The more important or serious the characteristic, the greater the attention it should receive from the quality system. Many companies utilize formal systems to classify the seriousness of the characteristic. These systems use inspection, quality planning, and written specifications, among others, to determine the classification level of the characteristic in question.

There are two lists which need to be classified: (1) quality characteristics derived from the specifications and (2) defects due to nonconformance during manufacturing and field failures during use. Normally one system of classification can be applicable to both lists. However, the lists are usually published separately since their usage in an organization may differ significantly between departments. Regardless of how a specific organization sets up its classification scheme, the overriding concern is the grouping of characteristics and defects into categories which reflect the seriousness or priority of the characteristics or defects.

The basic system of definitions was developed in the 1920s in the Bell System. One system classifies defects as Class A, B, C, or D[5]:

Class A defects.	Very serious, and will surely cause operating failure of the unit in service which cannot be readily corrected on the job
Class B defects.	Serious, and will probably, but not surely, cause Class A operating failure of the unit in service
Class C defects.	Moderately serious, and will probably cause operating failure of the unit in service
Class D defects.	Not serious, and will not cause operating failure of the unit in service

A similar commonly used system for classifying defects according to their seriousness is contained in MIL-STD-105E.[6] This method classifies defects into three classes:

Critical defect.	"A defect that judgment and experience indicate is likely to result in hazardous or unsafe conditions for individuals using, maintaining, or depending upon the product. . . . "
Major defect.	"A defect, other than critical, that is likely to result in failure, or to reduce materially the usability of the unit or product for its intended purpose."
Minor defect.	"A defect that is not likely to reduce materially the usability of the unit or product for its intended purpose, or is a departure from established standards having little bearing on the effective use or operation of the unit."

A similar classification scheme[7] adds a fourth classification as follows:

Incidental defect.	A defect which "will have no unsatisfactory effect on customer quality."

The ASQ Statistics Division's classification system[8] is also based upon the seriousness of the defect:

Class 1	*Very serious.*	"Leads directly to severe injury or catastrophic economic loss."
Class 2	*Serious.*	"Leads directly to significant injury or significant economic loss."
Class 3	*Major.*	"Related to major problems with respect to intended normal, or reasonably foreseeable, use."
Class 4	*Minor.*	"Related to minor problems with respect to intended normal, or reasonably foreseeable, use."

The MIL-STD-105E goes on to classify defectives according to the defect classification system (e.g., a critical defective contains one or more critical defects).

Classification can be a long, tedious process, but it is one that must be performed. By-products of this effort include identification of misconceptions and confusion among departments, and recognition of potential characteristics or defects that would otherwise remain undiscovered.

A key problem area that may arise involves the reluctance of personnel to "downgrade" characteristics and defects. In some people's eyes every characteristic or defect is critical. Care must be taken to properly categorize the seriousness of each item; otherwise the list will be useless as the critical category will contain the majority, if not all, of the identified characteristics and defects. Remember, the better the classification scheme, the shorter the inspection time, resulting in faster turnarounds, quicker delivery to customers, and reduced costs.

IDENTIFICATION OF MATERIALS AND STATUS

Materials can be identified either as discrete units, i.e., an engine, a washing machine, etc.; or as a collection of discrete units—a lot. Material can also exist in bulk, such as food or chemicals. In the case of bulk items, we usually refer to some or all of the bulk as a lot, while a unit is referred to as a specimen.

An important aspect of material packaging is content identification, tracking, and handling instructions.[9] Typical information included on a package is manufacturer, product, type of container, count, customer identification, manufacturer lot number, and special handling instructions. Other information can include the date, shift, and machine on which the material was produced. Increasingly this information is provided in scannable (e.g., bar code) format. Large commercial purchasers frequently specify exactly where the label is to be placed and what information it is to contain. Some customers require that the contents be identified by a code designation for proprietary purposes.

Some information is often made part of the product itself. Plastic molded parts frequently have part number, cavity number, and manufacturing date molded into the part. Formed metal parts sometimes have similar information stamped into the piece. In other cases serial numbers and other information are included either as an integral part of the unit or on labels affixed to the units.

Customers increasingly demand that suppliers provide quality information with lots of material. In some cases this consists of control charts documenting the state of the process during production of the lot. In other cases it is documentation of inspection under a specified sampling plan to an agreed-upon AQL or LTPD. A certificate of conformance to specifications may also be required. The standards for lot quality are usually contained in the inspection plans and sampling criteria published by the organization's quality control department. Chapter 5 contains a detailed discussion of sampling plans and procedures.

The status of all materials in a facility must be evident. For example, it should be evident to everyone that a particular lot of materials is awaiting inspection before being released for use in production. There are a number of approaches to material control, and usually more than one approach is used in an organization.

For uncertified or new suppliers, incoming materials are usually segregated into a separate holding area until they pass incoming inspection. Once they pass this inspection, a label or stamp is affixed to the packages and a move ticket authorizes the material to be stocked. Materials which fail to pass the incoming inspection should be marked and held in a separate secured storage area pending final disposition. For certified suppliers, materials may bypass incoming inspection and move directly to the materials warehouse or production area.

Material identification, control, handling, storage, packaging, preservation, and delivery are explicit parts of the ANSI/ASQC Q-9000 standards.[10] This is a further indication of the importance of these topics in maintaining and improving the performance of a quality system.

LOT TRACEABILITY

As discussed in Chapter 6, product traceability systems provide the ability to identify and track the genealogy of a product or part backward to its point of origin. Traceability is needed to assure lot uniformity in materials, to avoid mix-ups of look-alike materials, to aid in proper sequential usage of perishable materials, to simplify investigation of nonconforming material, and to aid in the location of material involved in product recalls. Traceability is also an explicit part of the ANSI/ASQC Q-9000 standards (e.g., paragraph 4.8 in ANSI/ISO/ASQC Q9001-1994).[11]

While there are instances where complete traceability is required (e.g., pharmaceuticals), most commercial products limit traceability to safety-oriented qualities and to those components which are decisive in achieving overall fitness for use. Traceability is accomplished using part identification numbers (for unique identification) or lot numbers, where specific identification is either unwarranted or not possible (e.g., drug lots). Traceability is facilitated when relevant information is included in a machine readable format (e.g., bar code).

MATERIALS SEGREGATION PRACTICES

Any time an inspector determines a lot of materials to be nonconforming, the materials should be clearly labeled to identify them as nonconforming. This often involves placing a red "hold" tag on the lot. The material should then be moved to a secured area of the facility which is reserved for nonconforming material. All reasonable effort should be taken to ensure that nonconforming material is segregated, labeled, and secured to ensure it will not be accidentally used in the process.

The inspector prepares a nonconforming report which is distributed to various departments and personnel. Distribution should, at a minimum, include schedulers who may have to make up for the lost material, and an investigator who is assigned to collect the type of information needed as inputs for the fitness-for-use decision maker. The final-disposition decision for nonconforming materials is frequently made by a materials review board.

MATERIALS REVIEW BOARD CRITERIA AND PROCEDURES

A Materials Review Board (MRB) is charged with the disposition of nonconforming product. A board may consist of a quality engineer, process engineer, purchasing representative, and production representative. The board generally has 3 choices available to it relative to the nonconforming material: Ship (or use as is), don't ship (or don't use as is), and corrective action. ANSI/ISO/ASQC Q9001-1994[12] lists 4 actions which may be taken relative to nonconforming product: (1) Rework to meet the specified requirements, (2) accept with or without repair by concession, (3) regrade for alternative applications, or (4) reject or scrap.

The decision to "ship or use as is" manifests in several different ways. First, the designer may allow a waiver in the specifications for the material in question, thereby putting the lot into a state of conformance. Second, the intended customer may allow a waiver, which in essence supersedes the material specifications. Third, for noncritical items, the quality control department may grant a waiver based on fitness-for-use decision criteria. Fourth, the MRB may grant a waiver. This waiver is based on the facts and conclusions of the investigator and requires the unanimous consent of the members of the MRB. A special case of a waiver involves approving the material for use for other than the original intended purpose or as a substitute for a lower grade of material. Finally, a waiver may be granted by upper management in conjunction with a recommendation from the MRB. Upper management becomes involved in cases of a critical nature where human safety or large sums of money are involved. Note that in none of the cases is the material designation changed from nonconforming to conforming. Rather a waiver is granted to the nonconforming lot allowing it to be used. This should be noted in the traceability system in case of future problems. In the case of purchased materials, the decision to waive certain quality requirements should always be promptly communicated to the supplier and a report of corrective action to prevent recurrence requested.

A "don't ship or don't use as is" decision may result from the investigation of the nonconforming material. When a don't-ship decision is made, the MRB must determine the most economical way to dispose of the nonconforming material. Choices for materials manufactured in-house include sort, repair, downgrade, and scrap. Purchased materials are usually returned to the supplier.

The third MRB decision alternative is "corrective action" (sometimes called rework). Sometimes the most economical decision is to accept the material and to initiate actions to correct the nonconformancies. In some cases this involves sorting; in other cases additional processing is required. The additional processing may take the form of replacing defective components, tightening loose connections, adding an additional spot weld, or similar actions.

In addition to the need to dispose of the nonconforming material, there is a need to prevent reoccurrence. The prevention process usually takes 1 of 2 paths, depending on the type of nonconformance. The first path involves nonconformance which occurs in some isolated, sporadic way within a traditionally well-behaved process. These problems may be due to human error or incorrect calibration of equipment, for example. For such cases, it is usually possible to identify the cause of the nonconformance and restore the process to its normal mode of operation. In statistical process control, this type of problem is referred to as an *assignable cause* and no changes to the fundamental nature of the process are required. The second path involves "repeat offenders." These cases point to fundamental stability problems in the process which require root cause analysis and correction if the nonconformance is to be eliminated.

Purchasing involvement in MRB actions is important because the purchasing staff members are the principle contacts between the organization and its suppliers. Purchasing is also usually responsible for negotiating the allocation of costs associated with nonconforming purchased materials.[13] Usually the supplier of nonconforming materials will be held responsible for transportation costs to and from the rejection point, testing costs, and rework costs associated with nonconforming lots. In some cases, contingent costs (e.g., production downtime, overtime) are also charged to the supplier.

SUMMARY

Inadequate work instructions or work instructions that are not adhered to are sources of defects and worker confusion and dissatisfaction. Clearly defined work instructions are therefore important aspects of the quality system. All defects do not result in the same risk. Defect classification schemes provide ways to classify defects according to the seriousness of their likely consequences. Clear identification of materials and their status helps assure that materials will be used appropriately. The ability to trace a product back to its constituent components provides a means of troubleshooting problems and also provides a rational basis for product recalls. The proper handling of nonconforming materials is important. Materials segregation practices and materials review boards are key components of the system to handle nonconforming materials.

DISCUSSION QUESTIONS

1. What are work instructions and why are they important?
2. What would be the foremost characteristics of an acceptable sampling plan for critical defects?
3. Should sampling procedures differ for critical, major, and minor defects? Discuss.
4. A manufacturer approaches a customer and asks which of the 237 dimensions on the blueprint are critical. The customer replies that it expects the product to be in conformance to all the dimensional specifications—therefore they are all critical. Is there a better approach the manufacturer could have taken with the customer? Discuss.
5. What are some of the categories of information which might be important to include on product packaging? When would it be appropriate and desirable to include this information on the product itself?
6. Why might lot traceability be more important in pharmaceutical manufacturing than in cement manufacturing?
7. An inspector determines at receiving inspection that a lot of raw materials is nonconforming. Discuss the actions that should be taken next.
8. What are the responsibilities of a Materials Review Board?

NOTES

1. ANSI/ASQC Q1-1986, p. 2.
2. ANSI/ASQC Q9000-1-1994, p. 6.
3. Shingo, Shigeo. *Zero Quality Control: Source Inspection and the Poka-yoke System.* Cambridge, MA: Productivity Press, 1986, pp. 28–29.
4. Ibid., p. 30.
5. Dodge, H. F. "A Method of Rating Manufactured Product." *The Bell System Technical Journal,* vol. 7, April 1928, pp. 350–368.
6. MIL-STD-105E, 1989, p. 2.
7. Feigenbaum, A. V. *Total Quality Control,* 3rd ed. New York: McGraw-Hill, 1983, p. 253.
8. American Society for Quality Control Statistics Division. *Glossary & Tables for Statistical Quality Control.* Milwaukee, WI: ASQC Quality Press, 1983, pp. 13–14.
9. Bowersox, D. J., & D. J. Closs. *Logistical Management, The Integrated Supply Chain Process.* New York: McGraw-Hill, 1996, pp. 444–445.
10. ANSI/ISO/ASQC Q9001-1994, pp. 4–9.
11. Ibid., p. 5.
12. Ibid., p. 7.
13. Leenders, M. R., & H. E. Fearon. *Purchasing and Supply Management,* 11th ed. Chicago: Irwin, 1997, pp. 165–166.

SUGGESTED READINGS

American Society for Quality Control Statistics Division. *Glossary & Tables for Statistical Quality Control.* Milwaukee, WI: ASQC Quality Press, 1983.

Bowersox, D. J., & D. J. Closs. *Logistical Management, The Integrated Supply Chain Process.* New York: McGraw-Hill, 1996.

Feigenbaum, A. V. *Total Quality Control,* 3rd ed. New York: McGraw-Hill, 1983.

Leenders, M. R., & H. E. Fearon. *Purchasing and Supply Management,* 11th ed. Chicago: Irwin, 1997, Chapter 4, pp. 128–171.

MIL-STD-105E, *Sampling Procedures and Tables for Inspection by Attributes.* Washington, DC: Government Printing Office, 1989.

Quality System Requirements QS-9000, 2nd ed. February 1995 (fourth printing, July 1996).

CHAPTER 10

Quality Management Principles

CHAPTER OBJECTIVES

This chapter introduces the following topics:

- Human resource management
- Motivation theories
- Employee involvement and teams
- Professional conduct and ethics
- Quality planning
- Supplier management

INTRODUCTION

Employees (human resources) are integral parts of the quality system of any organization. However, they are often treated as *just* the "hands" of the organization—that is, the part of the organization where actual work is accomplished. The modern view is that employees are more than just "hands," and human resource management is directed toward making employees true partners with management in the effective operation of the enterprise.

Quality professionals are part of the human resources of the enterprise. All employees must adhere to the rules, regulations, and policies of the organization which employs them. But certified quality professionals are also subject to the professional and ethical standards of the quality discipline.

Quality planning is one leg of Juran's quality trilogy.[1] Quality control and quality improvement without quality planning is as effective as a three-legged stool with one leg missing.

The modern view of the quality system includes the firm's suppliers' suppliers and the firm's customers' customers and everything in between. Supplier selection and supplier management are critical functions which, if ignored or mismanaged, can seriously impair an organization's ability to achieve its quality goals.

HUMAN RESOURCE MANAGEMENT

"Human resource management refers to the practices and policies you need to carry out the people or personnel aspects of your management job."[2] This section will examine two facets of human resource management: motivation theories and group dynamics.

Motivation Theories

Managers are charged with motivating their employees to work to achieve the goals of the organization as efficiently and effectively as possible. Managers then, by definition, accomplish their objectives through the work of others. For this reason it is incumbent upon managers to understand how to effectively motivate their employees.

Early insight into the motivation of workers resulted from studies conducted in the 1920s at the Hawthorne Plant of Western Electric. The initial studies were guided by the principles of scientific management—that there is "one best way" of doing a job—and focused on determining the effect of illumination on worker productivity. During the course of the experiments, it was found that productivity increased for both the experimental and control groups regardless of the level of illumination. When these experiments were abandoned, the report concluded that the most important variable in the study was "the psychology of the individual."[3]

Further studies at Hawthorne examined factors other than illumination levels. For example, the relay assembly experiments at Hawthorne found that the supervisor's style and the formation of small groups to build *esprit de corps* had a greater impact than pay in increasing worker productivity.

There were no theories at that time to explain the results of the Hawthorne Studies. Subsequently, theories were developed which attempted to explain motivation and how it contributes to performance. Four of these, often referred to as *classic theories of motivation,* are Maslow's Hierarchy of Needs, McGregor's Theory X and Theory Y, McClelland's Acquired Needs Theory, and Herzberg's Two Factor Theory. These classic theories provide insight into what motivates people. The influence of these theories on Deming is evident in his 14 points.

According to Maslow, there are 5 levels of motivators arranged in a hierarchy,[4] as shown in Figure 10.1. Higher-level needs are motivators only after lower-level needs have been satisfied. According to this theory, attempting to appeal to employees' ego needs while the employees are still striving to meet their physiological needs will be unsuccessful. For example, attempting to motivate minimum wage employees with promises of inflated job titles would not be expected to be the most effective strategy according to Maslow's theory.

McGregor[5] defines two approaches to management. The *classic* approach arises from Taylor's scientific management and is called Theory X. According to Theory X, workers inherently dislike work and must be coerced, controlled, and threatened in order to motivate them to work to achieve organizational objectives. Theory X suggests that workers actively avoid responsibility and that the worker's desire for security is the primary motivator. At the other extreme is Theory Y, which is derived from participatory approaches to management. Theory Y suggests that work is a natural activity for humans, that workers will actively work to achieve

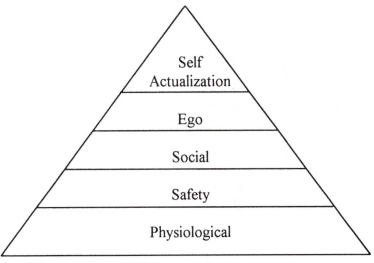

FIGURE 10.1   Maslow's hierarchy of needs.

goals to which they are committed, and that workers possess considerable ingenuity and imagination which are waiting to be tapped.

McClelland[6] suggests that workers have distinct motivational profiles. These profiles consist of the relative strengths of their needs for achievement (n ACH), affiliation (n AFF), and power (n POW). The implication of McClelland's theory is that understanding a particular employee's profile is the first step to designing motivational incentives for the employee. According to McClelland's theory, it is unlikely that the same incentive system will have the same effect on Employee A in Figure 10.2 as on Employee B. Employee A has high power, moderate achievement,

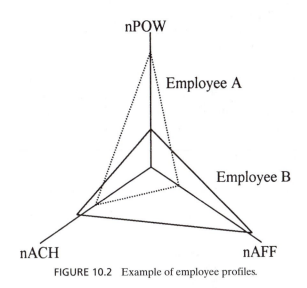

FIGURE 10.2   Example of employee profiles.

and low affiliation needs, while Employee B has low power, moderate achievement, and high affiliation needs.

Herzberg's[7] theory proposes that job satisfaction and job dissatisfaction are *not* two extremes of a single continuum. Rather there are two separate continuums. One has job satisfaction and no job satisfaction at the extremes; the other has job dissatisfaction and no job dissatisfaction at the extremes. Needs which when satisfied can lead to job satisfaction are called *motivators* (see Table 10.1). The other category of needs, called *hygiene* needs, can only lead to no job dissatisfaction. According to this theory, increasing pay or improving supervision can only decrease the level of worker job dissatisfaction. These actions will not result in increased worker job satisfaction.

Managers often find that these classic theories are oversimplified and sometimes contradictory. Today's manager faces a complex and dynamic environment. Employees are not all the same. No one theory can possibly deal with all the environmental factors. No *single* theory can provide the *prescription* for motivating *all* employees in *every* situation. Taken together, however, they can be useful to today's manager.

Integration of the Classic Motivational Theories

Wilkinson, Orth, and Benfari[8] provide a motivational model which integrates the classic theories in a way that enables the manager to adjust to changing social and organizational environments and differences among people. The integrated theory results in 8 conclusions:[9]

1. Herzberg's dissatisfiers are similar to Maslow's first two levels of need plus some small increment in each of the top three needs in his hierarchy.
2. These dissatisfiers tend to be related to the autocratic structured management style of Taylor or McGregor's Theory X.
3. Morse and Lorsch have identified this autocratic style as more effective for routine tasks.
4. Herzberg's satisfiers are similar to Maslow's top three levels of need.
5. McClelland's achievement, power and affiliation needs are a different mix of Maslow's top three levels of need.
6. [Herzberg's] satisfiers are related to the participative management style described by McGregor as Theory Y.
7. [McGregor's Theory Y] style, according to Morse and Lorsch, appears more effective for tasks with high levels of complexity.
8. The nature of the people and of the tasks being performed causes higher and higher levels of dependency, diversity, uncertainty, complexity, education, and professionalism. Therefore, the greater the observed difference between reactive and proactive behavior, and the greater the applicability of Multiple Influences.

TABLE 10.1   Examples of Herzberg's 2 Factors

Motivators	Hygiene Factors
Recognition	Pay
Responsibility	Security
Achievement	Supervisors
Personal growth	Working conditions

The integrated, multiple influences model can assist managers in adjusting managerial style to "the realities of human motivation in the workplace" and provide guidance for "how to proceed in developing work systems, given the social and organizational environment and the nature of people."[10]

Process Theories of Motivation

The classic motivational theories do not provide much information about how motivation actually occurs. Process theories of motivation attempt to explain how behavior is influenced.

Vroom's Expectancy Theory[11] defines the 4 primary variables of motivation as choice, expectancy, instrumentality, and valence. People are motivated to make choices about how they are to behave. That choice is influenced by their expectation of achieving rewards that satisfy given needs. Low expectations of reward are unlikely to greatly influence choice. Instrumentality is the probability assigned by the individual that a particular performance will lead to a specific reward. Valence is the value that the individual places on the specific reward. Vroom theorized that expectancy, instrumentality, and valence were related to motivation as follows:

$$\text{Motivation} = f(\text{expectancy} \times \text{instrumentality} \times \text{valence})$$

Porter and Lawler[12] extended expectancy theory by distinguishing between the effects of intrinsic rewards (e.g., recognition, achievement) and extrinsic rewards (e.g., advancement, salary increases). Porter and Lawler found that satisfaction was related to actual performance and the real outcomes resulting from that performance.

Managers must be careful when setting up reward systems to motivate specific behavior. Careful consideration must be given to the ramifications of motivating certain behaviors. For example, a bonus promised to a purchasing manager based on expenditures on raw materials as a percentage of sales might motivate the purchase of low-cost, low-quality materials. A better approach, although much harder to measure, might be to base the bonus on total cost of ownership of the materials (purchase price + inspection cost + failure cost due to materials + effect of materials on production efficiency + . . .).

Employee Involvement and Teams—Group Dynamics

Employee involvement (EI) develops naturally from the classic motivation theories and is a key tenet of total quality management. Employee involvement varies among organizations from information sharing, where management makes the decisions and then communicates the decisions to the employees, to total self-direction, where managers facilitate total self-management in an all-team organization.[13] The use of formal groups or teams is a frequent manifestation of EI in organizations.

Many different types of groups or teams are utilized in organizations. Temporary teams form for a particular, limited purpose and disband when that purpose is achieved. Examples of temporary teams include problem-solving teams, product design teams, and systems integration teams. Permanent groups include quality circles, management teams, and self-managed work teams.

One recent study identified the importance of time and training in team development.[14] Other studies have identified 4 factors as being important influences on group effectiveness.[15] These factors are group size, spatial constraints, group cohesiveness, and group norms. Group effectiveness tends to decrease when groups become too large. Ishikawa[16] explicitly recognized this in his definition of a quality circle as "a *small* group which voluntarily performs quality control activities within a single workshop." The American Society for Quality (ASQ) is more specific in its definition, specifying "small" as "10 or fewer."[17]

As the physical distance between workers increases, group effectiveness tends to decrease. This means that work station layouts which place workers in close proximity to each other can increase work group effectiveness. For example, a U-shaped layout will likely result in better communication and group effectiveness than a straight-line layout.

Group cohesiveness is the "degree to which group members form a strong collective unit reflecting a feeling of oneness."[18] This factor interacts with group size in that smaller groups tend to be more cohesive. The more threatening the external environment in which the group is working, the greater the tendency toward cohesiveness. This can be seen in military basic training units where unit cohesiveness is rapidly developed because all the unit members are immersed in a very hostile environment (everyone hates the drill instructor). High group status and similarity among members are other important factors in developing cohesiveness.

Group norms, the standards for group behavior, develop over time. Greater commitment to group norms is a reflection of greater group cohesiveness. The more congruent that group's norms are with the personal norms of the members, the more cohesive the group.

The Care and Feeding of Teams

Research has shown that the behavior of employees changes when they are formed into teams. One study[19] by Marks et al. reported that productivity and absenteeism improved when employees participated in quality circles. Griffin[20] documented improvements in job satisfaction, organizational commitment, and job performance when employees participated in quality circles. However, his study determined that these improvements tend to be short term, and they tend to disappear after about 18 months.

After an initial burst of enthusiasm, quality circles often tend to "wind down" as the most obvious problems have been addressed. Among the keys to sustained success are continuous and visible management involvement, legitimate recognition, and effective communication. Token efforts will not achieve long-term results.

PROFESSIONAL CONDUCT AND ETHICS

The American Society for Quality (formerly ASQC) requires that applicants for certification pledge to uphold the ASQC Code of Ethics shown in Figure 10.3. The Code of Ethics specifies that quality professionals have multiple constituencies to whom they owe the obligation of fair and ethical standards of professional behavior. This obligation begins with the employer or client who pays the quality professional, but also extends equally to the public, fellow professionals, and to the Society which certifies the professional.

CODE OF ETHICS[21]

To uphold and advance the honor and dignity of the profession, and in keeping with high standards of ethical conduct, **I acknowledge that I:**

Fundamental Principles

I.   Will be honest and impartial; will serve with devotion my employer, my clients, and the public.

II.   Will strive to increase the competence and prestige of the profession.

III.   Will use my knowledge and skill for the advancement of human welfare and in promoting the safety and reliability of products for public use.

IV.   Will earnestly endeavor to aid the work of the Society.

Relations With the Public

1.1   Will do whatever I can to promote the reliability and safety of all products that come within my jurisdiction.

1.2   Will endeavor to extend public knowledge of the work of the Society and its members that relates to the public welfare.

1.3   Will be dignified and modest in explaining my work and merit.

1.4   Will preface any public statements that I may issue by clearly indicating on whose behalf they are made.

Relations With Employers and Clients

2.1   Will act in professional matters as a faithful agent or trustee for each employer or client.

2.2   Will inform each client or employer of any business connections, interests, or affiliations that might influence my judgment or impair the equitable character of my services.

2.3   Will indicate to my employer or client the adverse consequences to be expected if my professional judgment is overruled.

2.4   Will not disclose information concerning the business affairs or technical processes of any present or former employer or client without his or her consent.

2.5   Will not accept compensation from more than one party for the same service without the consent of all parties. If employed, I will engage in supplementary employment of consulting practice only with the consent of my employer.

Relations With Peers

3.1   Will take care that credit for the work of others is given to those to whom it is due.

3.2   Will endeavor to aid the professional development and advancement of those in my employ or under my supervision.

3.3   Will not compete unfairly with others; will extend my friendship and confidence to all associates and those with whom I have business relations.

Copyright ASQC 1995, reprinted with permission

FIGURE 10.3   The code of ethics[21] of the American Society for Quality Control. (Copyright ASQC 1995, reprinted with permission.)

Having obligations to multiple constituencies creates the possibility for conflicting pressures upon the quality professional. Sometimes a professional may be tempted to simply tell the employers or clients what they want to hear rather than providing them with the plain unadulterated truth. While this may appear to be expedient in the short run, it can create grave consequences in the long run. An employer or client may base a decision on the inaccurate information provided—and the results are likely to be less than desired and could be catastrophic. The professional's credibility is now subject to question. A professional without credibility cannot be effective. It is better to endure the short-term discomfort that may come with providing objective and accurate information than to take the easy way out and shade the truth.

In cases which involve safety or health issues, quality professionals have a moral and ethical and possibly a legal responsibility that goes beyond the obligation to the employer or client. As recent "whistleblower" cases have shown, the ramifications of living up to one's responsibilities can be painful.

QUALITY PLANNING

Juran's quality trilogy consists of quality planning, quality control, and quality improvement. Juran defines quality planning as "the process for preparing to meet quality goals" and identifies the end result as "a process capable of meeting quality goals under operating conditions."[22] In this section, planning activities will be divided into long-term, operational, and project.

Long-Term Planning

Long-range quality planning is part of the strategic planning process (see Figure 10.4) for an organization and is driven by the organization's mission statement. The organization's mission statement should describe its purpose, customers, products and services, markets, philosophy, and basic technology.[23] Included in most

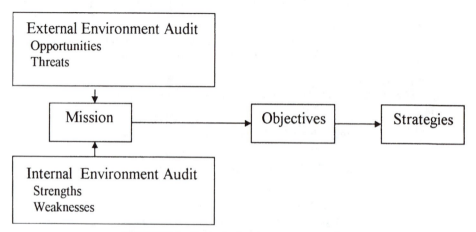

FIGURE 10.4   Strategic planning process overview.

mission statements is some indication of the importance of quality in the organization's mission.

A SWOT analysis[24] (*s*trengths, *w*eaknesses, *o*pportunities, *t*hreats) is used in the first stages of the planning process. Analysis of an organization's strengths and weaknesses is often referred to as an internal environmental audit. Quality considerations such as quality costs and extent of training would be included in the internal environmental audit. Analysis of the opportunities and threats to the organization is often referred to as an external environmental audit. Quality considerations such as product liability, customer complaints, and competitive product features would be included in the external environmental audit.

After the internal strengths and weaknesses and external opportunities and threats have been identified, strategic objectives are developed followed by strategies designed to enable the organization to achieve its objectives. Although the strategic planning process typically takes place at the highest levels of the organization, the operations and quality areas of the organization should have input to the process. Firms, such as Motorola, have identified their operations and quality areas as internal strengths. Part of Motorola's competitive strategy is to leverage these internal strengths.

Operational Planning

Each part of the organization is responsible for developing operational plans which are based upon the strategic plan and which are designed to effect the strategic plan. Operational plans have a much shorter time horizon than strategic plans and are more specific in nature. Figure 10.5 illustrates the relationship between strategic and operational plans.

Strategic Objective
Example: To be known as the highest quality producer of electronic components in the world.

↓

Strategy
Example: To use only the highest quality raw materials available in the production of our products.

↓

Operational Plan
Example Operational Objective:
By the beginning of Q1 1998, to purchase raw materials only from preferred suppliers who have met all the standards in the supplier qualification manual.
> Develop qualification criteria
> Develop schedule for qualifying suppliers

FIGURE 10.5   Example of the relationship between strategic and operational plans.

The operational plan for the quality organization should address the following questions:[25]

1. What specific elements of quality work need to be done?
2. When . . . does each element of work need to be done?
3. How is it to be done . . . ?
4. Who does it . . . ?
5. Where is it to be done . . . ?
6. What tools or equipment are to be used?
7. What are the inputs to the work . . . ?
8. What are the outputs? Do any decisions have to be made . . . ?
9. Is any record of the action to be made . . . ?
10. What are the alternative courses of action to be taken, depending on certain differences in the product quality encountered?
11. What are the criteria for these courses of action?
12. Is any time limit imposed on the work . . . ?

The result of the quality operational planning process must be clearly documented so that the plan can be communicated to everyone who has a role to play in its implementation. One form of output is the quality control manual which guides the day-to-day activities of the quality organization.

Project Planning

Every organization encounters nonroutine projects which must be accomplished. An example of such a project would be the selection, purchase, and installation of new equipment for a testing laboratory. Projects typically go through a life cycle which consists of 5 phases:[26]

1. *Concept.* Recognition of need for project.
2. *Feasibility analysis.* Examination of expected costs, benefits, and risks.
3. *Planning.* Specifies the details of the work and estimates for necessary human resources, time, and cost.
4. *Execution.* Time when the project is done.
5. *Termination.* Closure is achieved. Project resources are reassigned.

Spending time on the early phases of a project is known as *front-loading* the project. Time invested in Phases 2 and 3 results in fewer problems in Phase 4 and a higher probability for the project being successfully completed on time and on budget.

Among the tools available for assisting in project planning and control are Gantt charts and activity network diagrams, also known as PERT/CPM. Gantt charts are more appropriate for relatively simple projects. They enable a project manager to schedule project activities in a graphical form which facilitates monitoring project progress. A Gantt chart for the establishment of a decentralized testing site is shown in Figure 10.6.

Activity network diagrams (PERT and CPM) were discussed in Chapter 3. They are more appropriate for more complex projects. PERT and CPM have the added advantage over Gantt charts of clearly showing the precedence relationships

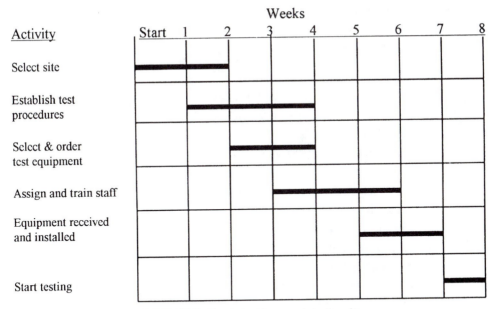

FIGURE 10.6   Gantt chart for remote testing site.

among project activities—that is, which activities must be completed before another activity can begin. PERT and CPM, unlike Gantt charts, also allow for easy identification of the critical path of the project.

SUPPLIER MANAGEMENT

Evidence for the changing nature of the purchasing function is everywhere. From Deming's point number 4—end the practice of awarding business on the basis of price tag alone—to moving purchasing from a tactical function to a strategic function, the change is evident. Because high-quality inputs are required in order to produce high-quality outputs from any productive system, quality is inextricably linked to the strategic purchasing function.

Supplier Selection

The trend today is toward doing business with a smaller number of suppliers who are carefully selected and with whom close ties are established. Partnering arrangements—"explicit or implicit arrangement by which selected parties gain more benefits by cooperating in a long-term, win-win relationship than by pursuing a short-term, win-lose arrangement"[27]—with suppliers are becoming more common.

The focus of such partnerships is on obtaining the *best buy*.[28] Best buy is a multidimensional concept that involves selecting the product for purchase which has the best combination of technical factors (e.g., specifications, reliability) and procurement factors (e.g., price, delivery, service). It reflects the total cost of owner-ship of a purchased item over its useful life. Life-cycle costing is an approach to measuring the total cost of ownership.

Selection of suppliers who can provide the best buy frequently is based upon 4 major factors:[29]

1. Technical or engineering capability
   Level of engineering technology
   R&D capability
2. Manufacturing or distribution capability
   Supplier location
   Quality systems
   Cleanliness of facility
3. Financial strength
   Ability to finance activities over long term
4. Management capability
   Progressive management
   Management stability
   Management attitudes

These factors are usually addressed using a formal supplier evaluation proce-dure which is designed to answer the questions:[30]

1. Is this supplier capable of supplying the purchaser's requirements satisfactorily in both the short and long run?
2. Is this supplier motivated to supply these requirements in the way the purchaser expects in the short and long term?

Sometimes third-party audits are used in addition to or instead of on-site sup-plier audits. Registration to the ISO 9000 standards is required by many European companies. The big three automobile manufacturers require certification to the QS 9000 standards. Motorola requires that its suppliers apply for the Malcolm Baldrige National Quality Award.

Careful selection of long-term supplier-partners is just the first step. Blindly staying with a supplier that is not continuously improving the value it adds to the relationship is not effective. The effectiveness of the relationship must be evaluated, the results of the evaluation must be shared, and both parties must work to continu-ously improve the relationship.

Supplier Evaluation

Evaluation of existing suppliers is a continuous process and is conducted using a variety of methods. Incoming inspection of purchased products is one commonly used means of ensuring that raw materials and purchased products meet specifica-tions. Routinely recording by supplier the results of incoming inspections provides one means of evaluating supplier performance over time.

However, the modern view of incoming inspection is that none should be nec-essary. Emphasis should be placed on selecting suppliers that are capable of doing things right the first time and requiring those suppliers to provide documentation (e.g., SPC control charts) showing that their products meet specifications.

Formal supplier evaluation systems recognize that supplier performance is multidimensional. The National Association of Purchasing Management[31] recommends rating suppliers in three areas of performance: quality, price, and service. Each area is weighted depending on market conditions. Hickman and Hickman[32] recommend a similar system using delivery performance, quality performance, and cost containment.

These rating systems focus on the suppliers' output. Many modern companies go beyond evaluation of output to evaluation of the suppliers' system. This is frequently done using a supplier audit. A quality audit is a formal and systematic assessment of suppliers and is covered in Chapter 14. The reason for evaluating the suppliers' system is that a capable system, operating in control, under good management is very likely to produce acceptable products on time and at the lowest possible price.

SUMMARY

Human resources are an integral part of a quality system. A quality engineer must be as proficient at dealing with this "soft" part of the system as with the "hard" parts—that is, the technical parts—of the system. Proficiency in dealing with the human aspects comes in part from understanding motivational theory and in part from recognizing that people differ one from another and that no one motivational plan is effective for everyone.

Quality professionals are bound by a code of ethics. This code of ethics recognizes that there are multiple constituencies to whom they owe the obligation of fair and ethical standards of professional behavior.

Quality control and quality improvement cannot be effective without quality planning. The quality professional has an important role to play in the long-term strategic planning of the organization. Quality professionals have the primary responsibility for developing the operational quality plan for the organization.

High-quality products and services cannot be produced by any organization without high-quality inputs. For this reason, supplier evaluation and supplier management are important factors in helping an organization meet its quality objectives.

DISCUSSION QUESTIONS

1. Discuss the significance of the Hawthorne Studies.
2. Compare Maslow's Hierarchy of Needs Theory to Herzberg's Two Factor Theory.
3. Discuss the influence that the classical motivational theories had on Deming's 14 points.
4. What is the difference between a motivator and a hygiene factor?
5. Might there ever be a conflict between a quality professional's ethical responsibility to society at large and loyalty to one's employer? Discuss.
6. Discuss the importance of credibility to a quality professional.

7. What is a SWOT analysis?

8. Compare the project management tools Gantt charts and PERT/CPM. What are the advantages and disadvantages of each?

9. What is meant by the term *best buy?*

10. Discuss the benefits of supplier partnering.

11. Might there be risks associated with supplier partnering? Discuss.

PROBLEMS

1. Construct a Gantt chart for the process of preparing for a final examination.

2. Construct a Gantt chart for the process of hosting a dinner party. You plan to send out written invitations three weeks prior to the date of the party with an RSVP date one week prior to the date of the party.

3. Develop guidelines for an appropriate incentive system for each of the two employees shown in Figure 10.2. Assume that both are professional/managerial-level employees. In what ways could the two incentive systems be the same? In what ways should they be different?

NOTES

1. Juran, J. M. "The Quality Trilogy." *Quality Progress,* vol. 9, no. 8, 1986, pp. 19–24. Reprinted in Sower, V., J. Motwani, & M. Savoie, *Classic Readings in Operations Management.* Ft. Worth, TX: Dryden, 1995, pp. 277–287.

2. Dessler, G. *Human Resource Management.* Upper Saddle River, NJ: Prentice Hall, 1997, p. 2.

3. Snow, C. E. *Tech Engineering News,* November 1927.

4. Maslow, A. H. *Motivation and Personality.* New York: McGraw-Hill, 1964.

5. McGregor, D. *The Human Side of Enterprise.* New York: McGraw-Hill, 1960.

6. McClelland, D. C. *The Achieving Society.* New York: Van Nostrand, 1961.

7. Herzberg, F. *Work and the Nature of Man.* New York: World Publishing, 1966.

8. Wilkinson, H. E., C. D. Orth, & R. C. Benfari. "Motivation Theories: An Integrated Operational Model." *SAM Advanced Management Journal,* Autumn 1986, pp. 24–31.

9. Wilkinson, pp. 29–30.

10. Ibid., p. 31.

11. Vroom, V. H. *Work and Motivation.* New York: Wiley, 1964.

12. Porter, L. W., & E. E. Lawler. *Managerial Attitudes and Performance.* Homewood, IL: Irwin, 1968.

13. Orsburn, J. D., L. Moran, E. Musselwhite, & J. H. Zenger. *Self-Directed Work Teams.* Homewood, IL: Business One Irwin, 1990, p. 34.

14. Banker, R. D., J. M. Field, R. G. Schroeder, & K. K. Sinha. "Impact of Work Teams on Manufacturing Performance: A Longitudinal Study." *Academy of Management Journal,* vol. 39, 1996, pp. 867–890.

15. Bedeian, A. G. *Management,* 3rd ed. Ft. Worth, TX: Dryden, 1993, pp. 506–515.

16. Ishikawa, K. *Quality Control Circles at Work.* Tokyo: Asian Productivity Organization, 1984, p. 4.

17. Bemowski, K. "The Quality Glossary." *Quality Progress,* February 1992, p. 26.

18. Bedeian, p. 507.

19. Marks, M. L., P. H. Mirvis, E. J. Hackett, & J. F. Grady. "Employee Participation in a Quality Circle Program: Impact on Quality of Work Life, Productivity, and Absenteeism." *Journal of Applied Psychology,* February 1986, pp. 61–69.

20. Griffin, R. W. "Consequences of Quality Circles in an Industrial Setting: A Longitudinal Assessment," *Academy of Management Journal,* June 1988, pp. 338–358.

21. ASQC, *Certified Quality Engineer.* Milwaukee, WI: ASQC, 1995, p. 8.

22. Juran, in Sower et al., p. 280.

23. David, F. R. *Strategic Management,* 6th ed. Upper Saddle River, NJ: Prentice Hall, 1997, p. 80.

24. Bedeian, pp. 157–158.

25. Feigenbaum, A. V. *Total Quality Control,* 3rd ed. New York: McGraw-Hill, 1991, p. 249.

26. Stevenson, W. J. *Production/Operations Management,* 5th ed. Chicago: Irwin, 1996, Chapter 16, pp. 756–805.

27. Hutchins, G. *Purchasing Strategies for Total Quality.* Homewood, IL: Business One Irwin, 1992, pp. 6–7.

28. Leenders, M. R., & H. E. Fearon. *Purchasing & Supply Management,* 11th ed. Chicago: Irwin, 1997, pp. 141–143.

29. Leenders & Fearon, pp. 232–235.

30. Ibid., p. 233.

31. Juran, J. M., & F. M. Gryna. *Quality Control Handbook,* 4th ed. New York: McGraw-Hill, 1988, p. 15.42.

32. Hickman, T. K., & W. M. Hickman. *Global Purchasing.* Homewood, Il: Business One Irwin, 1992, p. 210.

SUGGESTED READINGS

Human Resource Management

Deming, W. E. *Out of the Crisis.* Cambridge, MA: MIT Press, 1986, Chapter 8, pp. 248–275.

Dessler, G. *Human Resource Management.* Upper Saddle River, NJ: Prentice-Hall, 1997.

Evans, J. R., & W. M. Lindsay. *The Management and Control of Quality,* 3rd ed. Minneapolis: West, 1996, Chapters 10 and 11, pp. 392–482.

Ishikawa, K. *Quality Control Circles at Work.* Tokyo: Asian Productivity Organization, 1984.

Wilkinson, H. E., C. D. Orth, & R. C. Benfari. "Motivation Theories: An Integrated Operational Model." *SAM Advanced Management Journal,* Autumn 1986, pp. 24–31.

Professional Conduct and Ethics

ASQC, *Certified Quality Engineer.* Milwaukee, WI: ASQC, 1995, p. 8.

Quality Planning

Bedeian, A. G. *Management.* Ft. Worth, TX: Dryden, 1993, Chapter 17, pp. 496–521.

Deming, W. E. *Out of the Crisis.* Cambridge, MA: MIT Press, 1986.

Evans, J. R., & W. M. Lindsay. *The Management and Control of Quality,* 3rd ed. Minneapolis: West, 1996, Chapter 6, pp. 186–226.

Feigenbaum, A. V. *Total Quality Control,* 3rd ed. New York: McGraw-Hill, 1991.

Juran, J. M. *Juran's Quality Control Handbook,* 4th ed. New York: McGraw-Hill, 1988, Chapter 6, pp. 6.1–6.52, and Chapter 16, pp. 16.1–16.59.

Juran, J. M. "The Quality Trilogy." *Quality Progress,* vol. 9, no. 8, 1986, pp. 19–24. Reprinted in Sower, V., J. Motwani, & M. Savoie. *Classic Readings in Operations Management.* Ft. Worth, TX: Dryden, 1995, pp. 277–287.

Juran, J. M. & F. M. Gryna. *Quality Planning and Analysis,* 3rd ed. New York: McGraw-Hill, 1993.

Shtub, A., J. F. Bard, & S. Globerson. *Project Management Engineering, Technology, and Implementation.* Englewood Cliffs, NJ: Prentice-Hall, 1994.

Sower, V., J. Motwani, & M. Savoie. *Classic Readings in Operations Management.* Ft. Worth, TX: Dryden, 1995.

Spinner, M. P. *Elements of Project Management,* 2nd ed. Englewood Cliffs, NJ: Prentice-Hall, 1992.

Stevenson, W. J. *Production/Operations Management,* 5th ed. Chicago: Irwin, 1996.

Williams, P. B. *Getting a Project Done on Time—Managing People, Time, and Results.* New York: American Management Association, 1996.

Supplier Management

Deming, W. E. *Out of the Crisis.* Cambridge, MA: MIT Press, 1986, Chapter 2, pp. 18–96, and Chapter 15, pp. 407–464.

Hutchins, G. *Purchasing Strategies for Total Quality.* Homewood, IL: Business One Irwin, 1992.

Juran, J. M. *Juran's Quality Control Handbook,* 4th ed. New York: McGraw-Hill, 1988, Chapter 15, pp. 15.1–15.46.

CHAPTER 11

Human Factors

CHAPTER OBJECTIVES

This chapter introduces the following topics:

- Barriers to quality improvement efforts
- Organization and implementation of quality teams
- Principles of team leadership and facilitation
- Team dynamics management and conflict resolution

INTRODUCTION

Continuous quality improvement is continuous change. Many who have tried to institute change in any type of organization believe that the natural tendency of humans is resistance to change. There is evidence that change can be managed in ways that encourage people to buy into the change process. Efforts to manage the quality improvement process should begin with an understanding of some of the barriers to that process and approaches to dealing with those barriers.

From the Hawthorne Studies, Maslow's Hierarchy of Needs, and Hertzberg's Two-factor Theory (discussed in Chapter 10) to Stephen Covey's Maturity Continuum,[1] there have been many motivational theories and principles developed and applied to individual workers. Teams introduce a new dimension to the management process. In order to fulfill their charter, team leaders and team members must be educated in the rudiments of team dynamics. When team members realize that some conflict is normal and they and their leaders understand how to productively manage that conflict, the team's performance will be enhanced.

BARRIERS TO QUALITY IMPROVEMENT EFFORTS

Barriers to effective quality improvement efforts take many forms. Examples of common barriers are failure to correctly understand customers' requirements, failure to understand the capability of the production system, failure to track defects, failure to repair suboptimized processes, and failure to track quality costs. Deming assigns most of the blame for these barriers to management. His 14 points are written for management: " . . . no one else in the company can work effectively on quality and productivity unless it is obvious that the top people (management) are working on their obligations."[2] In Deming's view, most of these barriers are the result of ineffective management.

Even when top management is committed and involved, there can be significant barriers to quality improvement efforts. These can often be traced to a lack of communication.

Communication of quality begins at the very top of the organization. Top management must set a course and make a commitment to a defined level of quality today, and commit to continuous improvement for tomorrow. This commitment and direction must be clearly communicated throughout the organization. By clearly communicated, we mean that each employee must recognize the quality goals of the organization, and must clearly understand how the job he or she does impacts the quality of the organization's goods and services.

Once the quality goals have been communicated, employees must receive training on the tools and techniques used to measure and ensure the quality of the good or service. This training may take a number of different forms—from self-paced learning to formal classroom instruction.

Once trained, employees must integrate the training into the day-to-day operations of the organization. Management must be present in each of these steps to ensure the employees have the support and resources needed to fully achieve and maintain the targeted quality levels.

ORGANIZATION AND IMPLEMENTATION OF QUALITY TEAMS

Quality teams are designed to exploit the synergy created when multiple people focus their attention on a single problem. Optimal team size is 5 to 8,[3,4] and the focus is usually concentrated on a single problem or effort. Quality teams may be implemented within a department or functional area or cover a broad spectrum of the organization (often referred to as cross-functional teams).

Some examples of the types of teams that are used are:[5]

Example	**Scope**
Corrective action team	Short term, single purpose
Quality circle	Long term, multiple-task focus
Focus group	Short term, single-task focus
Self-managing	Daily operations
Process action team	Short term, but regularly formed

Regardless of the makeup, these teams share certain characteristics which help to ensure their success. (See Table 11.1)

TABLE 11.1   Characteristics of Quality Teams

- Number of members is 5 to 8
- Work from a team charter that clearly defines the problem, mission, and evaluation criteria
- Have a specific focus as identified in the team charter
- May be self-directed or have a team leader

PRINCIPLES OF TEAM LEADERSHIP AND FACILITATION

> *Wearing the same shirts doesn't make you a team.*
> —Vince Lombardi

What Is a Team?

A team is a group of people assembled to focus their knowledge, experience, and skills on a specific task.

Who Makes Up a Team?

A team is made up of a team leader, team members, and a facilitator. Each plays a unique role in helping the team achieve its goals.

Roles and Responsibilities of the Team Leader

Roles of a team leader include coach, mentor, and active participant. The ways in which these roles are effected will vary according to the nature of the group—its readiness for empowerment and its stage of development.[6] For example, a more directive leadership style might be more appropriate in the early stages of team development, while a more supportive leadership style would be appropriate as the team matures.

Coach. The team leader is a coach. The team leader is not there to direct, but to guide. Just as an athletic coach trains his or her charges, the team leader must make sure that the team members are capable of performing the duties requested of them. Team members with all the necessary tools to solve a problem are a rare find. Therefore, the team leader must be ready to solicit the training necessary to provide the team members with the tools needed to accomplish the task.

Mentor. The team leader is the first-level source of information for the team members. Even though in many cases, the team leader knows little more than the team members about the problem, the team members will look to him or her for guidance and direction. The team leader must provide as much input as possible to the team members—not in the form of "giving away answers" but in the form of questions and focus.

Active participant. In addition to all the other roles and responsibilities associated with being a team leader, he or she must remain an active participant in the team. The team leader is the head of the team and must be ready to support the members as they tackle difficult problems. The most important thing to remember is to lead by example, not with words! In other words, walk the talk.

Responsibilities of a team leader include effective communication, team building, win-win negotiations, and conflict resolution.

With regard to effective communication, it is the role of the team leader to ensure that all team members have an equal opportunity to voice their views. No one person should be allowed to dominate the meeting. The environment should be conducive to open, timely, and honest communication without fear of retribution from other members of the team.

With regard to team building, it is the role of the team leader to take the group of individuals assembled at the first meeting and turn them into a successful team. Attributes of a high-performance team (see Table 11.2) include:

1. Mission alignment
2. Participative leadership
3. Shared responsibility
4. Open communications
5. Focus on problem elimination
6. Dedication to change
7. Welcome diversity

With regard to win-win negotiations, the team leader must use collaborative efforts to reach consensus and win-win decisions with the team. Failure to achieve consensus is most often manifested by voting and compromising. It is the role of the team leader to ensure that all team members are in agreement about the problem to be solved and the solution method to be utilized.

When conflict occurs (and it will!) the team leader must be prepared to mediate the dispute. *It is not the job of the team leader to assume the role of judge and jury.* Rather, the team leader should facilitate discussion between all members of the team (not just the conflicting members) regarding the best way to proceed.

It would be a mistake, however, to assume that no conflict within a team is a strength. "Teams that lack open conflict are dying entities. . . . groups that have any vitality at all, any ideas, any instincts for growth will have conflicts."[7] It is the proper management of that conflict that can make it a strength instead of a weakness for the team.

Selecting Team Members

It is preferable that team members be volunteers. However, it is the job of the team leader to select the members for the team. With the help of the team's facilitator, the team leader should look for members who meet all or most of the criteria shown in Table 11.3.

Roles and Responsibilities of the Team Members

Team members are responsible for developing the team's work plan, including establishing action items and follow-up responsibilities. Team members are also responsible for establishing the meeting schedule based on the magnitude of the assignment and the time limit and for assigning a recorder. Remember, recording is not the responsibility of the facilitator!

Finally, team members must execute the work plan. Execution includes conducting the necessary research and analyses, developing conclusions, identifying solutions and alternatives, and making recommendations, producing the deliverable, presenting the deliverable to the client, and celebrating the achievement.

TABLE 11.2   Attributes of a High Performance Team

1. Mission alignment:
   - Clear statement of team:
     —Purpose
     —Functions served
     —Values
     —Vision
   - Buy in by members
   - Constantly communicated internally and externally
   - Can be improved by
     —Developing a vision
     —Setting goals

2. Participative leadership
   - Set the example
   - Eliminate artificial barriers
   - Free up and empower creativity
   - Coach, counsel, and encourage
   - Provide rapid feedback
   - Can be improved by:
     —Understanding leadership style
     —Improving supervision skills

3. Shared responsibility
   - Top performance is responsibility of all
   - Members are interdependent
   - Clear responsibilities and authorities
   - Recognition and rewards shared by all
   - Can be improved by:
     —Clarifying roles
     —Improving decision making
     —Involving workers in problem solving

4. Open communications
   - Begin at the top
   - Driven up, down, and sideways
   - Require learning to listen
   - Build climate of trust
   - Can be improved by:
     —Resolving conflict
     —Listening
     —Giving feedback

5. Focus on problem elimination
   - Eliminate—don't compromise
   - Establish specific goals
   - Attack the process
   - Tap job knowledge and creativity
   - Target root causes
   - Measure progress
   - Celebrate success
   - Can be improved by:
     —Identifying issues
     —Forming focus groups
     —Using a problem-solving process
     —Finding solutions

TABLE 11.2   *(continued)*

6. Dedication to change
   - Change is the continuum
   - Anticipate it
   - Plan for it
   - Thrive on it
   - Two types:
     —Change due to inspiration
     —Change due to desperation
   - Can be improved by:
     —Understanding the technology of change
     —Using the proper tools to manage it
7. Welcome diversity
   - Recognize and complement each other's strengths and weaknesses
   - Develop *synergy:* The simultaneous actions of separate entities which together have greater total effect than the sum of their individual effects.
   - Can be improved by:
     —Learning about each other
     —Learning about yourself
     —Sharing of information, ideas, and experiences

Roles and Responsibilities of the Facilitator

The facilitator is there to aid the team leader. Team facilitators are *not* there to run the meetings, identify the problem, or develop the solution! The team facilitator will keep the team focused on the assignment as defined in the charter by the customer.

TABLE 11.3   Team member selection criteria

- People skills:
  —Open communicator
  —Good listener
  —Self-motivated
- Personal characteristics
  —Participative
  —Enthusiastic
  —Cooperative
  —Sense of humor
  —Meets commitments
  —Team player
  —Experienced in subject area
  —Constructively challenges the status quo
- Readiness
  —Available to attend meetings
  —Available to do research/collect data
  —Willing to make a contribution

Some of the roles and responsibilities associated with the facilitator include:

- Availability to answer questions and provide guidance
- Attending the kick-off meeting for the team
- Attending meetings of first-time team leaders
- Helping the team leader to develop the agenda for the first meeting including developing the work plan
- Developing the meeting schedule and identifying the target date for presenting the deliverable
- Keeping the team focused on the assignment and discouraging digression
- Serving as a liaison between the team and the client
- Aiding in the technical review of reports
- Helping in assembling and distributing the report to management
- Helping the team prepare to do its briefing
- Preparing management to receive a report from the team
- Providing help in politically sensitive situations (e.g., dealing with a team member's boss who reneges on the time commitment agreed to with the team member)

Critical Action Items in the Team Life Cycle

There are critical actions that must be taken by any team wishing to be successful. These can be broken down into items done before the project is undertaken (preliminary), items done while the project is under way (ongoing), and items done when the project is completed (final). Each of these areas is listed in Table 11.4.

What Is a Team Charter?

The charter will identify the deliverable and its timeframe. It defines the "what and why," not the "how to." A team charter includes the:

> Name of the team
> Statement of the problem
> Scope of the assignment
> Deliverable to be produced
> Time limit for the assignment

General Information and Guidelines for Teams

The following are basic guidelines for developing and operating teams. The guidelines are generic and may be customized to your organization as required. Recognize, however, that successful teams will meet these guidelines in one form or another.

- The more clearly the problem is stated, the better the problem can be understood.
- The more specific the scope of the assignment, the narrower the focus with fewer deviations from the assignment.
- The charter should spell out what needs to be done. The team's work plan will spell out how it will be done.

TABLE 11.4   Critical Action Items in the Team Life Cycle

Preliminary Action Items
- Identify the problem or area to be addressed
- Select team members with the facilitator's assistance
  —Look for volunteers
- Obtain the support and commitment from the team member's manager and the team members
- Schedule the first meeting
  —Make introductions and brainstorm the team's guidelines
  —Work with the team to prepare a charter

Ongoing Action Items
- Handle meeting room logistics
- Prepare and distribute the meeting minutes and agenda for the next meeting
- Provide the customer with periodic status reports

Final Action Items
- Present an initial briefing to management on possible solutions
  —Include lessons learned by the team
- Get feedback from management on which solution to implement
  —Written response to the team leader
- Implement solution
- Provide management with a final briefing on performance of solution
- Incorporate management comments into the final briefing
- Distribute final draft to all upper management

- Select people with the most knowledge, experience, and skill in the topic or subject that you can find.
- Select only experienced facilitators; weak facilitators are detrimental to the team's performance.
- Limit the number of team members from 5 to 8.
- Get a commitment of time and availability for potential team members from the team member's manager; otherwise find someone else.
- Establish a time limit for the assignment.
- The team meeting schedule is driven by the duration of the work plan activities and the time limit established by the customer. Teams should meet as often as necessary, but should never meet "just to have a meeting."
- The team should call upon "topical" or "subject matter" experts for consultation and clarification when necessary.
- Trust, mutual respect, and recognition of each team member's contributions are the guiding principles of the team.

TEAM DYNAMICS MANAGEMENT AND CONFLICT RESOLUTION

Calling a group or work unit a team implies that it has a particular process of working together, one in which members identify and fully use one another's resources and facilitate their mutual interdependence toward more effective problem solving and task accomplishment. Therefore, team building is an effort in which a team:

- Studies its own process of working together
- Acts to create a climate in which members' energies are directed toward problem solving
- Maximizes the use of all members' resources for this process

Team-building components include:

1. Mission
   - Define the overall mission or objective for which the team has been formed.
2. Organization
   - Select the right people.
   - Establish external interfaces.
   - Clearly define responsibility and authority.
   - Clarify individual roles.
3. Leadership
   - Designate a leader.
   - Establish and follow ground rules.
   - Give rewards for contributions.
   - Ensure appropriate control for maturity and motivation of workers.
4. Commitment
   - Gladly accept responsibility.
   - Take pride in quality work.
5. Goals
   - Define long- and short-range goals necessary to accomplish the mission.
   - Ensure that each goal is:
        Clear and specific
        Measurable
        Achievable
        Prioritized
        Communicated to team members
        Trackable
        Periodically revised, as necessary
6. Communication
   - Balanced participation.
   - Listen to ideas.
   - Ensure that mutual trust exists.
   - Limit interruptions.
7. Delegation
   - To the lowest level possible.
   - Focus on methods that lead to results.
   - Implement using specific guidelines or standard procedures.
   - Identify available resources (human, financial, technical, and organizational).
   - Identify accountability and standards to be used in evaluating results.
   - Identify consequences of performance and nonperformance.
8. Meetings
   - Set up a meeting schedule.
   - Hold additional meetings only when clearly necessary.

- Define specific outcomes for the meeting.
- Invite those who can make a specific contribution.
- Prepare, distribute, and follow a specific agenda.
- Monitor and facilitate discussion to achieve the desired outcome.
- Summarize and record decisions, actions, responsible parties, and due dates.
- Review the meeting process with an eye toward improvement.
- Follow up to ensure meeting outcomes are executed.

9. Problem solving and decision making
   - Identify problems.
   - Identify and evaluate alternatives.
   - Encourage participation from all members.
   - Seek consensus on decisions.
   - Ensure timely decisions.
   - Assign action items to specific team members.

10. Conflict resolution
    - Identify disagreements before they escalate.
    - Challenge ideas and processes, not individuals.
    - Address conflict; don't avoid it.

11. Evaluation
    - Achieve goals.
    - Evaluate the process.
    - Be open to feedback.
    - Be willing to change the process and content as necessary.

Stages of Group Development

As a team *forms, adds,* or *subtracts* members, it goes through 4 stages of group development:[8]

1. Forming
2. Storming
3. Norming
4. Performing

Forming

This stage is the transition from individual to member status. It's also a period of testing behavior and dependence on formal or informal leadership. Members discover what behaviors are acceptable to the group.

Characteristics of the team
- Reluctant participation (quiet group)
- Suspicion and fear
- Anxiety about the new situation
- Testing of leader and members
- Minimal work accomplished

Team member behaviors

- Almost all comments are directed to the leader.
- Direction and clarification are sought.
- Status is accorded to group members based on their roles outside the group.
- Members fail to listen, resulting in non sequitur statements.
- Issues are discussed superficially, with much ambiguity.

Team member concerns

- Who am I in this group?
- Who are the others?
- Will I be accepted?
- Will he or she value me?
- Is the leader competent?
- Will I be capable?
- Who is the leader?
- What is my role?
- What tasks will I have?

Team leader behaviors

- Provide structure by holding regular meetings and assisting in task and role clarification.
- Encourage participation by all, domination by none.
- Facilitate learning about one another's areas of expertise and preferred working modes.
- Share all relevant information.
- Encourage members to ask questions of you and one another.

Helpful methods for leading a team in this stage

- Use icebreakers.
- Agree upon a set of meeting guidelines.
- Plan agendas.
- Create an environment for shared responsibilities.
- Follow up.

Storming

Members recognize the extent of the task demand and respond emotionally to the perceived requirements. As a way of expressing their individuality, they often become hostile or overbearing as they jostle for positions within the group.

Characteristics of the team

- Resistance to the task
- Increased tension
- Concern about individual roles and status; i.e., What's in it for me?
- Minimal work accomplished
- Conflict over control among the group's members and with the leader

Team member behaviors
- Attempts are made to gain influence.
- Subgroups and coalitions form, with possible conflict among them.
- The leader is tested and challenged (possibly covertly).
- Members judge and evaluate one another and the leader, resulting in ideas being shot down.
- Task avoidance.

Team member concerns
- How much autonomy will I have?
- Will I have influence over others?
- What is my place in the pecking order?
- Personal level: Whom do I like? Who likes me?
- Issues level: Do I have some support in here?

Team leader behaviors
- Engage in joint problem solving; have members give reasons why idea is useful and how to improve it.
- Establish a norm supporting the expression of different viewpoints.
- Discuss the group's decision-making responsibility appropriately.
- Encourage members to state how they feel as well as what they think when they obviously have feelings about an issue.
- Provide group members with the resources needed to do their jobs, to the extent possible (when this is not possible, explain why).

Helpful methods
- Refer to agreed-upon meeting guidelines
- Use consensus exercises
- Explain the stages of group development
- Conduct review of meeting, including critique

Norming

Members accept the team, its idiosyncrasies, and their own roles within that group. Emotional conflict lessens, and the task is accepted.

Characteristics of the team
- Group formation and solidarity
- Sense of team cohesiveness
- Sharing among the group (open discussion)
- Attempt to achieve maximum harmony
- Constructively expressed emotions
- Moderate work accomplished

Team member behaviors

- Members, with one another's support, can disagree with the leader.
- The group laughs together; members have fun; some jokes made at the leader's expense.
- A sense of "we-ness" and attention to group norms is present.
- The group feels superior to other groups in the organization.
- Members do not challenge one another as much as the leader would like.

Team member concerns

- How close should I be to the group members?
- Can we accomplish our tasks successfully?
- How do we compare with other groups?
- What is my relationship to the leader?

Team leader behaviors

- Talk openly about your own issues and concerns.
- Have group members manage agenda items, particularly those in which you have a high stake.
- Give a request for both positive and constructive negative feedback in the group.
- Assign challenging problems for consensus decisions (e.g., budget allocations).
- Delegate as much as the members are capable of handling; help them as necessary.

Helpful methods

- Adhere to the agenda.
- Reinforce team behaviors.

Performing

Because the team has established its interpersonal norms, it is now capable of diagnosing problems and making decisions using consensus.

Characteristics of the team

- Constructive self-change occurs.
- Team tends to check its own behavior.
- Maximum work is accomplished.
- Differentiation and productivity.

Team member behaviors

- Roles are clear, and each person's contribution is distinctive.
- Members take the initiative and accept one another's initiatives.
- Open discussion and acceptance of differences among members in their backgrounds and modes of operation.

- Challenging one another leads to creative problem solving.
- Members seek feedback from one another and from the leader to improve their performances.

Team member concerns

- Concerns of earlier stages have been resolved.

Team leader behaviors

- Jointly set goals that are challenging.
- Look for new opportunities to increase the group's scope.
- Question assumptions and traditional ways of behaving.
- Develop mechanisms for ongoing self-assessment by the group.
- Appreciate each member's contribution.
- Develop members to their fullest potential through task assignments and feedback.

Helpful methods

- Include critique in agenda.
- Encourage questioning of decisions.
- Promote motivational activities.
- Watch for group resistance to completing the process.

Creating a Win-win Situation

Teams make many decisions as they progress through the process; the key is to make them *effectively*. The two components involved in reaching an effective decision are quality and acceptance.

Quality refers to how good the decision is or how well it meets the needs of the problem. Here the team looks at different alternatives to determine how well they correct the situation. Using a problem-solving process will help to determine the best "quality" decision.

Acceptance refers to how well the decision is accepted by the affected group. It is necessary to know that the decision will be actively supported by all involved. After all, there are many ways to do the same thing. The optimum choice should be an alternative on which the team can reach consensus.

Teams reach an effective decision by balancing how well each alternative corrects the situation (quality) with how well it will be accepted and supported by the group (acceptance):

$$E = Q \times A$$

Consensus. A team reaches consensus through a collaborative effort. Consensus implies the voluntary giving of consent. Therefore, a team reaches consensus when each member decides to actively support the decision. This does not mean that everyone totally agrees, but that everyone will support the decision which has been made by the group.

Consensus is a *win-win method.* It guarantees that no one will lose because the final decision is not made until everyone can live with it. This assures buy-in from each individual, which gives everyone ownership in the decision and commitment to implementation.

Consensus is achieved through the team members' active discussion of the issues surrounding the decision. Each person must bring his or her knowledge and experience into the discussion. Of course, this process takes time, and consensus can sometimes be difficult to attain.

The following guidelines can help the team achieve consensus. Each team member should:

- Consider his or her position on the subject prior to the meeting.
- Obtain any data possible to support that position.
- Recognize the obligation to share his or her opinion with the group.
- Be willing to listen to the opinions and thoughts of every other team member.
- Be open to changing his or her personal position.
- Encourage differences of opinion in order to clarify issues.
- Avoid conflict-inducing techniques (i.e., voting, compromising, etc.).

SUMMARY

Barriers exist which inhibit quality improvement efforts. Often these barriers share a common cause—poor communication. The responsibility for removing the barriers rests with management.

Simply gathering several people together does not create a team. Roles and responsibilities must be fulfilled in order to turn a group of people into a team. Groups move through stages from forming to performing. This is a natural process, but each stage requires its own type of leadership. The ultimate objective is to create a team which produces high-quality decisions which are accepted by the affected groups.

DISCUSSION QUESTIONS

1. Discuss what Deming means when he says that most of the barriers to quality improvement efforts are management's responsibility.
2. What are some actions that could be taken to improve communication of quality within an organization?
3. What are the key roles and responsibilities of a team leader?
4. What does the word *synergy* mean as it applies to teams?
5. Is conflict within a team always bad? Discuss.
6. Compare the roles and responsibilities of team leader and team facilitator.
7. What are some ways to move a team out of the storming stage to the norming stage?
8. What are some ways to achieve consensus?
9. Does consensus mean that everyone on the team must agree completely with all decisions made by the team? Discuss.

NOTES

1. Covey, S. R. *The Seven Habits of Highly Successful People.* New York: Simon & Schuster, 1986.
2. Deming, W. E. "Improvement of Quality and Productivity through Action by Management." *National Productivity Review,* vol. 1, no. 1, Winter 1981–1982, pp. 12–22. Reprinted in Sower, V. E., J. Motwani, & M. J. Savoie. *Classic Readings in Operations Management.* Ft. Worth, TX: Dryden, 1995, p. 237.
3. Ishikawa, K. *Quality Control Circles at Work.* Tokyo: Asian Productivity Organization, 1984, p. 4.
4. Bemowski, K. "The Quality Glossary." *Quality Progress,* February 1992, p. 26.
5. Brocka, B., & M. S. Brocka. *Quality Management, Implementing the Best Ideas of the Masters.* Burr Ridge, IL: Irwin, 1992, p. 147.
6. Johnson, R. S. *TQM: Leadership for the Quality Transformation.* Milwaukee, WI: ASQC Quality Press, 1993, p. 92.
7. Harvey, T. R., & B. Drolet. *Building Teams, Building People.* Lancaster, PA: Technomic Publishing Co., 1994, pp. 20–21.
8. Plovnick, M., R. Fry, & I. Rubin. "New Developments in O.D. Technology: Programmed Team Development." *Training and Development Journal,* April 1975.

SUGGESTED READINGS

Brocka, B., & M. S. Brocka. *Quality Management, Implementing the Best Ideas of the Masters.* Burr Ridge, IL: Irwin, 1992.

Deming, W. E. "Improvement of Quality and Productivity through Action by Management." *National Productivity Review,* vol. 1, no. 1, Winter 1981–1982, pp. 12–22. Reprinted in Sower, V. E., J. Motwani, & M. J. Savoie. *Classic Readings in Operations Management.* Ft. Worth, TX: Dryden, 1995, pp. 231–247.

Ishikawa, K. *Quality Control Circles at Work.* Tokyo: Asian Productivity Organization, 1984.

Johnson, R. S. TQM: *Leadership for the Quality Transformation.* Milwaukee, WI: ASQC Quality Press, 1993.

Lindsay, W. M., & J. A. Petrick. *Total Quality and Organization Development.* Boca Raton, FL: St. Lucia Press, 1997.

CHAPTER 12
Quality Costs

CHAPTER OBJECTIVES

This chapter introduces the following topics:

- The goal of a quality cost system
- The categories of quality costs
- Quality cost data collection, interpretation, and reporting

INTRODUCTION

The quality cost concept was formalized in the 1950s. Armand Feigenbaum, in his 1956 article which launched the concept of total quality control, discussed 3 categories of quality costs: prevention costs, appraisal costs, and failure costs. He argued that "the ultimate end result is that total quality control brings about a sizable reduction in overall quality costs, and a major alteration in the proportions of the three cost segments."[1] Twenty years later, Philip Crosby wrote that "quality is measured by the cost of quality which . . . is the expense of nonconformance—the cost of doing things wrong."[2]

The 3 quality cost categories (ASQ subdivides failure costs into internal and external failure costs, yielding 4 categories) can be used to evaluate a quality system and facilitate efforts directed toward improving the performance of that system. A routine and systematic approach to collecting and classifying quality costs is considered to be an important part of a modern quality system.

THE GOAL OF A QUALITY COST SYSTEM

Many companies do a poor job of tracking their costs of quality. Often only customer returns (cost of warranty in Deming's terms[3]) are tracked and recorded as quality costs. The costs of providing test and inspection facilities and personnel are lumped into overhead. Scrap costs are booked as a material cost variance. Rework costs are recorded as a labor variance or sometimes even included as part of the standard labor cost. Such an accounting system provides "visible figures"[4] which understate the true cost of quality. These flawed data produce flawed decisions.

According to Crosby the goal of a quality cost system is to provide a means of showing management "that reducing the cost of quality is in fact an opportunity to increase profits without raising sales, buying equipment, or hiring new people."[5] In addition to getting management's attention, a cost of quality system also "provides a measurement base for seeing how quality improvement is doing."[6]

The American Society for Quality (ASQ) incorporates both aspects and broadens them by specifying that the goal "of any quality cost system . . . is to facilitate quality improvement efforts that will lead to operating cost reduction opportunities."[7] Assigning specific costs of quality to categories provides another means of monitoring quality improvement. The quality cost categories are the subject of the next section.

THE CATEGORIES OF QUALITY COSTS

Historically (and as noted earlier), quality costs are divided into 3 main categories: *prevention* costs, *appraisal* costs, and *failure* costs. ASQ subdivides failure costs into *internal* and *external failure* costs, resulting in 4 categories.[8]

Prevention costs are "the costs of all activities specifically designed to prevent poor quality in products and services."[9] ASQ defines prevention costs as "costs incurred to keep failure and appraisal costs to a minimum."[10] Costs falling into this category include those associated with quality planning activities, quality improvement councils, design of quality systems, and supplier evaluation. A principle associated with quality cost systems is that dollars spent in prevention are worth more than those spent in the other categories because these are the only dollars spent to prevent the production of poor-quality products and services. Effective investment in prevention minimizes the added costs of appraisal, rework, and warranty claims resulting from the production of poor-quality goods and services.

Appraisal costs are defined as "the costs associated with measuring, evaluating, or auditing products or services to assure conformance to quality standards and performance requirements."[11] Appraisal costs include the costs of incoming inspection, in-process inspection, outgoing inspection, test instrument maintenance, and costs associated with gathering and analyzing product and process measurement data.

Internal failure costs are defined as "the costs resulting from products or services not conforming to requirements or customer/user needs (which) occur prior to delivery or shipment . . . to the customer."[12] Included in internal failure costs are costs associated with scrap and rework, costs of determining the causes of nonconformance and necessary corrective actions to prevent their recurrence, and costs of lost production time due to nonconforming products and services.

External failure costs are defined as "the costs resulting from products or services not conforming to requirements or customer/user needs (which) occur after delivery or shipment of the product, and during or after furnishing of a service, to the customer."[13] External failure costs include costs associated with servicing products under warranty, costs of returned products, liability costs associated with defective products or services, and costs associated with recalls of potentially defective product.

Deming referred to these external failure costs as "costs of warranty." According to Deming, costs of warranty are "unknown and unknowable." He illustrates this point by citing a 1983 survey that showed that a satisfied car owner is likely to buy 4 more cars of the same make over the following 12 years. A dissatisfied owner will

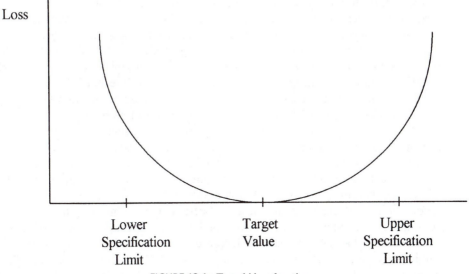

FIGURE 12.1   Taguchi loss function.

share his or her complaints with an average of 16 other people.[14] The lost profit (cost effect) resulting from these potential customers who now might not consider this make of automobile is extremely difficult to determine.

Crosby does not share the same despair that these costs are unknowable. According to Crosby, "those who assume that some tasks are just plain unmeasureable [are wrong.] Anything can be measured if you have to do it."[15]

Taguchi's[16] work suggests that failure costs are traditionally understated. He developed a loss function that shows that there is a cost (loss) incurred when products conform to specifications but do not fall exactly on the target value. (See Chapter 6 for further discussion.) The loss increases the farther away the actual value is from the target value (see Figure 12.1). An illustration of this concept involves the production of gold-plated contacts for use in automobile air bags. Contacts where the gold plating is applied to the high side of the specification create extra material costs for the manufacturer and may result in a tolerance buildup problem for the customer. Contacts plated on the low side of the specification may suffer from reduced reliability under certain field conditions. In both cases, the plating thickness is within the specification limits but not on the target value. Quality cost systems which only track the costs of nonconforming products and services miss the extra costs associated with failing to produce products on the target value.

QUALITY COST DATA COLLECTION

Collection of quality cost data usually begins with an analysis of data already being collected by cost accounting. Much of the cost of quality data is probably already being collected, but is classified into budget categories instead of quality cost categories. With the assistance of the cost accountant, the quality engineer can identify a substantial portion of the quality cost information. For example, salaries for inspectors, QC technicians, and others whose primary function involves sampling, inspection and testing of incoming materials, work in progress, and finished goods can be broken out of the indirect salaries budget category and identified as appraisal costs. Indirect time reported by direct labor personnel to accomplish rework can be identified in the labor variance accounts and be classified as internal failure costs. Scrap costs listed in a material usage variance account can be identified as internal failure costs. Customer returns listed in a returns and allowances budget account can be identified as external failure costs. Money spent for employee training in quality principles and methods can be extracted from indirect cost categories and identified as prevention costs. (See Table 12.1 for an example of a cost-of-quality report.)

The collaboration with the cost accounting function cannot end with the identification of certain quality costs. A system must be developed to routinely track and report the cost-of-quality data. These cost-of-quality systems are most effective (as are budget systems) when they report actual dollars and also those dollars related to an appropriate base. An increase or decrease in total cost of quality does not tell the whole story unless, for example, sales are constant. If sales are rising and all other things are equal, quality costs would be expected to rise proportionally. Reporting

TABLE 12.1   Example of a Cost-of-Quality Report

	This Month			Last Month		
Cost	Amount	% of Total	% of Sales	Amount	% of Total	% of Sales
Prevention costs						
Quality planning seminar	11,000			500		
QA manager's salary	6,000			6,000		
QA engineering	28,000			27,000		
Process capability studies	4,000			7,000		
QIS costs	4,500			5,500		
SPC training	3,500			8,500		
Total	$ 57,000	36.8%	2.59%	$ 54,500	33.9%	2.10%
Appraisal costs						
Test laboratory	24,000			26,000		
Gage calibration and R&R	2,000			1,000		
Receiving inspection	6,000			6,500		
Process inspection	18,000			19,500		
Total	$ 50,000	32.3%	2.27%	$ 53,000	33.0%	2.04%
Internal failure costs						
Scrap	19,500			21,500		
Rework	14,000			13,300		
Downgrade costs	6,500			7,400		
Total	$ 40,000	25.8%	1.82%	$ 42,200	26.4%	1.62%
External failure costs						
Returned goods	4,400			6,300		
Warranty repair costs	3,700			4,800		
Total	$ 8,100	5.2%	0.37%	$ 11,100	6.9%	0.43%
Total quality costs	$ 155,000		7.05%	160,800		6.18%
Sales	$2,200,000			$2,600,000		

quality costs as a percentage of sales provides a better (if still incomplete) picture of real trends in quality costs.

In a dynamic product pricing environment, a sales base might not be the most appropriate. Fluctuations in price will affect sales and in turn affect quality costs as a percentage of sales. In this case a production unit base might make more sense.

Some quality costs do not show up immediately. Customer returns resulting from a production problem might not begin to show up for months after the problem has been identified and corrected. The quality cost system must provide sufficient detail to be able to account for this lag.

QUALITY COST INTERPRETATION AND REPORTING

ANSI/ASQC Q9004-1-1994 stresses the importance of "reporting quality-system activities and effectiveness in financial terms (so that) management will receive the results in a common business language from all departments."[17] The state of a firm's quality system is reflected in the way in which costs are distributed among the cost-of-quality (COQ) categories. This cost distribution is also helpful in identifying ways in which quality dollars might be spent more effectively. Figure 12.2a illustrates changes in one firm's cost-of-quality distribution over time. In this illustration, the firm reacted to increasing external failure costs simply by increasing the number of

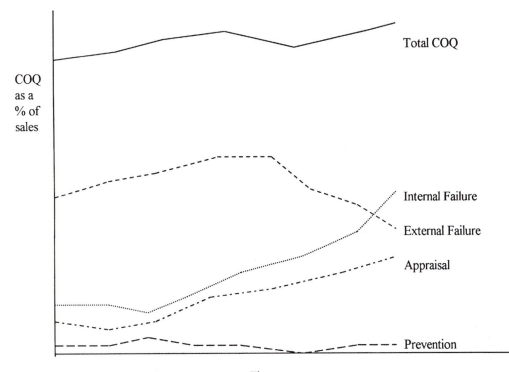

Time

FIGURE 12.2a   Cost-of-quality distribution over time.

inspectors (appraisal cost). Increased inspection detected more nonconforming parts which increased the internal failure cost. While external failure costs were decreased, the total cost of quality was not reduced.

Figure 12.2b shows a different reaction to the same situation. In this case the firm responded to increasing external failure costs by spending time and money to discover the root cause of the problem and to improve the quality system to correct the problem and prevent its recurrence. While internal failure costs and appraisal costs increased initially, they declined over time as the quality system was improved. And over time, the total cost of quality declined.

Prevention costs can be viewed as a form of investment rather than as a cost since dollars allocated here work to prevent the production of nonconforming products or services. Appraisal costs detect nonconforming products after they are produced, and failure costs account for the nonconforming products produced. Since it is cheaper to do things right the first time, it is logical to seek to increase prevention costs as a proportion of total quality costs. The question of what proportions are appropriate for each category is best addressed in relative terms. How does this period's distribution compare with last period's? How does our distribution compare with best-of-class companies? Over time, increasing prevention costs coupled with decreasing costs in the other 3 categories and decreasing total cost of quality can be an indication of an improving quality system. And each dollar saved in total COQ reduction translates into an additional dollar of earnings.

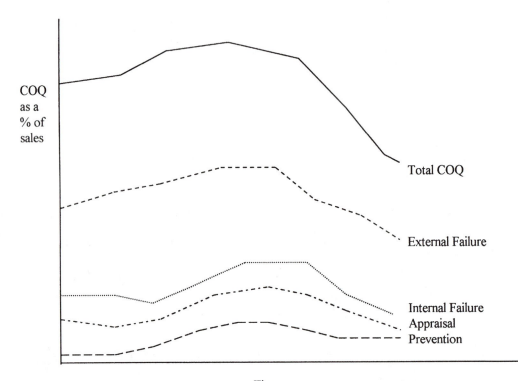

FIGURE 12.2b   Cost-of-quality distribution over time.

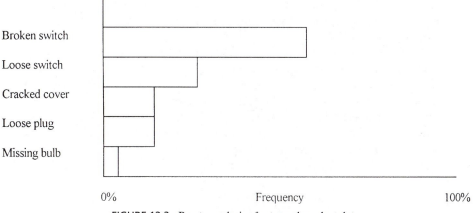

FIGURE 12.3 Pareto analysis of returned product data.

The quality improvement tools discussed in Chapter 3 can be employed to analyze cost-of-quality data and to provide direction for improvement efforts based upon that analysis. In a situation where total costs of quality are increasing due primarily to an increase in external failure costs (Figure 12.2a, close to origin), Pareto analysis of the returned goods and warranty service data would reveal the most frequent reasons for failure. Figure 12.3 clearly shows that most of the customer returns are associated with the switch—with "broken switch" being the single most frequently occurring problem. Cause and effect analysis (Figure 12.4) is

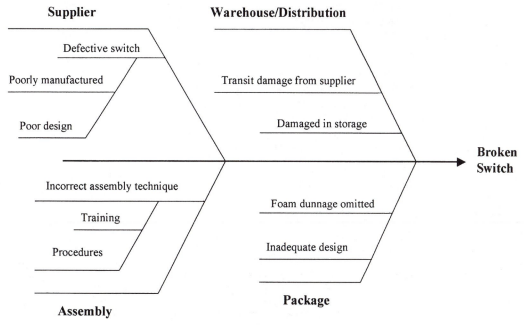

FIGURE 12.4 Cause and effect analysis—broken switch.

undertaken to determine possible causes for broken switches. Each cause is investigated, and the principal root cause of the increasing external failure costs can be identified. Effective corrective action can now be directed toward the specific root cause of the problem.

In this example, the root cause was determined to be supplier-related—a high proportion of nonconforming switches was being received from the supplier. Investigation showed that the problem resulted from poor manufacturing practices in the supplier's facility. Initially, total COQ increased as the firm worked with the supplier to correct the problems. After the problem was corrected, both internal and external failure costs decreased substantially while prevention costs increased as the firm adopted a supplier certification program to improve the quality system to prevent recurrence of this type of problem. The total COQ was substantially decreased.

SUMMARY

This chapter has discussed the quality cost system and its component categories of quality costs: prevention, appraisal, internal failure, and external failure. The purpose of a quality cost system is to guide continuous improvement efforts and to provide a measurement base to evaluate the effectiveness of those efforts. An effective continuous improvement program guided by the cost-of-quality system will result in reduced total quality costs and increased profit.

DISCUSSION QUESTIONS

1. Of what value is a cost-of-quality system to an organization?
2. Why might there be some initial conflict between an organization's cost accounting and quality engineering departments in starting a cost-of-quality program?
3. Why does Deming refer to external failure costs as "unknown and unknowable"?
4. How do Taguchi's ideas about quality costs differ from the traditional view?
5. As an organization's cost-of-quality program matures, how would you expect the ratios among the 4 cost-of-quality categories to change?
6. Discuss how the tools of quality can be used in conjunction with a cost-of-quality system for continuous improvement.

PROBLEMS

1. Classify the following quality costs:

Cost	Amount
Product recall cost	$10,500
Rework rejected outgoing lot	2,500
Freight for rejected goods from customer	450
TQM training class for operators	3,000
Quality engineers' salary	12,000
In-process inspection	5,600
Downtime due to rejected parts	4,500
Quality audit of supplier	1,500

2. If sales for the period are $1,400,000, calculate the quality costs in Problem 1 as a percentage of sales. What conclusions can be drawn? What are the advantages and disadvantages of reporting quality costs as a percentage of sales?

NOTES

1. Feigenbaum, A. "Total Quality Control." *Harvard Business Review,* vol. 34, no. 6, 1956, pp. 93–101. Reprinted in Sower, V., J. Motwani, & M. Savoie. *Classic Readings in Operations Management.* Ft. Worth, TX: Dryden, 1995, pp. 307–321.
2. Crosby, P. B. *Quality Is Free.* New York: McGraw-Hill, 1979, p. 15.
3. Deming, W. E. *Out of the Crisis.* Cambridge, MA: MIT Center for Advanced Engineering Study, 1982, p. 123.
4. Ibid.
5. Crosby, p. 103.
6. Ibid., p. 104.
7. Campanella, J. (ed.). *Principles of Quality Costs,* 2nd ed. Milwaukee, WI: ASQC Quality Press, 1990, p. 12.
8. Bemowski, K. "The Quality Glossary." *Quality Progress,* vol. 25, no. 2, 1992, p. 21.
9. Campanella, p. 22.
10. Bemowski, p. 21.
11. Campanella, p. 23.
12. Ibid.
13. Ibid.
14. Deming, pp. 121–123.
15. Crosby, p. 16.
16. Taguchi, G. *Introduction to Quality Engineering.* Tokyo: Asian Productivity Organization, 1986, p. 1.
17. ANSI/ASQC Q9004-1-1994, p. 7.

SUGGESTED READINGS

ANSI/ASQC Q9004-1-1994, Section 6, pp. 7–8.

Campanella, J. (ed.). *Principles of Quality Costs,* 2nd ed. Milwaukee, WI: ASQC Quality Press, 1990.

Crosby, P. B. *Quality Is Free.* New York: McGraw-Hill, 1979.

Deming, W. E. *Out of the Crisis.* Cambridge, MA: MIT Center for Advanced Engineering Study, 1982.

Feigenbaum, A. "Total Quality Control." *Harvard Business Review,* vol. 34, no. 6, 1956, pp. 93–101. Reprinted in Sower, V., J. Motwani, & M. Savoie. *Classic Readings in Operations Management.* Ft. Worth, TX: Dryden, 1995, pp. 307–321.

MIL-STD-1520C.

MIL-Q-9858A.

Taguchi, G. *Introduction to Quality Engineering.* Tokyo: Asian Productivity Organization, 1986.

CHAPTER 13

Quality Systems

CHAPTER OBJECTIVES

This chapter introduces the following topics:

- Elements of a quality system
- Scope and objectives of quality information systems
- Techniques for ensuring data accuracy and integrity
- Management systems for improving quality
- Quality documentation systems
- Problem identification, analysis, reporting, and corrective action system

INTRODUCTION

A system can be defined as any set of interdependent parts performing a specific function or set of functions. A quality system is defined as "the collective plans, activities and events that are provided to ensure that a product, process, or service will satisfy given needs."[1] A quality system is more than the sum of processes. "To be effective, the quality system needs coordination and compatibility of its component processes, and definition of their interfaces."[2]

This chapter examines the development and operation of a quality system for an organization. Included in this chapter are the elements of a quality system, elements of a quality information system, the scope and objectives of quality information systems, techniques for ensuring data accuracy and integrity, management systems for improving quality, quality documentation systems, and problem identification, analysis, reporting, and corrective action systems.

Information systems are systems designed to transmit data and information from one place to another and store the data for future access and retrieval. Information systems may be manual or electronic. For instance both a filing cabinet and a computer hard disk are forms of data storage and retrieval systems. E-mail, memos, notices, and Post-it™ notes are all forms of information transmission mediums.

Quality Information Systems (QISs) may be electronic, manual, or any combination of the two. They range from formal, detailed systems such as ISO 9000 to verbal feedback. The size and type of quality information system required by a particular organization is determined by the people who will use it. Never forget, the best system in the world, unused, is no better than having no system at all. There-fore, it is important that the people in an organization who will use the QIS are involved in the identification, recommendation, selection, and implementation of the quality system.

ELEMENTS OF A QUALITY SYSTEM

The basic elements of a quality system include the following:

- Definition of the job to be performed (job description or work instructions)
- The criteria by which the job will be evaluated
- Some method of gathering data on job performance
- A storage medium by which historical data can be saved for future analysis and trending
- A feedback system by which the results of the data can be communicated back to the person or persons responsible for the job

The functional elements of a quality management system may include the quality management program itself, product design, product specification, an inspection/test plan, purchasing, receiving, work-in-process inspection, nonconformance control, final inspection, inspection and testing of equipment, packaging and shipping, and customer service.

The primary evidence that a quality system has been designed is the quality manual. This manual, at a minimum, provides evidence that:

- A process has been defined.
- The procedures are approved.
- The procedures are under control.[3]

SCOPE AND OBJECTIVES OF QUALITY INFORMATION SYSTEMS

Quality information systems are part of and support the overall quality system in ensuring that desired quality is being achieved in an organization. To develop an effective system, we must analyze the quality needs of the organization and define an information system to meet those needs. This analysis and design process is driven from an organizational perspective, is an organizational improvement process, and is based on an understanding of the organization's objectives, structure, and processes with regard to quality.

There are 3 key components to the development of a quality information system:

- *Data:* Raw facts about things
- *Data flows:* Data in motion from one place in the system to another
- *Processing logic:* Steps by which data are transformed or moved and a description of the events that trigger these steps

Each of these components must be designed and analyzed so that the right information is provided to the right person at the right time in the right format to ensure that a quality product or service is provided to the customer.

To ensure proper design of the system, we utilize a systems development life cycle (SDLC), developed for the analysis and design of information systems. While there are several different versions of the SDLC, we use the 6-step process defined in Figure 13.1. Utilizing this process ensures that we design a system capable of meeting the needs of our quality assurance process.

1. **Identifying the Project**
   Purpose: Develop a preliminary understanding of the business situation
   Deliverable: A formal request to conduct a project to design and develop an information system solution to the business problem identified

2. **Project Initiation and Planning**
   Purpose: State business situation and how information systems might help solve a problem or make an opportunity possible
   Deliverable: Written request to study possible changes to an existing system or development of a new system

3. **Analysis**
   Purpose: Analyze the business situation thoroughly to:
   • determine requirements for a new or enhanced IS,
   • structure requirements for clarity and consistency,
   • select among competing systems features those that best meet user requirements within development constraints
   Deliverable: functional specifications for a system that meets user requirements and is feasible to develop and implement

4. **Logical Design**
   Purpose: To elicit and structure all information requirements for the new system
   Deliverable: A detailed and highly structured set of functional specs for the system (includes all data, forms, reports, computer displays, and processing rules for all aspects of the system). Must be agreed to by all affected parties (stakeholders)

5. **Physical Design**
   Purpose: to develop all technology and organizational specifications for the new information system
   Deliverables: program and database structures, technology purchases, physical site plans, and organizational redesigns

6. **Implementation and Maintenance**
   Purpose: to program the system, build all data files, test the new system, install system components, convert and cease operation of prior systems, train users, and turn over the system to operations
   Deliverables: programs that work accurately and to specifications, documentation, training materials, and project reviews.

FIGURE 13.1 Steps in the systems development life cycle.

TECHNIQUES FOR ENSURING DATA ACCURACY AND INTEGRITY

Quality systems must be checked and verified on a regular basis. The most common technique for ensuring data accuracy and integrity is to randomly pull a unit of product after it has completed its quality checks and then perform the checks manually. These manual checks are then compared with the quality system numbers. If the numbers match, the system is collecting accurate, valid data. If the numbers do not match, further tests must be performed both manually and with the system to identify the root cause(s) of the discrepancies. Once identified, a plan is developed to address the problem, the solution is implemented, and further checks are used to verify that the system is operating in an acceptable mode.

Process control charts (see Chapter 3), for example, help to control processes by presenting process data on an ongoing basis. In a process that is under control, a process control chart provides information to the operator, supervisor, or quality control person regarding variation of output around a desired goal. It is an early warning device for potential problems that may arise when the process deviates significantly from the desired output level. Once a problem is noted, root cause analysis (see Chapter 3) can be used to determine the cause of the deviation and to develop corrective actions.

MANAGEMENT SYSTEMS FOR IMPROVING QUALITY

ISO 9000, ANSI/ASQC Q 9000 (ISO's U.S. equivalent), and the Malcolm Baldrige National Quality Award (discussed in Chapter 14) are systems which seek to formalize the quality control process. Each approaches the process from a different perspective, but with the same goal: to provide a framework through which a quality control program can be identified, designed, developed, implemented, and enhanced to improve the overall performance of an organization. Guidelines and criteria for ISO 9000 and the Malcolm Baldrige National Quality Award are provided in Chapter 14.

QUALITY DOCUMENTATION SYSTEMS

Quality documentation systems begin with the quality manual and include all process documentation and procedures and end on the production floor with such things as color-coded stickers which, when placed on a product, indicate the type and seriousness of defects found. Regardless of the size, complexity, or formalization of the program, each quality documentation system must be designed to provide an audit trail that can be used to verify that quality defects are being identified and noted, and that corrective action is being taken and followed up to ensure the continuous improvement of the product and process.

> Documentation is important for quality improvement. When procedures are documented, deployed, and implemented, it is possible to determine with confidence how things are done currently and to measure current performance. Then reliable measurement of the effect of a change is enhanced. Moreover, documented standard operating procedures are essential for maintaining the gains from quality-improvement activities.[4]

Most systems utilize a series of standard forms for reporting quality problems. Figure 13.2 shows an example of a quality control reporting form. Note that Part 1

PART 1: DEFECT REPORT

Date: _____   Time: _____   Location: _____

Type of   ☐ Non-conformance to spec   ☐ damaged parts
Defect: ☐ process out of control   ☐ incorrect raw material

Comments: _____

_____

_____

_____

Signature: _____   Date: _____

PART 2: CORRECTIVE ACTION REPORT

Date Received: _____   Time Received: _____

Type of   ☐ non-conformance to spec   ☐ damaged parts
Defect: ☐ process out of control   ☐ incorrect raw material

If different than in Part 1, please comment: _____

_____

Corrective Action Taken: _____

_____

_____

By Whom: _____

_____

Date: _____   Time: _____   Location: _____

Signature: _____   Date: _____

PART 3: FOLLOW UP

Date: _____   Time: _____   Location: _____

Assigned Person: _____

Findings: _____

_____

_____

_____

Signature: _____   Date: _____

Source: M. J. Savoie & Associates, Dallas, Texas. Used by permission.

FIGURE 13.2   Sample quality control reporting form.

of the form has a place to report the type of defect; the time, date, and location where the defect occurred; a place for comments from the person who identified the defect; and a place for that person to sign.

Once Part 1 of the form is completed, it is filed in the quality information system and routed to the appropriate party for action. Part 2 of the form provides places for the time and date when the form was received, the person to whom the problem was assigned, the corrective action taken, and when, where, and by whom.

Part 3 of the form allows for a follow-up check on the problem area to ensure that the corrective action is having the desired effect. Once again it notes the time and date of the follow-up, who performed it, and what he or she found.

PROBLEM IDENTIFICATION, ANALYSIS, REPORTING, AND CORRECTIVE ACTION SYSTEM

With the advent of computerized data collection and storage, vast amounts of data are available for analysis. However, the ability to turn the data into usable information is dependent on our ability to

- Understand and accurately track the data.
- Analyze the data using statistical analysis to determine its significance.
- Report our findings in a clear, concise manner that is understandable by the intended recipient.
- Formulate and implement corrective actions that fix nonconformance and enhance the overall quality of the system.

The larger and more complex the systems being investigated, the more formal this system should be. Superfluous reports need to be identified and eliminated so that critical information can be received, analyzed, and acted on in a timely manner. The ability to quickly respond to quality control issues can minimize, and in some cases eliminate, the problem.

Reporting can take either a vertical or horizontal path through the organization. On a vertical path, reports are "sent up the chain" so that the supervisor, managers, and executives can be made aware of the quality issues in the facility. This reporting sequence is critical to the strategic quality management process. Only by knowing the problems that are occurring, the action that is being taken to correct the problem, and the results of this action can management truly plan for improving the overall quality of the organization and its processes.

A horizontal path allows quality issues to be passed "up and down the line" to those people who will be directly affected by the nonconformance. By sharing data horizontally, problems can be addressed at the root cause of occurrence, and the effects of the nonconformance can be seen by all affected parties. Quality circles were an initial attempt to address quality issues at the line level. They have evolved into the quality teams of today, which may be either functional or cross-functional. In many cases, these teams have evolved to include customers as well as suppliers in order to obtain the best possible quality across the "cradle-to-grave" life cycle of the product.

SUMMARY

This chapter has looked at quality systems and quality information systems and their various elements. We began by discussing the key elements of a quality system so as to better understand what is meant by the term *quality information system.* Next, we identified some of the key functional elements required in order to have a comprehensive quality system. The next two sections of the chapter discussed the scope and objectives of quality information systems and the techniques used to ensure data accuracy and integrity. Management systems for improving quality were discussed briefly, with the reader referred to Chapter 14 for further discussion and examples. Finally, quality documentation systems, as well as problem identification, analysis, reporting, and corrective action systems, were discussed. A sample quality reporting form was provided as an example of the type of data collection required to ensure an accurate and complete assessment of a quality control issue.

DISCUSSION QUESTIONS

1. Define the term *system.*
2. What are the purposes of a quality information system.
3. List and discuss the key elements of a quality system.
4. List and discuss the functional elements of a quality information system.
5. List and discuss the 3 key components for developing a quality information system.
6. List and define the steps of the systems development life cycle.
7. Discuss the most common method for assessing the accuracy and integrity of quality data.
8. Name three quality management systems guidelines discussed in the chapter.
9. What are the purposes of quality documentation systems?
10. What is meant by vertical and horizontal reporting paths in an organization? Give examples of each with regard to a quality information system.

NOTES

1. ANSI/ASQC Q1-1986, p. 2.
2. ANSI/ASQC Q9000-1-1994, p. 5.
3. Ibid., p. 6.
4. Ibid.

SUGGESTED READINGS

ANSI/ASQC Q1-1986.

ANSI/ASQC Q9000-1-1994.

Hoffer, J. A., J. F. George, & J. S. Valacich. *Modern Systems Analysis and Design.* Reading, MA: Benjamin/Cummings Publishing Company, 1996.

Juran, J. M., & F. M. Gryna, *Quality Planning and Analysis,* 3rd ed. New York: McGraw-Hill, 1980, pp. 577–589.

Rabbitt, J. T., & P. A. Bergh. *The ISO 9000 Book,* 2nd ed. New York: Quality Resources, 1994.

Sinha, M. N., & W. O. Willborn. *The Management of Quality Assurance.* New York: Wiley, 1985, pp. 472–495.

CHAPTER 14

Quality Auditing

CHAPTER OBJECTIVES

This chapter introduces the following topics:

- The objectives of quality audits
- The types of quality audits
- The quality audit process
- ISO 9000 and the Malcolm Baldrige National Quality Award

INTRODUCTION

Quality audits are a part of the evaluation and assessment process that managers use to uncover areas for improvement. When used appropriately, audit findings can serve to focus the organization on the areas most in need of attention. When used as the basis for punitive measures, they can further divide an already troubled organization.

ISO 8402 and ANSI/ASQC Q10011-1-1994 define a quality audit as "a systematic and independent examination to determine whether quality activities and related results comply with planned arrangements and whether these arrangements are implemented effectively and are suitable to achieve objectives."[1] ANSI/ASQC Q1-1986 defines a quality audit as "a systematic examination of the acts and decisions by people with respect to quality in order to independently verify or evaluate and report degree of compliance to the operational requirements of the quality program, or the specifications or contract requirements of the product or service."[2]

Quality audits, then, are by definition a form of management audit.[3] It is also evident that a quality audit cannot be performed unless the desired state has been fully documented. Unless the ideal state has been defined, it is impossible to determine through an audit the degree to which that undefined state has been attained.

Quality audits may be either internal (Q10011-1-1994, 3.4a) or external (Q10011-1-1994, 3.4b–d). Internal audits (first-party audits) are performed within the auditee's own organization. Internal auditors may be organizational employees or outsiders hired by the organization. External audits include supplier certification, regulatory compliance (e.g., FDA regulations), standards compliance (e.g., UL standards), and registration audits (e.g., ISO 9001 registration). External auditors may be either employees of the client organization (second party) or employees of an independent agency (third party) authorized to perform the audit.

The knowledge gained from an independent internal audit of a quality system can provide management with information necessary to improve that program. That same knowledge can be gained through an independent external audit. However, since an outside party conducts an external audit, external audits often are viewed in a more negative light. There often is much at stake in an external audit. ISO/Q-9000 registration or remaining on the preferred supplier list of a major customer may hang in the balance. This can sometimes lead to a defensive posture on the part of the auditee. Management must take appropriate measures to avoid such a reaction.

SPECIFIC TYPES OF QUALITY AUDITS

There are several different approaches to classifying audits. Tunner[4] describes 3 generic types of quality audit:

1. Policy audit
2. Practice audit
3. Product audit

A policy audit compares written policies and procedures with standards and specifications. A practice audit checks actual practices against established procedures. A product audit evaluates the performance of a product relative to its specifications.

Mills[5] subdivides quality audits based upon 4 dimensions:

1. The purpose of the audit—"Why?"
   a. Suitability quality audit.
   b. Conformity quality audit.
2. The object of the audit—"What?"
   a. Quality program audit.
   b. Quality system audit.
3. The nature of the audit—"Who?"
   a. Internal quality audit.
   b. External quality audit.
4. The method of the audit—"How?"
   a. Comprehensive quality system audit.
   b. Selected quality program element audit.

Various permutations and combinations of these dimensions constitute specific types of audits.[6] For example, an ISO/Q-9000 audit is a comprehensive suitability and conformity quality audit of a quality system by an external auditor.

Arter[7] characterizes audits based upon the identity of the auditor (the individual performing the audit) and auditee (the organization being audited):

1. First-party audit
2. Second-party audit
3. Third-party audit

A first-party audit is an internal audit—the auditor and auditee are in the same organization. A second-party audit would be an external audit if your organization is the auditor. An example would be where your organization conducts an audit of a supplier. A second-party audit also would be an external audit if your organization is the auditee. An example would be where your organization is audited by a customer. A third-party audit is performed by someone other than either the customer or the supplier. An example of a third-party audit would be an ISO 9000 audit performed by an accredited registrar.

PERFORMING A QUALITY SYSTEM AUDIT

ANSI/ASQC Q1-1986 lists the responsibilities of the auditor, the client (the individual requesting the audit), and the auditee.[8] It also provides a flow chart documenting the entire audit process.[9]

The audit client responsibilities include:[10]

- Initiate audit, define reference standards, receive audit report.
- Abstain from an undue interference with audit activities.
- Determine follow-up action.

Auditee responsibilities include:[11]

- Appoint a responsible person to accompany the auditor(s).
- Provide access to facilities and evidential material requested by the auditor.
- Provide adequate working facilities at the audit site.
- Cooperate with the auditors.
- Attend meetings called by the auditor.
- Review audit findings to ensure a factual report.
- Take corrective action when required by the client.
- Abstain from any undue interference with the audit.

Auditor responsibilities include:[12]

- Comply with applicable audit standards.
- Clarify and articulate the audit objective.
- Effectively and efficiently plan and implement the audit.
- Report the audit results.
- Audit results of corrective action(s), if requested by the client.
- Retain and safeguard audit working papers.
- Maintain independence from the organization being audited.

The steps involved in performing a quality audit, as defined by ANSI/ASQC Q1-1986, are initiation, planning, implementation, and reporting.[13] The Eli Lilly internal audit process is defined somewhat differently.[14] Lilly's approach defines auditing as a cycle consisting of 5 basic steps:

- Preparation
  Audit plan
  Audit program

- Conduct
  Opening meeting
  Fieldwork, examination, daily update
  Closing meeting
- Writing/review
  Draft detailed audit report
- Reporting
  Audit report
- Follow-up
  Follow-up audit (when applicable)

Lilly has found this approach facilitates understanding, cooperation, and partnership between the quality assurance function and its customers while providing management with unbiased information.

Particular attention must be directed to the proper conduct of internal audits. Internal quality audits performed by representatives of the quality assurance department can perpetuate the "quality department as policeman" stereotype. Rice[15] suggests that attention to establishing and maintaining clear lines of communication between auditor and auditee is key. This includes discussing deficiencies with the auditee prior to making a decision that will impact the organization. Proper preparation so that the auditor understands the auditee's procedures prior to the start of the audit is also important. An auditor's ability to see things from the auditee's perspective is helpful in heading off potential conflict. Focusing on problems and not individuals helps avoid defensive responses to audit findings. Taking the time to build a good working relationship will help ensure that even differences of opinion can be handled in an objective manner, and that the audit will have the desired effect of helping the auditee improve the operation.

ISO 9000 AND THE MALCOLM BALDRIGE NATIONAL QUALITY AWARD

Two of the main frameworks of requirements or criteria used in the United States for auditing quality systems are the ANSI/ASQC Q9000 (ISO 9000) standards and the Malcolm Baldrige National Quality Award (MBNQA) Criteria for Performance Excellence. Even organizations which have no intention of being registered to the ISO 9000 standards or applying for the MBNQA often use these standards and criteria as the basis for audits of their systems.

ISO 9000

ISO 9000, the International Standards, and ANSI/ASQC Q9000, the American National Standards, are a set of standards which "describe what elements quality systems should encompass but not how a specific organization implements these elements.[16] The United States Q9000 standards are identical to the International ISO 9000 standards. The U.S. standards are issued by the American National

Standards Institute (ANSI) and the American Society for Quality (ASQ). The international standards are issued by the International Organization for Standardization (ISO). ANSI is the U.S. member body of the ISO.

An organization seeking registration to one of the ISO 9000 standards would undergo an external audit by a registrar. The ISO 9001 standards are the most comprehensive, covering quality assurance in design, development, production, installation, and servicing. ISO 9002 covers quality assurance in production, installation, and servicing. ISO 9003 is a model for quality assurance in final inspection and test. An outline of the quality system requirements for ISO 9001 is given in Figure 14.1.

QS-9000 is a specialized standard developed in 1994 by the U.S. big three automobile manufacturers. It is applicable to those internal and external suppliers to Chrysler Corp., Ford Motor Corp., and General Motors Corp. who supply production materials, production and service parts, heat treating, painting, and plating and other finishing services.[17] QS-9000 is interdependent with ISO 9000. The QS-9000 standard is based on the 1994 edition of ISO 9001 and includes all the ISO 9001 requirements plus other requirements that are particular to the automotive industry. Some of these additional requirements are similar to Malcolm Baldrige National Quality Award concepts. The process of becoming registered to QS-9000 is similar to that for ISO 9000.

A recent survey conducted by the Automotive Industry Action Committee found that the average cost for a supplier to become registered to QS-9000 is $118,100. Average costs for selected certification activities include:

Preparation	$36,900
Consulting/training	$26,000
Registrar	$18,300
Software	$ 5,100

The suppliers estimated the average benefit of being registered to be $304,300.[18]

Malcolm Baldrige National Quality Award

"The Malcolm Baldrige National Quality Award is an annual award to recognize U.S. companies for performance excellence."[19] Organizations are eligible to compete for the award in 3 categories: manufacturing companies, service companies, and small business. The National Institute of Standards and Technology (NIST), U.S. Department of Commerce, manages the MBNQA program, and the American Society for Quality administers the program. Winners of the MBNQA since its inception in 1988 are listed in Figure 14.2.

Seven categories constitute the MBNQA criteria. These are outlined in Figure 14.3.

Many of the states have established quality awards which in most cases parallel the MBNQA criteria, but each has its own objectives and criteria. The Texas Quality Award, for example, is "patterned after the Malcolm Baldrige National Quality Award criteria, (and) is an annual recognition of Texas organizations that excel in quality management and quality achievement. Public or private businesses, government agencies, public and private educational organizations, and nonprofit organizations located in Texas are eligible to apply for the Award."[21]

4.1   Management Responsibility
           4.1.1   Quality Policy
           4.1.2   Organization
                    4.1.2.1   Responsibility and Authority
                    4.1.2.2   Resources
                    4.1.2.3   Management Representative
           4.1.3   Management Review

4.2   Quality System
           4.2.1   General
           4.2.2   Quality System Procedures
           4.2.3   Quality Planning

4.3   Contract Review
           4.3.1   General
           4.3.2   Review
           4.3.3   Amendment to Contract
           4.3.4   Records

4.4   Design Control
           4.4.1   General
           4.4.2   Design and Development Planning
           4.4.3   Organizational and Technical Interfaces
           4.4.4   Design Input
           4.4.5   Design Output
           4.4.6   Design Review
           4.4.7   Design Verification
           4.4.8   Design Validation
           4.4.9   Design Changes

4.5   Document and Data Control
           4.5.1   General
           4.5.2   Document and Data Approval and Issue
           4.5.3   Document and Data Changes

4.6   Purchasing
           4.6.1   General
           4.6.2   Evaluation of Subcontractors
           4.6.3   Purchasing Data
           4.6.4   Verfication of Purchased Product
                    4.6.4.1   Supplier Verification at Subcontractor's Premises
                    4.6.4.2   Customer Verification of Subcontracted Product

4.7   Control of Customer-Supplied Product

4.8   Product Identification and Traceability

FIGURE 14.1   ISO 9001 quality system requirement outline.

4.9 Process Control

4.10 Inspection and Testing
- 4.10.1 General
- 4.10.2 Receiving Inspection and Testing
- 4.10.3 In-Process Inspection and Testing
- 4.10.4 Final Inspection and Testing
- 4.10.5 Inspection and Test Records

4.11 Control of Inspection, Measuring, and Test Equipment
- 4.11.2 Control Procedure

4.12 Inspection and Test Status

4.13 Control of Nonconforming Product
- 4.13.1 General
- 4.13.2 Review and Disposition of Nonconforming Product

4.14 Corrective and Preventive Action
- 4.14.1 General
- 4.14.2 Corrective Action
- 4.14.3 Preventive Action

4.15 Handling, Storage, Packaging, Preservation, and Delivery
- 4.15.1 General
- 4.15.2 Handling
- 4.15.3 Storage
- 4.15.4 Packaging
- 4.15.5 Preservation
- 4.15.6 Delivery

4.16 Control of Quality Records

4.17 Internal Quality Audits

4.18 Training

4.19 Servicing

4.20 Statistical Techniques
- 4.20.1 Identification of Need
- 4.20.2 Procedures

FIGURE 14.1 *(continued)*

1988
Motorola, Inc.
Commercial Nuclear Fuel Division of Westinghouse Electric Co.
Globe Metallurgical, Inc.

1989
Millikin & Co.
Xerox Corp. Business Products and Systems

1990
Cadillac Motor Car Division
IBM Rochester
Federal Express Corp.
Wallace Co., Inc.

1991
Solectron Corp.
Zytec Corp.
Marlow Industries

1992
AT&T Network Systems Group/Transmission systems Business Unit
Texas Instruments, Inc. Defense Systems and Electronics Group
AT&T Universal Card Services
The Ritz-Carlton Hotel Co.
Granite Rock Co.

1993
Eastman Chemical Co.
Ames Rubber Co.

1994
AT&T Consumer Communications Services
GTE Directories Corp.
Wainwright Industries, Inc.

1995
Armstrong World Industries Building Products Operation
Corning Telecommunications Products Division

1996
ADAC Laboratories
Dana Commercial Credit Corp.
Custom Research, Inc.
Trident Precision Manufacturing, Inc.

1997
3M Dental Products Division
Solectron Corp.
Merrill Lynch Credit Corp.
Xerox Business Services

FIGURE 14.2   Winners of the Malcolm Baldrige National Quality Award.

1   Leadership
     1.1   Leadership System
     1.2   Company Responsibility and Citizenship

2   Strategic Planning
     2.1   Strategy Development Process
     2.2   Company Strategy

3   Customer and Market Focus
     3.1   Customer and Market Knowledge
     3.2   Customer Satisfaction and Relationship Enhancement

4   Information and Analysis
     4.1   Selection and Use of Information and Data
     4.2   Selection and Use of Comparative Information and Data
     4.3   Analysis and Review of Company Performance

5   Human Resource Development and Management
     5.1   Work Systems
     5.2   Employee Education, Training, and Development
     5.3   Employee Well-Being and Satisfaction

6   Process Management
     6.1   Management of Product and Service Processes
     6.2   Management of Support Processes
     6.3   Management of Supplier and Partnering Processes

7   Business Results
     7.1   Customer Satisfaction Results
     7.2   Financial and Market Results
     7.3   Human Resource Results
     7.4   Supplier and Partner Results
     7.5   Company Specific Results

FIGURE 14.3   Outline of 1997 MBNQA criteria.[20]

Many countries also have established national awards for quality. Japan established the first of these, the Deming Prize, in 1951. The Canada Awards for Excellence and the European Quality Award, covering countries in the European Community, are other examples.

SUMMARY

Quality audits are a form of management audit. Effective quality audits can be an invaluable tool to managers for improving quality. Care must be taken to ensure that the audits are properly conducted and that the findings are appropriately utilized. Poorly executed audits provide incomplete or inaccurate information upon which to base future decisions. Using audit results in a punitive fashion can result in a nonproductive, defensive reaction instead of quality improvement. The ISO 9000 (ANSI/ASQC Q9000) and MBNQA standards and criteria are the two most frequently used audit standards in the United States.

DISCUSSION QUESTIONS

1. Discuss the differences between a first-party, second-party, and third-party audit.
2. Might there be differences in the reception by managers and employees of an internal versus an external audit report? Discuss.
3. Discuss the differences in responsibilities of client, auditor, and auditee in performing a quality system audit.
4. Discuss the similarities and differences between the audit steps in ANSI/ASQC Q1-1986 and those used by Eli Lilly.
5. Discuss ways that an internal auditor might avoid the "quality department as policeman" stereotype.
6. Contrast the ANSI/ASQC Q9000-ISO 9000 standards and the Malcolm Baldrige National Quality Award criteria. Are the purposes of these two frameworks the same?

NOTES

1. ANSI/ASQC Q10011-1-1994, p. 1.
2. ANSI/ASQC Q1-1986, pp. 1–2.
3. Arter, D. R. *Quality Audits for Improved Performance,* 2nd ed. Milwaukee, WI: ASQC Quality Press, 1994, p. 2.
4. Tunner, J. R. *A Quality Technology Primer for Managers.* Milwaukee, WI: ASQC Quality Press, 1990.
5. Mills, C. *The Quality Audit: A Management Evaluation Tool.* Milwaukee, WI: ASQC Quality Press, 1989, pp. 25–34.
6. Ibid.
7. Arter, pp. 4–5.
8. ANSI/ASQC Q1-1986, pp. 2–4.
9. Ibid., pp. 9–13.
10. Ibid., p. 3.
11. Ibid., pp. 3–4.
12. Ibid., p. 2.
13. Ibid., p. 4.
14. Bishara, R., & M. Wyrick, "A Systematic Approach to Quality Assurance Auditing." *Quality Progress,* vol. 27, no. 12, December 1994, pp. 67–70.
15. Rice, C. "How to Conduct an Internal Quality Audit and Still Have Friends." *Quality Progress,* vol. 27, no. 6, June 1994, pp. 39–41.
16. ANSI/ASQC Q9000-1-1994, p. vii.
17. http://www.asq.org/standcert/9000.html.

18. *Quality Digest,* vol. 17, no. 8, August 1997, p. 10.

19. *Malcolm Baldrige National Quality Award 1997 Criteria for Performance Excellence.* Milwaukee, WI: ASQC, 1997, p. 1.

20. Ibid., p. 2.

21. *Quality Texas Facts.* Austin, TX: Quality Texas, 1996.

SUGGESTED READINGS

ANSI/ASQC Q1-1986.

ANSI/ASQC Q9000-1-1994.

ANSI/ASQC Q9001-1994.

ANSI/ASQC Q9002-1994.

ANSI/ASQC Q9003-1994.

ANSI/ASQC Q9004-1-1994.

Arter, D. R. *Quality Audits for Improved Performance,* 2nd ed. Milwaukee, WI: ASQC Quality Press, 1994.

Bishara, R., & M. Wyrick. "A Systematic Approach to Quality Assurance Auditing." *Quality Progress,* vol. 27, no. 12, December 1994, pp. 67–60.

Evans, J. R., & W. Lindsay. *The Management and Control of Quality,* 3rd ed. Minneapolis: West, 1996, pp. 484–518.

Fiorentino, R., & M. Perigord. "Going from an Investigative to a Formative Auditor." *Quality Progress,* vol. 27, no. 10, October 1994, pp. 61–65.

Malcolm Baldrige National Quality Award 1997 Criteria for Performance Excellence. Milwaukee, WI: ASQC, 1997.

Mills, C. A. *The Quality Audit: A Management Evaluation Tool.* Milwaukee, WI: ASQC Quality Press, 1989.

Quality System Requirements QS-9000, 2nd ed. February 1995 (fourth printing July 1996).

Rice, C. "How to Conduct an Internal Quality Audit and Still Have Friends." *Quality Progress,* vol. 27, no. 6, June 1994, pp. 39–41.

Tunner, J. R. *A Quality Technology Primer for Managers.* Milwaukee, WI: ASQC Quality Press, 1990.

CASE III THE TURKELL STUD MILL

The Turkell Stud Mill is part of an international wood products corporation headquartered in the United States. The Turkell Mill produces dimensional lumber used in the construction industry. Your quality consulting firm has been engaged to assist Turkell in improving its incoming log inspection process. The General Manager estimates that the mill incurs losses in excess of $100,000 per year due to overpayment for logs.

Turkell purchases its logs primarily from independent loggers. These loggers transport logs they cut to Turkell on trucks which contain from 20 to 50 logs. Because all Turkell's products have a nominal length of 8 feet, they cut the logs into 8-foot 9-inch blocks before milling. Logs whose length is not a multiple of 8 feet 9 inches contain unusable wood which must be chipped and sold to one of the company's paper mills. The value of the chips is a small fraction of the value of the studs produced from usable lengths.

The problem is that the company has found that it is not feasible to inspect every log as received. Incoming logs may contain up to 4 blocks (35 feet). Trucks may contain up to 50 logs. With the current inspection procedure, only the logs on the outside of the shipment (face logs) can be accurately measured for length. The only way to accurately measure the length of all logs in a shipment is to "spread them"—that is, to unload the truck in the inspection area. This process is expensive and too time consuming to be feasible.

Currently, when a truckload of logs arrives at the mill, all the logs receive an end inspection for cracks, decay, and similar defects and the end diameter is measured. Four outside (face) logs are measured for length using a tape measure. An adjustment is made for any of the 4 measured logs which is not a block multiple. A block shorter than 8 feet 9 inches is value-adjusted. If all the 4 logs measured require adjustment, the load is spread and all the logs are measured. Using the lengths obtained from the sample of 4 logs, the end diameters, and a "taper factor," the number of board feet in the shipment is determined. The payment to the logger is calculated on the basis of the number of board feet in the load.

Based upon information obtained from the 6 previous month's milling operation, it is believed that 4.23 percent of the incoming logs are shorter than block length. Incoming inspection records from the same period indicate that about 10 percent of the short blocks are found and the appropriate adjustment made. The value lost by failing to adjust for a short block is about $9. The mill purchases between 250,000 and 300,000 logs per year.

There are other lumber mills in the area to which the loggers can sell their logs. The Turkell Mill General Manager is concerned that if the inspection time per load is significantly increased, or if a new inspection process is perceived by the loggers to be unfair, he will lose many of his suppliers to other mills. He has asked that you evaluate the situation and make recommendations for reducing losses due to short blocks that are missed at incoming inspection.

Appendices

APPENDIX A

Table of 4-Digit Random Numbers				
9301	9230	4867	0187	0816
5940	0570	0928	5713	8673
1946	7308	6931	2841	1919
0537	9197	0743	4714	6096
1816	4086	0715	6195	8700
6202	7127	5954	9829	4855
0244	6758	6637	6566	6365
0891	5979	9763	7810	6287
7515	0854	1741	6595	0046
1325	7991	1112	2058	7569
0721	3172	8962	2091	0473
4433	2218	1901	7107	9716
4468	8196	0488	3589	4992
0223	0292	1896	8921	9520
7252	5788	8036	0469	6751
7663	8327	2893	7572	6988
8802	0494	5366	7901	7360
7643	4017	6199	1368	2370
6223	5258	0812	9480	0843
9552	0478	0011	3984	9297

Note: Generated using NWA Quality Analyst.™

APPENDIX B

Areas under the Standard Normal Distribution Curve From $-\infty$ to $+z$

z	.00	.01	.02	.03	.04	.05	.06	.07	.08	.09
.0	.5000	.5040	.5080	.5120	.5160	.5199	.5239	.5279	.5319	.5359
.1	.5398	.5438	.5478	.5517	.5557	.5596	.5636	.5675	.5714	.5753
.2	.5793	.5832	.5871	.5910	.5948	.5987	.6036	.6064	.6103	.6141
.3	.6179	.6217	.6255	.6293	.6331	.6368	.6406	.6443	.6480	.6517
.4	.6554	.6591	.6628	.6664	.6700	.6736	.6772	.6808	.6844	.6879
.5	.6915	.6950	.6985	.7019	.7054	.7088	.7123	.7157	.7190	.7224
.6	.7257	.7291	.7324	.7357	.7389	.7422	.7454	.7486	.7517	.7549
.7	.7580	.7611	.7642	.7673	.7703	.7734	.7764	.7794	.7823	.7852
.8	.7881	.7910	.7939	.7967	.7995	.8023	.8051	.8078	.8106	.8133
.9	.8159	.8186	.8212	.8238	.8264	.8289	.8315	.8340	.8365	.8389
1.0	.8413	.8438	.8461	.8485	.8508	.8531	.8554	.8577	.8599	.8621
1.1	.8643	.8665	.8686	.8708	.8729	.8749	.8770	.8790	.8810	.8830
1.2	.8849	.8869	.8888	.8907	.8925	.8944	.8962	.8980	.8997	.9015
1.3	.9032	.9049	.9066	.9082	.9099	.9115	.9131	.9147	.9162	.9177
1.4	.9192	.9207	.9222	.9236	.9251	.9265	.9279	.9292	.9306	.9319
1.5	.9332	.9345	.9357	.9370	.9382	.9394	.9406	.9418	.9429	.9441
1.6	.9452	.9463	.9474	.9484	.9495	.9505	.9515	.9525	.9535	.9545
1.7	.9554	.9564	.9573	.9582	.9591	.9599	.9608	.9616	.9625	.9633
1.8	.9641	.9649	.9656	.9664	.9671	.9678	.9686	.9693	.9699	.9706
1.9	.9713	.9719	.9726	.9732	.9738	.9744	.9750	.9756	.9761	.9767
2.0	.9772	.9778	.9783	.9788	.9793	.9798	.9803	.9808	.9812	.9817
2.1	.9821	.9826	.9830	.9834	.9838	.9842	.9846	.9850	.9854	.9857
2.2	.9861	.9864	.9868	.9871	.9875	.9878	.9881	.9884	.9887	.9890
2.3	.9893	.9896	.9898	.9901	.9904	.9906	.9909	.9911	.9913	.9916
2.4	.9918	.9920	.9922	.9925	.9927	.9929	.9931	.9932	.9934	.9936
2.5	.9938	.9940	.9941	.9943	.9945	.9946	.9948	.9949	.9951	.9952
2.6	.9953	.9955	.9956	.9957	.9959	.9960	.9961	.9962	.9963	.9964
2.7	.9965	.9966	.9967	.9968	.9969	.9970	.9971	.9972	.9973	.9974
2.8	.9974	.9975	.9976	.9977	.9977	.9978	.9979	.9979	.9980	.9981
2.9	.9981	.9982	.9982	.9983	.9984	.9984	.9985	.9985	.9986	.9986
3.0	.9987	.9987	.9987	.9988	.9988	.9989	.9989	.9989	.9990	.9990
3.1	.9990	.9991	.9991	.9991	.9991	.9992	.9992	.9992	.9993	.9993
3.2	.9993	.9993	.9994	.9994	.9994	.9994	.9994	.9995	.9995	.9995
3.3	.9995	.9995	.9995	.9996	.9996	.9996	.9996	.9996	.9996	.9997
3.4	.9997	.9997	.9997	.9997	.9997	.9997	.9997	.9997	.9997	.9998

APPENDIX C

Partial F-Tables $F_{0.01, \nu_1, \nu_2}$

$\nu_2 \backslash \nu_1$	1	2	3	4	5	6	7	8	9	10	12	15	20
1	4052.0	4999.5	5403.0	5625.0	5764.0	5859.0	5928.0	5982.0	6022.0	6056.0	6106.0	6157.0	6209.0
2	98.50	99.00	99.17	99.25	99.30	99.33	99.36	99.37	99.39	99.40	99.42	99.43	99.45
3	34.12	30.82	29.46	28.71	28.24	27.91	27.67	27.49	27.35	27.23	27.05	26.87	26.69
4	21.20	18.00	16.69	15.98	15.52	15.21	14.98	14.80	14.66	14.55	14.37	14.20	14.02
5	16.26	13.27	12.06	11.39	10.97	10.67	10.46	10.29	10.16	10.05	9.89	9.72	9.55
6	13.75	10.92	9.78	9.15	8.75	8.47	8.26	8.10	7.98	7.87	7.72	7.56	7.40
7	12.25	9.55	8.45	7.85	7.46	7.19	6.99	6.84	6.72	6.62	6.47	6.31	6.16
8	11.26	8.65	7.59	7.01	6.63	6.37	6.18	6.03	5.91	5.81	5.67	5.52	5.36
9	10.56	8.02	6.99	6.42	6.06	5.80	5.61	5.47	5.35	5.26	5.11	4.96	4.81
10	10.04	7.56	6.55	5.99	5.64	5.39	5.20	5.06	4.94	4.85	4.71	4.56	4.41
11	9.65	7.21	6.22	5.67	5.32	5.07	4.89	4.74	4.63	4.54	4.40	4.25	4.10
12	9.33	6.93	5.95	5.41	5.06	4.82	4.64	4.50	4.39	4.30	4.16	4.01	3.86
13	9.07	6.70	5.74	5.21	4.86	4.62	4.44	4.30	4.19	4.10	3.96	3.82	3.66
14	8.86	6.51	5.56	5.04	4.69	4.46	4.28	4.14	4.03	3.94	3.80	3.66	3.51
15	8.68	6.36	5.42	4.89	4.56	4.32	4.14	4.00	3.89	3.80	3.67	3.52	3.37
16	8.53	6.23	5.29	4.77	4.44	4.20	4.03	3.89	3.78	3.69	3.55	3.41	3.26
17	8.40	6.11	5.18	4.67	4.34	4.10	3.93	3.79	3.68	3.59	3.46	3.31	3.16
18	8.29	6.01	5.09	4.58	4.25	4.01	3.84	3.71	3.60	3.51	3.37	3.23	3.08
19	8.18	5.93	5.01	4.50	4.17	3.94	3.77	3.63	3.52	3.43	3.30	3.15	3.00
20	8.10	5.85	4.94	4.43	4.10	3.87	3.70	3.56	3.46	3.37	3.23	3.09	2.94
21	8.02	5.78	4.87	4.37	4.04	3.81	3.64	3.51	3.40	3.31	3.17	3.03	2.88
22	7.95	5.72	4.82	4.31	3.99	3.76	3.59	3.45	3.35	3.26	3.12	2.98	2.83
23	7.88	5.66	4.76	4.26	3.94	3.71	3.54	3.41	3.30	3.21	3.07	2.93	2.78
24	7.82	5.61	4.72	4.22	3.90	3.67	3.50	3.36	3.26	3.17	3.03	2.89	2.74
25	7.77	5.57	4.68	4.18	3.85	3.63	3.46	3.32	3.22	3.13	2.99	2.85	2.70

Degrees of freedom for the numerator (ν_1).
Degrees of freedom for the denominator (ν_2).

Partial F-Tables $F_{0.05, v_1, v_2}$

v_2/v_1	1	2	3	4	5	6	7	8	9	10	12	15	20
1	161.4	199.5	215.7	224.6	230.2	234.0	236.8	238.9	240.5	241.9	243.9	245.9	248.0
2	18.51	19.00	19.16	19.25	19.30	19.33	19.35	19.37	19.38	19.40	19.41	19.43	19.45
3	10.13	9.55	9.28	9.12	9.01	8.94	8.89	8.85	8.81	8.79	8.74	8.70	8.66
4	7.71	6.94	6.59	6.39	6.26	6.16	6.09	6.04	6.00	5.96	5.91	5.86	5.80
5	6.61	5.79	5.41	5.19	5.05	4.95	4.88	4.82	4.77	4.74	4.68	4.62	4.56
6	5.99	5.14	4.76	4.53	4.39	4.28	4.21	4.15	4.10	4.06	4.00	3.94	3.87
7	5.59	4.74	4.35	4.12	3.97	3.87	3.79	3.73	3.68	3.64	3.57	3.51	3.44
8	5.32	4.46	4.07	3.84	3.69	3.58	3.50	3.44	3.39	3.35	3.28	3.22	3.15
9	5.12	4.26	3.86	3.63	3.48	3.37	3.29	3.23	3.18	3.14	3.07	3.01	2.94
10	4.96	4.10	3.71	3.48	3.33	3.22	3.14	3.07	3.02	2.98	2.91	2.85	2.77
11	4.84	3.98	3.59	3.36	3.20	3.09	3.01	2.95	2.90	2.85	2.79	2.72	2.65
12	4.75	3.89	3.49	3.26	3.11	3.00	2.91	2.85	2.80	2.75	2.69	2.62	2.54
13	4.67	3.81	3.41	3.18	3.03	2.92	2.83	2.77	2.71	2.67	2.60	2.53	2.46
14	4.60	3.74	3.34	3.11	2.96	2.85	2.76	2.70	2.65	2.60	2.53	2.46	2.39
15	4.54	3.68	3.29	3.06	2.90	2.79	2.71	2.64	2.59	2.54	2.48	2.40	2.33
16	4.49	3.63	3.24	3.01	2.85	2.74	2.66	2.59	2.54	2.49	2.42	2.35	2.28
17	4.45	3.59	3.20	2.96	2.81	2.70	2.61	2.55	2.49	2.45	2.38	2.31	2.23
18	4.41	3.55	3.16	2.93	2.77	2.66	2.58	2.51	2.46	2.41	2.34	2.27	2.19
19	4.38	3.52	3.13	2.90	2.74	2.63	2.54	2.48	2.42	2.38	2.31	2.23	2.16
20	4.35	3.49	3.10	2.87	2.71	2.60	2.51	2.45	2.39	2.35	2.28	2.20	2.12
21	4.32	3.47	3.07	2.84	2.68	2.57	2.49	2.42	2.37	2.32	2.25	2.18	2.10
22	4.30	3.44	3.05	2.82	2.66	2.55	2.46	2.40	2.34	2.30	2.23	2.15	2.07
23	4.28	3.42	3.03	2.80	2.64	2.53	2.44	2.37	2.32	2.27	2.20	2.13	2.05
24	4.26	3.40	3.01	2.78	2.62	2.51	2.42	2.36	2.30	2.25	2.18	2.11	2.03
25	4.24	3.39	2.99	2.76	2.60	2.49	2.40	2.34	2.28	2.24	2.16	2.09	2.01

Degrees of freedom for the numerator (v_1).
Degrees of freedom for the denominator (v_2).

APPENDIX D

Computerized Test Bank

PROGRAM REQUIREMENTS

The program will run on an IBM compatible PC that is running under either Windows 3.1, Windows 95, or a later version of Windows. The amount of hard drive disk storage required for the program and data files is 406,000 bytes. RAM memory requirements are the same as the minimum required for running Windows.

WINDOWS 95 OR LATER WINDOWS VERSION

Installation

The program and data files will be installed on a hard drive to be run under Windows 95. This example will use C: as the hard drive identifier; however, you can substitute the appropriate drive letter for your own computer. You will need to know the drive identifier for the CDROM. The example command will show drive X, and you will need to substitute the actual drive letter in the command below. This example will show how to copy the files from the CD to the hard drive.

Install on Hard Drive

1. Open a DOS session by clicking on START, then click on PROGRAMS, then click on a DOS session in the program list.
2. C: (or letter of the drive on which to install on your computer).
3. MD EXAM (this creates a subdirectory named EXAM on the hard drive of your computer).
4. CD EXAM (change directory to the new subdirectory).
5. COPY X:*.* (where X is the drive letter of the CDROM drive)

RUNNING THE PROGRAM

Select one of the following methods, based on whether you prefer to install and run the program from the PROGRAM LIST (reached via the START icon) or whether you prefer to install and run the program from an icon in a folder on the desktop.

Method 1. Using the Program List

1. Click on START with the *right* mouse button.
2. Click on OPEN.
3. Click on PROGRAMS folder with the *right* mouse button.
4. Go to Step 9 if you want to install into an existing folder.
5. Position the cursor on the blank space between existing folders.
6. Click with the *right* mouse button.
7. Select NEW.
8. Select FOLDER.
9. Click on the folder with the *right* mouse button.
10. Select OPEN.
11. Click inside the folder with the *right* mouse button.
12. Select NEW.
13. Select SHORTCUT.
14. Type C:\EXAM\EXAMMAIN.EXE in the COMMAND box (where C: is the hard drive identifier for the disk where the program is located) and press ENTER.
15. Close the folder (ALT-F4 or click on the upper right x).
16. Close PROGRAMS folder (ALT-F4 or click on the upper right x).
17. Close the START MENU folder (ALT-F4 or click on the upper right x).
18. Now, to run the program:
    A. Click on START.
    B. Click on PROGRAMS.
    C. Click on the folder name you used above.
    D. Click on the icon for EXAMMAIN.

Method 2. Using a Folder on the Desktop

1. If you want to use an existing folder, go to Step 6.
2. Position the cursor on a blank space on the desktop.
3. Click with the *right* mouse button.
4. Select NEW.
5. Select FOLDER.
6. Click on the folder with the *right* mouse button.
7. Select OPEN.
8. Click on the folder with the *right* mouse button.
9. Select NEW.
10. Select SHORTCUT.
11. Type C:\EXAM\EXAMMAIN.EXE in COMMAND box (where C: is the hard drive identifier for the disk where the program is installed) and press ENTER.

12. Close the folder (ALT-F4 or click on the upper right x).

13. Now, to run the program:

    A. Click on the folder.

    B. Click on the icon for EXAMMAIN.

WINDOWS 3.1

Installation on the Hard Drive

From a DOS session:

1. C: (where C is the drive letter where the program is to be installed)

2. MD EXAM (create a subdirectory named EXAM)

3. CD EXAM (change the directory to the new subdirectory)

4. COPY X:*.* (where X is the drive letter of the CDROM)

From a Windows session:

1. Open the Group Icon into which you want to install the program.

2. Click on FILE.

3. Click on NEW.

4. Click on Program Item.

5. For Description, enter QCE TUTORIAL.

6. For Command Line, enter EXAMMAIN.EXE.

7. For Working Directory, enter C:\EXAM (where C: is the hard drive identifier for the drive where the program is installed).

8. Click OK.

9. Now to run the program, double-click on the QCE TUTORIAL icon in the open Windows group.

USING THE PROGRAM

When the user runs the program, a main menu is presented. Entering the code for a chapter will present the questions in that chapter one by one. As each question is displayed, entering the appropriate code will allow the user to advance to the next question, back up to the previous question, print the question, display the explanation for the question, display a list of references for the question, and enter an answer for the question. As a question is displayed, the user should determine which of the five answers shown is correct and then enter the appropriate code. If the user needs to do research to determine the answer, the QUIT option allows exiting the program. If the user selects the wrong answer, a message is shown, and the user may then make another selection.

SCORING

There are two scoring options on the main menu. The first is Score by Chapter. The second is Score by Section. The first option will be explained first.

As you answer questions, the program will record and keep track of those questions that were answered correctly on the first attempt. The Score by Chapter function will first determine which chapter the user wants to score. The number of correct answers on first attempt and the total number of questions for the chapter are shown. If the number correct is not high enough to show mastery of the subject matter, the user is given the opportunity to print out the questions that were not answered correctly on the first attempt, to use in reviewing the subject matter.

The Score by Section function shows how many questions were answered correctly on the first attempt for a section of the body of knowledge. If not enough questions were answered correctly on the first attempt, the user can request a list of which chapters in the book to review.

There is also an option to reset the user score. Using this option will clear the log of all questions previously answered. Score will then start over following this function.

Exiting the program (the QUIT function) does not affect the user score. When the user runs the program the next time, all previous correct answers are kept. If at any time the user wants to remove all correct answers previously given, the Reset Score function may be used.

ADDITIONAL FILE

Also included is an Excel template for doing the Gauge R & R exercise shown in Figure 7.6 in the text. It will be located in the C:\EXAM subdirectory. You will need to use the Excel program to open the file.

BIBLIOGRAPHY

ANSI/ASQC A1–1987, Definitions, Symbols, Formulas, and Tables for Control Charts.

ANSI/ASQC A2–1987, Terms and Symbols for Acceptance Sampling.

ANSI/ASQC C1–1985, of General Requirements for a Quality Program.

ANSI/ASQC M1–1996, American National Standard Calibration Systems.

ANSI/ASQC Q1–1986, American National Standard Generic Guidelines for Auditing Quality Systems.

ANSI/ASQC Q10011–1–1994, American National Standard Guidelines for Auditing Quality Systems.

ANSI/ASQC Q9000–1–1994, American National Standard Quality Management and Quality Assurance Standards—Guidelines for Selection and Use.

ANSI/ISO/ASQC Q9001–1994, American National Standard Quality Systems—Model for Quality Assurance in Design, Development, Production, Installation, and Servicing.

ANSI/ASQC Q9002–1994, American National Standard Quality Systems—Model for Quality Assurance in Production, Installation, and Servicing.

ANSI/ASQC Q9003–1994, American National Standard Quality Systems—Model for Quality Assurance in Final Inspection and Test.

ANSI/ASQC Q9004–1–1994, American National Standard Quality Management and Quality System Elements—Guidelines.

ANSI/ASQC Z1.4–1993, American National Standard Sampling Procedures and Tables for Inspection by Attributes.

ANSI/ASQC Z1.9–1993, American National Standard Sampling Procedures and Tables for Inspection by Variables for Percent Nonconforming.

ANSI/ISO/ASQC A8402–1994, Quality Management and Quality Assurance_Vocabulary.

Arter, D. R. *Quality Audits for Improved Performance,* 2nd ed. Milwaukee, WI: ASQC Quality Press, 1994.

ASQC Automotive Division Statistical Process Control Manual Milwaukee, WI: ASQC Quality Press, 1986.

ASQC. *Certified Quality Engineer.* Milwaukee, WI: ASQC, 1995.

ASQC Quality Costs Committee, J. Campanella (ed.). *Principles of Quality Costs,* 2nd ed. Milwaukee, WI: ASQC Quality Press, 1990.

ASQC Statistics Division. *Glossary & Tables for Statistical Quality Control.* Milwaukee, WI: ASQC Quality Press, 1983.

ASTM, ASTM STP 15D ASTM Manual on Presentation of Data and Control Chart Analysis. Philadelphia: American Society for Testing and Materials, 1976.

Banker, R. D., J. M. Field, R. G. Schroeder, & K. K. Sinha. "Impact of Work Teams on Manufacturing Performance: A Longitudinal Study." *Academy of Management Journal,* vol. 39, 1996, pp. 867–890.

Barker, T. B. *Engineering Quality by Design.* New York: 1990.

Barrentine, L. B. *Concepts for R&R Studies.* Milwaukee, WI: ASQC Quality Press, 1991.

Bedeian, A. G. *Management,* 3rd ed. Ft. Worth, TX: Dryden, 1993.

Bemowski, K. "The Quality Glossary." *Quality Progress,* vol. 25, February 1992, pp. 18–29.

Bhote, K. R. *World Class Quality,* New York: AMACOM, 1991.

Bishara, R., & M. Wyrick. "A Systematic Approach to Quality Assurance Auditing." *Quality Progress,* vol. 27, no. 12, December 1994, pp. 67–70.

Bossert, J. L. *Supplier Management Handbook.* Milwaukee, WI: ASQC Quality Press, 1994.

Bowersox, D. J., & D. J. Closs. *Logistical Management, The Integrated Supply Chain Process.* New York: McGraw-Hill, 1996.

Box, G. E. P. *Statistics for Experimenters.* New York: Wiley, 1978.

Burr, I. "The Effect of Non-Normality on Constants for X-bar and R Charts." *Industrial Quality Control,* vol. 23, no. 9, March 1967, pp. 563–568.

Campanella, J. (ed.). *Principles of Quality Costs.* 2d ed. Milwaukee, WI: ASQC Quality Press, 1990.

Christensen, H. B., & the Statistics Instructional Development Team, Brigham Young University. *Statistics Step by Step.* Boston: Houghton Mifflin, 1977.

Conover, W. J. *Practical Nonparametric Statistics,* 2nd ed. New York: Wiley, 1980.

Covey, S. R. *The Seven Habits of Highly Successful People.* New York: Simon & Schuster, 1986.

Crosby, P. B. *Quality Is Free.* New York: McGraw-Hill, 1979.

David, F. R. *Strategic Management,* 6th ed. Upper Saddle River, NJ: Prentice Hall, 1997.

Deming, W. E. "Improvement of Quality and Productivity through Action by Management." *National Productivity Review,* vol. 1, no. 1, Winter 1981–1982, pp. 12–22. Reprinted in Sower, V. E., J. Motwani, & M. J. Savoie. *Classic Readings in Operations Management.* Ft. Worth, TX; Dryden, 1995, pp. 231–247.

Deming, W. E. *The New Economics.* Cambridge, MA: MIT Center for Advanced Engineering Study, 1993, p. 35.

Deming, W. E. *Out of the Crisis.* Cambridge, MA: Massachusetts Institute of Technology, 1986.

Dessler, G. *Human Resource Management.* Upper Saddle River, NJ: Prentice Hall, 1997.

Dodge, H. F. "A Method of Rating Manufactured Product." *The Bell System Technical Journal,* vol. 7, April 1928, pp. 350–368.

Dodge, H. F., & H. G. Romig. *Sampling Inspection Tables, Single and Double Sampling,* 2nd ed. New York: Wiley, 1959.

Duncan, A. J. *Quality Control and Industrial Statistics,* 5th ed. Homewood, IL: Irwin, 1986.

Enrick, N. L. *Quality Control and Reliability,* 7th ed. New York: Industrial Press, 1977.

Evans, J. R., & W. M. Lindsay. *The Management and Control of Quality,* 3rd ed. St Paul, MN: West, 1996.

Farago, F. T. *Handbook of Dimensional Measurement,* 3rd ed. New York: Industrial Press, 1994.

Feigenbaum, A. "Total Quality Control." *Harvard Business Review,* vol. 34, no. 6, 1956, pp. 93–101. Reprinted in Sower, V., J. Motwani, & M. Savoie. *Classic Readings in Operations Management.* Ft. Worth, TX: Dryden, 1995, pp. 307–321.

Feigenbaum, A. V. *Total Quality Control,* 3rd ed. New York: McGraw-Hill, 1991.

Fiorentino, R., & M. Perigord. "Going from an Investigative to a Formative Auditor." *Quality Progress,* vol. 27, no. 10, October 1994, pp. 61–65.

Frigon, N. L., & D. Mathews. *Practical Guide to Experimental Design.* New York: Wiley, 1997.

Galloway, D. *Mapping Work Processes*. Milwaukee, WI: ASQC Quality Press, 1994.

Gitlow, H., A. Oppenheim, & R. Oppenheim. *Quality Management,* 2d ed. Burr Ridge, IL: Irwin, 1995.

Grant, E. L., & R. S. Leavenworth. *Statistical Quality Control,* 7th ed. New York: McGraw-Hill, 1996.

Griffith, G. *Quality Technician's Handbook*. New York: Wiley, 1986.

Harvey, T. R., & B. Drolet. *Building Teams, Building People*. Lancaster, PA: Technomic Publishing Co., 1994.

Herzberg, F. *Work and the Nature of Man*. New York: World Publishing, 1966.

Hickman, T. K., & W. M. Hickman. *Global Purchasing*. Homewood, IL: Business One Irwin, 1992.

Hutchins, G. *Purchasing Strategies for Total Quality*. Homewood, IL Business One Irwin, 1992.

http://www.asq.org.

Ishikawa, K. *Guide to Quality Control*. White Plains, NY: Quality Resources, 1976.

Ishikawa, K. *Quality Control Circles at Work*. Tokyo: Asian Productivity Organization, 1984.

ISO 10012-1-1992, Quality Assurance Requirements for Measuring Equipment—Part 1: Metrological Confirmation System for Measuring Equipment.

ISO 5725-1,2,3-1994, Accuracy (Trueness and Precision) of Measurement Methods and Results.

Juran, J. "The Quality Trilogy." *Quality Progress,* vol. 19, August 1986, pp. 19–24. Reprinted in Sower V., J. Motwani, & M. Savoie. *Classic Readings in Operations Management*. Ft. Worth, TX: Dryden, 1995, pp. 277–287.

Juran, J. M. *Quality Control Handbook,* 4th ed. New York: McGraw-Hill, 1988.

Juran, J. M. & F. M. Gryna. *Quality Planning and Analysis,* 3rd ed. New York: McGraw-Hill, 1993.

Kenet, R., & S. Zacks. *Modern Industrial Statistics: The Design and Control of Quality and Reliability*. Pacific Grove, CA: Duxbury Press, 1998.

Kennedy, C. W., & D. E. Andrews. *Inspection and Gaging,* 5th ed. New York: Industrial Press, 1977.

Kolarik, W. J. *Creating Quality*. New York: McGraw-Hill, 1995.

Kvanli, A. H., C. S. Guynes, & R. J. Pavur. *Introduction to Business Statistics,* 4th ed. St Paul, MN: West, 1996.

Leenders, M. R., & H. E. Fearon. *Purchasing and Supply Management,* 11th ed. Chicago: Irwin, 1997.

Lochner, R. H., & J. E. Matar. *Designing for Quality*. Milwaukee, WI: ASQC Quality Press, 1990.

Malcolm Baldrige National Quality Award 1997 Criteria for Performance Excellence. Milwaukee, WI: ASQC, 1997.

Maslow, A. H. *Motivation and Personality*. New York: McGraw-Hill, 1964.

McClelland, D. C. *The Achieving Society*. New York: Van Nostrand, 1961.

McGregor, D. *The Human Side of Enterprise*. New York: McGraw-Hill, 1960.

McWilliams, T. P. *How to Use Sequential Statistical Methods*. Milwaukee, WI: ASQC Quality Press, 1989.

Measurement Systems Analysis, Reference Manual. Southfield, MI: Automotive Industry Action Group, 1995.

Mills, C. *The Quality Audit: A Management Evaluation Tool*. New York: McGraw-Hill, 1989.

MIL-STD-105E, *Military Standard Sampling Procedures and Tables for Inspection by Attributes.* Washington, DC: Government Printing Office, 1989.

MIL-STD-414, *Military Standard Sampling Procedures and Tables for Inspection by Variables for Percent Defective.* Washington, DC: Government Printing Office, 1957.

MIL-STD-1235B, *Military Standard Single- and Multi-Level Continuous Sampling Procedures and Table for Inspection by Attributes.* Washington, DC: Government Printing Office, 1981.

MIL-STD-1520C.

MIL-Q-9858A.

Montgomery, D. C. *Design and Analysis of Experiments,* 3rd ed. New York: Wiley, 1991.

Montgomery, D. C. *Introduction to Statistical Quality Control,* 3rd ed. New York: Wiley, 1996.

Montgomery, D. C., G. Runger, & N. Hubele. *Engineering Statistics.* New York: Wiley; 1998.

Morris, A. S. *Measurement and Calibration for Quality Assurance.* Englewood Cliffs, NJ: Prentice-Hall, 1991.

Orsburn, J. D., L. Moran, E. Musselwhite, & J. H. Zenger. *Self-Directed Work Teams.* Homewood, IL: Business One Irwin, 1990.

Osborn, A. *Applied Imagination,* 3d ed. New York: Scribner's, 1963.

Parnes, S., R. Noller, & A. Biondi (eds.). *Guide to Creative Action.* New York: Scribner's, 1977.

Pennella, C. R. *Managing the Metrology System.* Milwaukee, WI: ASQC Quality Press, 1992.

Plovnick, M., R. Fry, & I. Rubin. "New Developments in O.D. Technology: Programmed Team Development." *Training and Development Journal,* April 1975.

Pyzdek, T., & R. W. Berger (eds.). *Quality Engineering Handbook.* Milwaukee, WI: ASQC Quality Press, 1994.

Quality Digest, vol. 17, no. 8, August 1997, p. 10.

Quality System Requirements QS-9000, 2nd ed. February 1995 (fourth printing July 1996).

Rice, C. "How to Conduct an Internal Quality Audit and Still Have Friends." *Quality Progress,* vol. 27, no. 6, June 1994, pp. 39–41.

Russell, R. S., & B. W. Taylor. *Operations Management.* Upper Saddle River, NJ: Prentice Hall, 1998.

Shapiro, S. S. *How to Test Normality and Other Distributional Assumptions.* Milwaukee, WI: ASQC Quality Press, 1990.

Shewhart, W. *Economic Control of Quality of Manufactured Product.* New York: Van Nostrand, 1931.

Shewhart, W. "Excerpts from Economic Control of Manufactured Product" (1931) and "Excerpts from Statistical Method from the Viewpoint of Quality Control" (1939). Reprinted in Sower V., J. Motwani, & M. Savoie. *Classic Readings in Operations Management.* Ft. Worth, TX: Dryden, 1995, pp. 191–230.

Shingo, Shigeo. *Zero Quality Control: Source Inspection and the Poka-yoke System.* Cambridge, MA: Productivity Press, 1986.

Shtub, A., J. F. Bard, & S. Globerson. *Project Management Engineering, Technology, and Implementation,* Englewood Cliffs, NJ: Prentice Hall, 1994.

Snow, C. E. *Tech Engineering News,* November 1927.

Sower V., J. Motwani, & M. Savoie. *Classic Readings in Operations Management.* Ft. Worth, TX: Dryden, 1995.

Sower, V. E., J. Motwani, & M. Savoie. "Are Acceptance Sampling and Statistical Process Control Complementary or Incompatible?" *Quality Progress,* vol. 26, no. 9, September 1993, pp. 85–89.

Sower, V. E., J. Motwani, & M. Savoie. "Delta Charts for Short Run Statistical Process Control." *International Journal of Quality & Reliability Management,* vol. 11, no. 6, 1994, pp. 50–56.

Spinner, M. P. *Elements of Project Management,* 2nd ed. Englewood Cliffs, NJ: Prentice Hall, 1992.

Stevenson, W. J. *Production/Operations Management,* 5th ed. Chicago: Irwin, 1996.

Sullivan, L. "Quality Function Deployment." *Quality Progress,* vol. 19, no. 6, June 1986, pp. 39–50.

Suntag, C. *Inspection and Inspection Management.* Milwaukee, WI: ASQC Quality Press, 1993.

Taguchi, G. *Introduction to Quality Engineering.* Tokyo: Asian Productivity Organization, 1986.

Traver, R. W. "Measuring Equipment Repeatability—The Rubber Ruler." *1962 ASQC Annual Convention Transactions.* Milwaukee, WI: ASQC, 1962.

Tunner, J. R. *A Quality Technology Primer for Managers.* Milwaukee, WI: ASQC Quality Press, 1990.

Vining, G. G. *Statistical Methods for Engineers.* Pacific Grove, CA: Duxbury Press, 1998.

Walton, M. *The Deming Management Method.* New York: Perigee Books, 1986.

Western Electric. *Statistical Quality Control Handbook.* Indianapolis: Western Electric Co., 1956.

Wilkinson, H. E., C. D. Orth, & R. C. Benfari. "Motivation Theories: An Integrated Operational Model." *SAM Advanced Management Journal,* Autumn 1986, pp. 24–31.

Williams, P. B. *Getting a Project Done on Time—Managing People, Time, and Results.* New York: American Management Association, 1996.

Index